Ali Pasha

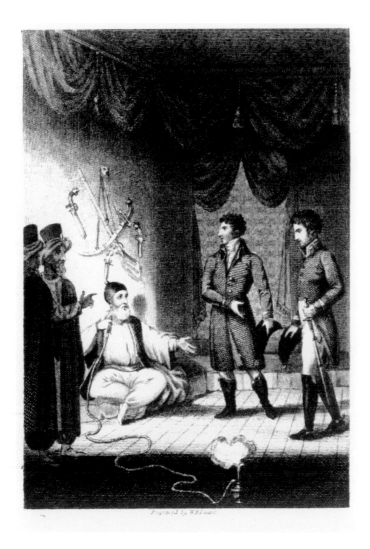

Yet in his lineaments ye cannot trace
While gentleness her Milder radiance throws
Along that aged venerable face
The deeds that lurk beneath, & stain him with disgrace

Fig. 1: Illustration from the English translation of the *History of Suli and Parga* by Christophoros Perraivos.

On my having paid him some slight compliment, Ali received me with so much courtesy of speech and of manner, that, had I not been certain, from general report, that he was a most barbarous and cruel man, and if, before entering his palace, I had not, in seeing fastened up on stakes some heads still dropping with blood, been a witness of his barbarity, I would have formed the most favourable opinion of him, and would have looked on him as the gentlest and most agreeable of men.

Carlo Gherardini, Italian translator of the *History of Suli and Parga*

Ali Pasha
Lion of Ioannina

The Remarkable Life of the Balkan Napoleon

By
Drs Quentin and Eugenia Russell

Pen & Sword
MILITARY

First published in Great Britain in 2017 by
Pen & Sword Military
an imprint of
Pen & Sword Books Ltd
47 Church Street
Barnsley
South Yorkshire
S70 2AS

ISBN 978 1 47387 720 7

A CIP catalogue record for this book is
available from the British Library.

Printed and bound in India by Replika Press Pvt. Ltd.

Pen & Sword Books Ltd incorporates the Imprints of Pen & Sword Archaeology, Atlas, Aviation, Battleground, Discovery, Family History, History, Maritime, Military, Naval, Politics, Railways, Select, Transport, True Crime, Fiction, Frontline Books, Leo Cooper, Praetorian Press, Seaforth Publishing, Wharncliffe and White Owl.

For a complete list of Pen & Sword titles please contact
PEN & SWORD BOOKS LIMITED
47 Church Street, Barnsley, South Yorkshire, S70 2AS, England
E-mail: enquiries@pen-and-sword.co.uk
Website: www.pen-and-sword.co.uk

Contents

List of Illustrations

Maps

The European territories of the Ottoman Empire in 1814 by John Thomson (1815).

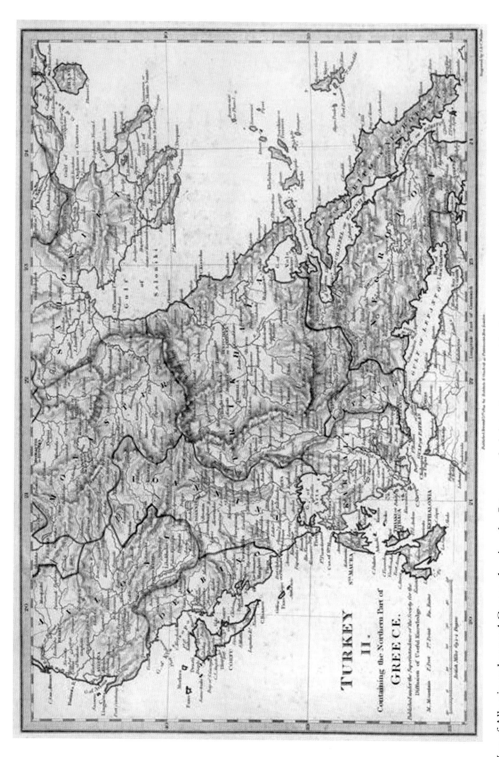

Map of Albania and central Greece showing the Ottoman administrative units with the contemporary place names.
Engraved by J & C Walker, published by Baldwin & Cradock, London, for the Society for the Diffusion of Useful Knowledge (1829).

Some Major Historical Events during the Life of Ali Pasha

1734–1739 Austro-Russian war with Turkey.

1739–1748 War of Jenkins's Ear between Britain and Spain.

1740 Empress Anne of Russia dies, 1741 Elizabeth seizes power from Ivan VI (a baby).

1740–1748 War of the Austrian Succession when Marie Theresa succeeds as Holy Roman Empress; Frederic II (the Great) of Prussia invades Silesia; France declares war on Britain and Austria (1744).

1754 Osman III succeeds Mahmud I as Sultan of the Ottoman Empire.

1754–1763 Anglo-French War in North America ('The French and Indian War'), from 1756, part of the Seven Years War: the struggle between Prussia and Austria becomes a world conflict fought between shifting alliances containing Britain and France in opposition. Treaty of Paris: Britain gains New France in North America and Florida from Spain, islands in the West Indies, Senegal and trading supremacy in India; Treaty of Hubertusburg maintains the status quo between Prussia and Austria.

1757 Mustafa III Sultan of the Ottoman Empire: a modernizer.

1760 George III succeeds his grandfather George II to the British throne.

1762 Peter III succeeds as Emperor of Russia; is murdered, accession of Catherine II, the Great (Ivan VI murdered 1764).

1766 Anglo-Russian treaty of friendship, commerce and navigation.

1767–1772 Ali Bey rebels against the Ottoman Empire and attempts to make Egypt independent, eventually driven into exile by his troops.

1768–1774 Russio-Turkish War; 1771 Austria allies with Turkey; Treaty of Küçük Kaynarca, Russia consolidates its gains at the expense of Turkey.

1773 Unrest in Britain's American colonies: Boston Tea Party, protest against tea duty.

1775–1783 American War of Independence: France, Spain and the Netherlands ally to the colonies; Treaty of Versailles, Britain recognizes their independence.

1774 Louis XVI succeeds Louis XV as King of France. Abdul Hamid I succeeds as Sultan.

1780 Emperor Joseph II succeeds Maria Theresa of Austria.

1786 Frederick William II succeeds Frederick the Great of Prussia.

1787–1792 Russio-Turkish War: Austria allies with Russia (1788–1790), Prussia with Turkey (1790-1792); Turkey defeated; 1789 the reformist Selim III becomes Sultan.

1789–1794 Short-lived Belgian Republic breaks from Austrian domination.

1789–1799 The French Revolution: 1792 France declared a Republic; 1793 execution of Louis XVI and Marie Antoinette, Louis XVII dies in prison (1795); Reign of Terror; Revolutionary army formed; The First Coalition (Austria, Spain, Great Britain, et al.) against France.

1790 Leopold II Holy Roman Emperor followed by Francis II (1792).

1796 Paul I succeeds Catherine the Great.

1797–1802 France's armies under Napoleon successful in Austria and Italy; Treaty of Campo Formio, Austria keeps Venice but Venetian territories that include the Ionian Islands go to France (1797); 1798 Napoleon victorious in Egypt but Nelson defeats the French Fleet (Battle of the Nile); Osman Pazvantoğlu Ottoman governor of Vidin (Bulgaria) sets up a rebel state (1798–1807); 1799 Napoleon returns to France, overthrows the Directory and sets up the Consulate. Russia and Turkey take the Ionian Islands. 1800 sees the French defeat the Austrians (Morengo). 1801 sees the British defeat the French at Copenhagen, Britain and Turkey defeat the French in Egypt; France makes peace with Austria, Spain, Portugal and Naples. Paul I of Russia murdered, succeeded by Alexander I. In 1802 Napoleon becomes Consul for life and President of the Italian Republic; Peace between Britain and France (Treaty of Amiens), Sri Lanka recognized as British colony.

1803–1815 Napoleonic Wars; 1804 Napoleon crowned Emperor; Serbia rises in revolt against Turkey. 1805 Alliance between Britain, Russia, Austria, Naples and Sweden; Battle of Trafalgar; Napoleon crowned king in Italy, deposes King of Naples, takes Venice and Ancona; Austria and Russia defeated (Austerlitz), Austria makes peace. Mehemet Ali Pasha takes control of Egypt. 1806 Napoleon abolishes the Holy Roman Empire (Francis II becomes Francis I of Austria), defeats Prussia (Jena), successful in Italy and Poland, invades Portugal (the Peninsular War 1807–14).

1806–1812 Russo-Turkish War.

1807 Napoleon routs the Russians (Friedland); Treaty of Tilsit, France and Russia become allies dividing Europe between them; France agrees to help Russia against Turkey if Russia joins against the British Empire; the Ionian Islands handed to the French; British expedition to Egypt. The janissaries depose Selim III in favour of Mustafa IV. 1808 Congress of Erfurt, Napoleon and Tsar Alexander I's secret plan to partition the Ottoman Empire breaks down over Constantinople and the Straits; France subdues Sweden and Spain, Russia invades

Finland, Moldavia and Wallachia. Selim III assassinated by Mustafa IV, in turn deposed and killed by Mahmud II. 1809 War between Austria and France; the British begin taking the Ionian Islands.

1810–1836 Spain loses control of its American colonies.

1812–15 Napoleon invades Russia, the retreat from Moscow; Treaty of Bucharest between Russia and Turkey grants Serbia autonomy, which Turkey ignores, second Serbian revolt 1815–17 leading to the semi-independent Principality of Serbia. 1814 Napoleon defeated, Louis XVIII becomes king; Treaty of Paris, Ionian Islands a British protectorate. 1815 Napoleon escapes from Elba, defeated at Waterloo; Congress of Vienna reverses all French gains.

1821–1832 Greek War of Independence.

Place Names

The places referred to in the contemporary literature have changed their names and spellings often on numerous occasions reflecting changes in ethnic distribution and political authority. Here are the common nineteenth century versions, their modern equivalents and other variants. The nineteenth century versions, which are used in the contemporary literature discussed in the book, are the names that the reader would require when delving deeper into those texts or conducting word searches. To facilitate further enquiry and study, we have mostly used those versions. When quotations from other authors are used, the spellings of those authors are preserved. Place names containing only small spelling differences and not a different name as such, e.g. Souli or Suli, Vostitsa or Vostizza, which the reader can easily identify, have been omitted for simplicity. This table provides information on additional and alternative names as well as the country to which each of these locations belong today.

Names used in the sources	Modern names
Adrianoupolis, Adrianople	Edirne (East Thrace, Turkey)
Agios Vasilis	Shen Vasil (Albania)
Argyrocastro (Argyro Kastro)	Gjirokastër (Albania)
Avlona, Valona (It.) Avlonya (Turk.)	Vlorë, Vlora (Albania)
Brusa, Proussa	Bursa (Turkey)
Buthrotum, Vouthroton	Butrint (Albania)
Chimara, Khimara	Himara, Himarë (Albania)
Constantinople	Istanbul (Turkey)
Durazzo (Dyrrachium, Epidamnos)	Durrës (Albania)
Elbasan (Neokastron)	Elbasan (Albania)
Ghardiki, Gardiki	Kardhiq (Albania)
Hormovo (Chormovo)	Hormovë (Albania)
Janina, Yannina	Ioannina (Greece)
Jassy	Iași, Iassy (Romania)
Karaferi	Veroia (Macedonia, Greece)
Klissura	Këlcyrë (Albania)
Korytsa	Korçë, Goritsa (Albania)

Leghorn	Livorno (Italy)
Lepanto	Naupactus, Nafpaktos (Greece)
Libokovo (Libkhobo)	Libohovë (Albania)
Moldavia	part of modern Romania, Ukraine and the Republic of Moldova
Moscopole (Bossigrad)	Voskopojë (Albania)
Monastir (Manastir, Voutelion)	Bitola (Former Yugoslavian Republic of Macedonia)
Morea, the	Peloponnese, Peloponnesos, Morias (colloquial) (Greece)
Navarino	Pylos (Greece)
Negosti	Naousa (Macedonia, Greece)
Negroponte (Chalkis, Euripos)	Euboea (Greece)
Nivitza	Nivice (Albania)
Ochrid (Achrida, Lychnidos)	Ohrid (Former Yugoslavian Republic of Macedonia)
Ostanitsa, Ostanizza	Aidonochori (Greece)
Paramithia (Ajdonat, Aghios Donatos)	Paramythia (Greece)
Patraziki (Neopatras, Neai Patrai, Patrai Helladikai)	Ypati (Greece)
Philippopolis (Filibe)	Plovdiv (Bulgaria)
Premeti	Përmet (Albania)
Ragusa	Dubrovnik (Croatia)
Rumeli, Rumelia	refers to either the administrative *eyalet* of the Balkans or Central Greece
Salona, La Sole	Amfissa (Greece)
Salonika	Thessalonika, Thessaloniki (Greece)
Saloniki (village)	Saloniki Paramythias (Greece)
Santi Quaranta (The Scala of the Forty Saints, Aghioi Saranda)	Saranda (Albania)
Scutari	Shkodër, Shkodra (Albania)
Septinsular Republic	**Ionian Islands** (Greece)
Corfu	Kerkyra, Korkyra
Paxos & Antipaxos	Paxos & Antipaxos (coll. Paxi)

Santa Maura	Leukas, Lefkada
Ithaka (Thiaki)	Ithaka, Ithaki
Cephalonia (Kephalonia)	Kefalonia, Kefallinia
Zante	Zakynthos
Cerigo, Carigo	Kythera
Spalatro	Split (Croatia)
Techovo	Karydia (Macedonia, Greece)
Tepelen, Tepalen, Tepelenë	Tepelena, Tepelenë (Albania)
Tilsit	Sovetsk (Russian Federation, formerly in East Prussia)
Tirhala	Trikkala, Trikala (Greece)
Tripolitza	Tripolis, Tripoli (Greece)
Vodena	Edessa (Macedonia, Greece)
Vostitsa, Vostizza, Votitza (Lagostica)	Aigio (Greece)
Vrachori	Agrinion (Greece)
Wallachia	part of Romania
Widin, Widdin	Vidin (Bulgaria)
Zitouni	Lamia (Greece)

The Principal Protagonists

Grand Tourists, Travellers and Diplomats

In essence the travellers and writers who saw Ali Pasha fall into two categories, before and after Byron. There were a number of foreigners in Ioannina at the turn of the century and the French and British had a significant presence. The first group of writers, few in number, were connected to diplomatic or military affairs. After Lord Byron's visit in 1809, Ioannina was established on the tourist trail and all the subsequent travel writers walk in the shadow of his poetic description and express philhellenic sentiments. Most of the precursors were French diplomats, soldiers and even prisoners. Notable among them are Guillaume de Vaudoncourt of the French Army who assisted Ali in his defences and François Pouqueville who had been captured by the Turks and became French ambassador to Ali, 1806–14. He travelled and made a study of Albania with his British counterpart William Leake. During 1801 Leake was in the employ of the Turks to help as a military attaché. In 1804 he made a survey of Albania for the British and Turkish allies, and from 1807 to 1810 he was British ambassador to Ali.

After Byron, Edward Gally Knight, a poetic imitator of Byron, traveller, activist for Greek liberation and later an MP, followed close in his footsteps. Sir Henry Holland, physician, was there between 1812 and 1813, at the same time as the Danish archaeologist Peter Oluf Brønsted whose excavating party in Greece had included the architect, Charles Robert Cockerell. Cockerell visited Epirus with the scholar, the Rev. Thomas Smart Hughes. His *Travels in Sicily, Greece, and Albania* (1820) was illustrated with drawings by Cockerell and translated into French and German. Another acquaintance of Cockerell's received by Ali Pasha was the French painter Louis Dupré who made a tour of Greece with three other English travellers in 1819, who also acted as his patrons and publishers. Dupré is particularly admired for his paintings of individuals and their costumes and weapons. An exception to the norm was Ibrahim Manzour, soldier of fortune and author, and convert to Islam otherwise known as Samson Cerfbeer de Médelsheim, born in Strasbourg. He wrote his own *Mémoires* of life at Ali's court from his experience as his military advisor from 1814 to 1817. Edward Everett was the first American to visit Ali's court in the early summer of 1819. A fervent philhellene and activist in the Greek cause, he travelled to Epirus during his tour of Europe and Turkey on completion of his studies at Göttingen University in Germany, he went on to become a diplomat, President of Harvard and a Secretary of State.

François Charles Hugues Laurent Pouqueville (1770–1838): French physician, diplomat, writer, explorer and ardent philhellene. A fierce critic of Ali Pasha and those who accepted his hospitality, such as Lord Byron, he had declared Napoleon as the forerunner of

Fig. 2: The artist crossing the Pindus Mountains from Ioannina to Trikkala in 1819 by Louis Dupré from his *Voyage â Athènes et â Constantinople* (1825).

the Greek freedom movement as early as 1805. He met Thomas Hughes in Ioannina and the two men became close friends and travelled Greece together. His writings on geography and topography were the basis for the work of many later French geographers and are comparable to that of Leake. His philhellenic writings were extremely influential and inspired painters such as Ary Scheffer and Francesco Hayez. Pouqueville was the recipient of the Order of the Redeemer of Greece.

William Martin Leake FRS (1777–1860): Brilliant topographer, military officer and traveller to the Greek lands. During his early military career he served in the West Indies. Later he acted as a land surveyor for the Royal Artillery within the Ottoman Empire, which gave him the opportunity to develop a deep interest in antiquities and topography. He was the first to record measurements of the Peloponnese for the purpose of creating accurate maps. His unique approach included an interaction between the physical reality of his day and his knowledge of Ancient Greek literature, especially the geographer Pausanias. Upon his retirement from the Army in 1815, Leake pursued his scientific interests further and helped establish the Royal Geographical Society. His highly regarded *Topography of Athens* was a groundbreaking work and his detailed and extensive travel writings continue to be studied as a valuable record of the period.

Lord George Gordon Byron (1788–1824): Author of *The Lament of Tasso*, *Prometheus*, *Childe Harold's Pilgrimage*, *The Giaour*, *Manfred*, *The Siege of Corinth* and the dramatic work *Cain*. He was seen as the embodiment of the Romantic ideal, hence the phrase Byronic hero. Samuel Taylor Coleridge saw in 'his eyes the open portals of the sun'. Byron was probably the most famous amongst the many philhellenes discussed in this book and much of his work was influenced and defined by Greece. When Byron died in Missolonghi the news spread like dynamite all over Europe and America, shocking public opinion and giving strength to the Greek fight for independence.

John Cameron 'Cam' Hobhouse (Lord Broughton, 1786–1869): Radical politician, author and close friend of Byron's from their Cambridge years. He accompanied Byron on his travels and recorded his experiences in *A Journey through Albania, and other provinces of Turkey in Europe and Asia, to Constantinople during the years 1809 and 1810*. He wrote notes for the Fourth Canto of *Childe Harold* and upon completion in 1818 Byron dedicated the entire poem to him in a long literary address that stressed that Hobhouse was 'a friend often tried and never found wanting'.

Sir Henry Holland FRS (1788–1873): Physician, traveller and writer. He travelled to Iceland and the Mediterranean and his travel writings gained him much attention. His expedition to Iceland took place in 1810 in the company of fellow-physician Richard Bright and the mineralogist and geologist George Mackenzie. They took the smallpox vaccine to Iceland and later Holland wrote a thesis on the diseases of Iceland in Latin for Edinburgh University. He served as consultant physician to several Prime Ministers, including George Canning, Physician in Ordinary to Queen Victoria and President of the Royal College of

Physicians, while also giving medical advice to his cousin, the novelist and short story writer Elizabeth Gaskell.

Rev. Thomas Smart Hughes (1786–1847): Important theologian, thinker and scholar of Greek. Hughes travelled through Greece with Charles Robert Cockerell, RA, who illustrated his well-known record of their journey *Travels to Greece and Albania*. Subsequently he authored several notable theological works and continued the *History of England* by David Hume and Tobias Smollett, producing volumes 14–21. Hughes wrote passionately about Greek freedom, especially after the Massacre of Chios. Hughes is the author of the poem *Belshazzar's Feast*, which inspired the apocalyptic vision of John Martin's eponymous painting.

Introduction

Anyone lucky enough to travel through the beautifully rugged mountain landscape of north-western Greece and southern Albania will soon be aware of numerous grey and forbidding fortifications dotting the landscape. Enquiries will reveal them to be, often as not, associated with a notorious local ruler known as Ali Pasha. The first time I heard this name was as a child holidaying in Greece. When our party was visiting Ioannina, then well off the tourist map, we took the short boat trip to the little island of Pamvotis, on the lake by which the city stands. At a little taverna, a traditional travelling musician serenaded us with the story of Ali's exploits, and the mystery of his name and its association with the place of his dramatic death, must have left as deep an impression on me as his deeds have on the local landscape. Ioannina, once Ali's capital, is full of his memory, and his reputation continues, as both hero and villain, in tales associated with local landmarks and in folk song. Ali is so ingrained into the fabric of the local culture that throughout the region it feels as though his ghost is following you around.

This region, once ancient Epirus, is split between modern Greece and Albania. Classical antiquities are less conspicuous here than in the Greek heartlands further south, but there is still a wealth of history to be seen: Byzantine, Crusader and Venetian. Then a void appears in the story, for the shadow of the Ottoman Empire falls across the land, and time seems to stand still. For almost 500 years Epirus is under the 'dead hand' of the Sultan's rule in Constantinople, and it is the almost timeless and larger than life Ali who emerges to fill this historical gap.

Ali Pasha lived around 200 years ago during the long period of Ottoman decline. Surprisingly, considering his obscure origins, Ali left more than just a mark on his native land. His exploitation of the Empire's weakness at this time brought him to the attention of the Western Powers and through travellers' tales and poetic fantasizing his exploits became the sensational matter of popular imagination and culture. For those of us in the West this period can be reconstructed within the framework of our conceptions of the Napoleonic wars and romanticism. For the descendants of those Europeans living under what was referred to as 'the Ottoman yoke' this is an enigmatic and different past, messy and contradictory, as defined as if crossing a border. Never has the quote, 'the past is a foreign country: they do things differently there' been more true.[1] For the overwhelmingly Orthodox Christian Greeks memories of Muslim Turkish occupation are bitter, and felt to be best forgotten. The Albanians too, both Christian and Muslim, were only too glad to gain independence and rid themselves of Turkish rule. Consequently, with the consciously nationalist creation of

---

[1] From *The Go-Between* by L P Hartley (1953).

Fig. 3: Ioannina and the lake, photo by Derek Smith.

modern identities much of this Ottoman related legacy has been cleansed away and, with it, Ali's memory too has been anaesthetized by being consigned to legend and folklore.

It is the purpose of this book to reimagine Ottoman Greece and Albania and its complex relationship with the rest of Europe, and to restore Ali Pasha to the prominence he once held, as a major player in the power struggles of Revolutionary and Napoleonic Europe.

In 1834 two young English adventurers, John Saville, Earl of Mexborough, and Alexander William Kinglake, arrived at Semlin, a town at the confluence of the River Sava with the Danube. The two old Etonians were on their way eastward to make a tour of the Levant, which today we might refer to as the eastern Mediterranean. Kinglake subsequently used the raw material from this trip as the basis for an idiosyncratic and fancifully ironic travel book, *Eothen or Traces of Travel Brought Home from the East*, which provides a window into the mindset of a certain type of nineteenth century traveller. What is interesting about Semlin is that at that time it stood at the border between Austro–Hungary and Serbia, and it marked not only a physical barrier but a mental watershed, for it was here, in central Europe, that the pair prepared to leave the sights and sounds of familiar life, where the women went unveiled, to cross from 'wheel-going Europe' into the 'Splendour and havoc of the East'.

Semlin was the German name for what is today the modern suburb of Zemun, absorbed by its neighbour across the Sava, the city of Belgrade, and despite it being no more than a 'cannon shot' from its castle to the opposite bank, Kinglake reports that there was 'no communion' between the two sides. Belgrade's own fortress was garrisoned by Turkish troops under the command of a local pasha. Although Serbia had gained semi-independence it still remained under the nominal rule of the Ottoman Empire. The border crossing therefore represented the fault line between two empires and two cultures. This transition into what was known as 'Turkey in Europe', was underlined by forced passage through the town's Quarantine Establishment (Lazaretto), for, according to Kinglake, the lands of the Ottoman Empire were almost perpetually in the grip of 'the Plague', marked by the flying of a yellow flag. Those returning into Austria-Hungary would also have to endure a fourteen-day stay in the 'odious Lazaretto'. Kinglake was writing for effect and his heightened reminiscences must be taken with a pinch of salt, but the threat of plague was real enough. When the non-sense poet and landscape painter, Edward Lear, arrived in Thessaloniki in 1848 on route to Mt Athos, he encountered the plague first-hand; the city so in its grip that he was obliged to take a more adventurous and circuitous route through the Ottoman Balkans by way of Macedonia, Albania, Epirus and Thessaly!

Travellers coming back from the East to Western Europe were always subjected to stays in quarantine. This reflected a difference in attitude; whereas Europeans thought plague was something that could be controlled, the Ottomans were fatalistic, attributing it to an act of God. Differences in religion were compounded with the feeling that, with advances in science and technology, Europe was becoming increasingly 'enlightened' while the Orient was already backward. Not until 1838 did Ottoman reforms impose their own quarantine, but this was partially as a way to restrict European influence. Such impediments empha-sized the crossing from one world to another. Ironically, even a visit to Greece, the birth-place of European civilization, necessitated such a shock to the system for the unprepared. Hans Christian Andersen, the children's author, records in his own Eastern travel memoir, *A Poets Bazaar*, how on arrival in the Bay of Piraeus in 1841, the passengers were obliged to spend three days on board ship in quarantine before setting foot in Athens. Southern Greece, which had only been officially liberated from Ottoman rule since 1832, was not yet 'westernized'. This ambiguity of place in the Balkans influenced the way western trav-ellers reacted to the local population, imbuing them with vices and virtues, often indis-criminately, depending on their own cultural prejudices. On his return journey, Andersen endured a further ten days in the prison-like quarantine quarters in Orsova, today on the Romanian bank of the Danube.

Since the Ottoman conquests of the fifteenth century, the Orient, then, had begun in Eastern Europe, and once there, you were in a land, Lear said, without pots and pans; a land where one sat on the floor to eat; a land of Turkish carpets, pashas, whirling dervishes, long *nargile* pipes, minarets, seraglios and camels; a land of *The Arabian Nights* peopled by European subjects. Since the translation from the Arabic of *The One Thousand and One Nights* at the beginning of the eighteenth century, the European imagination had been fired by Romantic visions of Eastern exoticism.[2] As the Ottoman Empire became less of a threat, its power eclipsed by the rise of its European rivals, this interest increased, so much so that 'Orientalism' became a fashion. Since the Second World War, the spread of westernization and its consequences have tarnished this romance, but for those of Kinglake's contemporaries

[2] Into French by Antoine Gallard between 1704 and 1717; the first anonymous English translation from Gallard in 1706.

who found Western manners stifling they would have shared his delight in being 'free from the stale civilization of Europe'. As Lord Byron had discovered, twenty-five years previously, to be 'free' was just a short hop across the Adriatic from Italy to 'Albania', where he was able to indulge his fantasies, while in the process becoming a celebrity. His fictionalized memoirs in verse of his Grand Tour, *Childe Harold's Pilgrimages*, were the publishing sensation that in the process introduced Ali Pasha to a wide audience.

With a little help from Byron, the colourful Ali dazzlingly emerged from the obscurity of a little known Ottoman backwater on Europe's doorstep, to hold its leaders and public in thrall. Even though the continent was busy tearing itself apart during what is loosely termed the Napoleonic wars, his sideshow fulfilled all Orientalist preconceptions; he was Ali Pasha, 'Aslan', the Lion of Ioannina, the epitome of the Oriental despot, fascinating and loathsome in equal measure. Fortuitous to emerge just at the right time in world affairs, and in the right place, he was both distrusted and courted. For a quixotic moment he held centre stage, seemingly indispensable to the schemes of the warring parties, only to disappear into the shadows again.

The contemporary view of the East, as a place both fearful and exotically enticing, so clouded the picture of Ali Pasha, that, even during his own lifetime, he is as elusive as any typical folklore hero, a Robin Hood or William Tell. Despite the marks left by the harsh experience of his uncompromising rule, his greatest legacy at first appeared to be to the world of the imagination; even when his moment was passed his fame lingered on in Europe throughout the nineteenth century. When the Balkans were finally freed from Turkish rule in the next century interest in their Ottoman history waned. For Western visitors to Greece, the classical past was more relevant; a past the locals were only too happy to promote. In the meantime, much of Ali's territory was, until recently, well off the tourist trail. Recent events in Albania and improvements in communications have made Ali's physical legacy accessible, and the Ottoman world of Turkey in Europe is distant enough to safely revisit. Modern conservation of the monuments of this period has helped to bring this past back to life. This renewed interest makes it possible to attempt a more dispassionate and hopefully objective unravelling of his true story from the fiction and an assessment of his impact. Present preoccupations with events in the Middle East make it a prescient time to look back on the political and cultural antecedents of the relationship between East and West.

Ali Pasha's story is entertaining in itself, with many anecdotes that have been embellished along the way, but it is nothing more than that unless put into a context. To establish the larger picture, his geographical and historical positioning gives a perspective on why Ali Pasha became so famous in his lifetime and infamous afterwards. From the tales about him it appears as though he emerged fully formed from the mountain mist. The conditions that allowed a former bandit leader to become the de facto ruler of nearly all Ottoman Albania and Greece, for much of the time thumbing his nose at the authority of the Sultan, were of their time and place, but they have modern parallels. The context helps us gain a view as to whether Ali's success as a political manoeuvrer was in part due to being in the right place at the right time, expediency, or skill, comparable to a modern-day Afghani warlord or a precursor of the archetypal Middle Eastern ruler, a Saddam Hussein of Iraq or a Bashar al-Assad of Syria, adept at playing off competing powers to maintain his position.[3] Ali's territorial expansion gained him a formidable military reputation, earning comparisons with the great General Napoleon himself; he was the 'Muslim Bonaparte' according to Lord Byron. This reputation as a war leader and wily diplomat was built largely on reports coming back to Europe from Western visitors to his court at Ioannina. These stories were the fuel for the legend.

It takes a leap of imagination for the modern traveller, especially of the armchair variety, to understand the obscurity from which Ali Pasha emerged. Our world has become so small, with every corner made accessible to us by intrepid writers and TV crews, that it is hard for us to conceive that a land within swimming distance of Corfu could be as remote as some tropical jungle hideaway to a native of Britain or France. If today, the land of Ali is off the familiar track, in the late eighteenth century it was virtually unknown, a forgotten land, described by the author of the *Decline and Fall of the Roman Empire*, Edward Gibbon, as 'a land within sight of Italy and less known than the interior of America'. Writing his history between the 1770s and 1780s Gibbon complained of the lack of adequate maps of the region, knowledge of which was only slowly emerging through the writings of travellers, the equivalent of explorers in more remote regions. A land of stunning beauty but unforgiving terrain and extremes of climate it had proved difficult for outsiders to penetrate and rulers to rule, and, as the Germans and Italians were to discover to their cost in the Second World War, perfect for guerilla warfare.

It was these travellers, Lord Byron among them, who were largely responsible for the legend of Ali Pasha. Once war with Napoleonic France put much of cultural Europe out of bounds for their Grand Tour, the wealthy and well-connected British had to venture further afield to lands in the main only previously visited by the intrepid and antiquarians. The war also made relations with the Ottoman Empire of greater significance, and the Balkans of strategic importance. Diplomatic and military intelligence was also required, and the British were not alone; the French were active in this area too. The tourists provided colourful first-hand impressions of Ali's court to feed the European appetite for the exotic, while serious travellers like Captain William Leake, who was involved in diplomatic service, gave a more sober account.

The earliest accounts of Ali Pasha relied heavily on this material, and before long his story had passed into literature, mainly influenced by the Romantic and Orientalist movements that were particularly fashionable in France. For the historian the problem is to disentangle the elements of embellishment in the first-hand accounts from any worthy factual material, and ascertain which sources are the most reliable. Modern scholarship has broadened the search for more reliable and varied sources. Rather than relying wholly on Western sources contemporary Greek writings and records from Ali's court are now available.

The physical remains of his rule that provide haunting attractions for the tourist help to paint a picture of the reality of life within his domains. Though mute in themselves, they

---

[3] Coincidentally both *aslan* (Turkish) and *assad* (Arabic) mean lion.

have left unequivocal evidence of his impact and are important in any gauge of his ability to govern. These remains are not only military, but some are cultural, architectural or utilitarian. It is to be recognized, however, that while assisting in trying to find the man behind the myth, any appraisal of his significance to history cannot ignore his larger than life persona. This would be telling only half the story. Even in his lifetime Ali had already passed into local legend. The stories and songs of his exploits still told and sung today are his living testament. This journey from local despot to part of the western Orientalist vision, how he became the epitome of the Oriental tyrant and a melodramatic hero/villain, immortalized in works of fiction and local folklore, is also part of his history.

To create the complete picture of the life of Ali Pasha of Ioannina it is necessary to have an overview that takes in and resolves all the strands: context, legend, history and finally legacy. The legacy of Ali is as much to do with perception as with reality, and therefore is as much cultural as historical. In Greece and Albania Ali lives on within the landscape and memory and though his memory may have faded in the West, it helped formulate, for better or worse, our modern perceptions of the East.

Quentin Russell

Chapter 1

Historical Background

The Region of Epirus

The historical regional identity of Ali Pasha's mountainous powerbase existed long before the present national borders. Known as Epirus from the classical period, by Ali's time it was commonly referred to as part of Albania. When Henry Holland travelled there in 1812 he described it thus:

> Albania, as a country, cannot be defined by any strict line of boundary; but it is rather determined in its outline by the language and other characters of the population. The country around Ioannina, and even Acarnania, though inhabited chiefly by Greeks, are often spoken of under this name; and at present, when annexed to the power of an Albanian ruler, not entirely without reason.

Defined by the spread of population, Holland suggested that Albania began in the south at the Suli Mountains (Paramythia), just north of the Gulf of Arta in present-day Greece, and followed a coastal strip until it reached its present border at Montenegro, which strictly speaking excluded Arta and Ioannina, Ali's capital. The division between north and south was often referred to as Upper and Lower Albania. Today the classical name of Epirus has been resurrected on both sides of the Greek/Albanian border, recognizing the historical region.

Facing the Ionian Sea and the island of Corfu to the west, Epirus is boarded to the east by the rugged Pindus Mountains, a continuation of the Dinaric Alps that form a spine down the centre of the Balkan Peninsula, through Albania and into central Greece. The range rises to over 2,600m (8,600ft) in a series of steep ridges running parallel to the coast, a formidable barrier of over 100km (62miles) to east-west movement between Epirus and Macedonia and Thessaly. From the Pindus to the coast is a high plateau dominated by a further number of smaller parallel ranges, cut by narrow river valleys and gorges. Particularly striking are the Ceraunian Mountains (Çika 2012m) in Albania, the high (Acroceraunian) western range of which isolates the coastal area of Himara, and the Paramythian plateau through the mountains (Koryla 1,658m and Chionistra 1644m) of which the mythical Acharon River cuts its gorge on its journey from the underworld. Lake Pamvotis, on whose shore the region's largest town, Ioannina, stands, is at an elevation of 460m (1500ft). The northern boundary of Epirus is marked by the Bay of Vlora in modern Albania and the southern by the Ambracian Gulf (or Gulf of Arta) in Greece.

Northern Epirus, today mainly in Albania, is divided from the south by the watershed between the River Vjosa and its tributary the Drino, which flows north into the Gulf of Vlora, and the Arachthos and Thiamis rivers flowing to the south into the Ambracian Gulf and west into the Ionian Sea respectively. The prevailing maritime westerly winds make Epirus the wettest region of Greece, and its mountainous terrain (less than 4 per cent lowland) and poor soils provide a harsh environment mainly suitable for pasture, especially sheep. While the high mountains are the home of brown bears and wolves, the coastal strip provides a slight respite where olives and fruit can be grown, but the river mouths are characterized by wetlands that in historical times were particularly marshy and malarial.

Ottoman Occupation

In 1479, Vonitsa, the last outpost of the Despotate of Epirus finally fell to the Turks. This defeat meant that all of mainland Greece, apart from a few coastal enclaves held by the Republic of Venice, was in the hands of the Ottoman emperor, Sultan Mehmed II the Conqueror. In classical times Epirus had been an energetic independent kingdom that under the ambitious Pyrrhus took on the emerging military power of the Roman Republic in a series of battles between 280 and 275 BC. Though he could defeat Rome in battle he was unable to win the war, hence the term 'Pyrrhic victory'. Eventually Epirus became part of the Roman and then Byzantine empires, but as Byzantine power waned it once again became an independent or semi-independent state, passing between Crusader, Frankish, Byzantine and Serbian

Fig. 4: The Pindus Mountains, photo by Derek Smith.

domination. The Ottoman armies began their slow march through the Balkans in 1362 when Sultan Murad I transferred his capital to Adrianople (in Thrace), renaming it Edirne. The long war of attrition picking away at Byzantium's diminishing territories finally came to an end in 1453 when Mehmed took the far greater prize of Constantinople after a fifty-three day siege, the last Byzantine emperor, Constantine XI Palaiologos, dying valiantly in the last-ditch attempt to defend the city walls.

In Epirus the Turkish vultures had already been circling for some time. To the north the Sanjak of Albania had been established by 1419, stretching as far as south as Argyrocastro (Gjirokastër), and in Epirus itself the major centres of Ioannina (1430) and Arta (1449) were already in Ottoman hands.[1] With the fall of Vonitsa began the 400 years or so of Turkish rule, but it was a rule that proved as hard to universally maintain as it was to impose. The mountains of Epirus were ideally suited to those willing to eke out a harsh but independent existence, and the coastal enclave of Himara isolated by the Acroceraunian range and the Zagora region in the high reaches of the Pindus retained an element of autonomy. Similarly remote Suli, hidden within the Paramythian Mountains, became a refuge for those escaping Ottoman rule. In the meantime the Italian city-states of Genoa and Venice (commonly referred to as Franks) had retained a territorial presence in the eastern Mediterranean dating from the Crusades and stubbornly tried to hold on to their Greek island and mainland possessions. Venice in particular was keen to maintain its maritime empire, the *Stato del Mar*, and was unafraid to take the war to the Turks. After the Turks occupied the Peloponnese, at that time referred to as the Morea, Venice tried to regain control on a number of occasions but with little lasting effect.

As a consequence of the Ottoman invasion a majority of the population of Albania converted to Islam, with a significant number of Albanians and Greeks following the Dervish Bektashi Order, a mystical Sufi branch of Islam that came to prominence in the fifteenth century, particularly in the Balkans. The divide between north and south Albania was, and still is, characterized by Catholic Christianity retaining a following amongst the Dheg dialect speakers of Albanian above the line of the River Shkumbin, and Orthodox Christianity being followed by the Tosk speakers and Greeks to the south, and by other minorities such as the Vlachs and Slavs.

The Decline of Ottoman Power and the Rise of the West

The tussles between Venice and the Ottomans became a sideshow in the main thrust of European affairs as the centres of power moved away from the Mediterranean. With the fall of Byzantium and the eclipse of Greek culture, the southern Balkans faded from view in the West. Seen as an isolated backwater it was not until the latter eighteenth and early nineteenth centuries that the region was thrust back into the mainstream. During this period the con-quered lands of Eastern Europe were known as 'Turkey in Europe'. After a period of dynamic expansion, Ottoman power peaked under Suleyman the Magnificent who took his armies as far west as the walls of Vienna (1529), but failed to take the city. At sea the Ottoman Fleet also

---

[1] Ottoman provinces, *eyalets* or *viyalets*, where divided into sanjaks and then further subdivided into *timars* (fiefs).

suffered a devastating defeat at the Battle of Lepanto (1573, modern Nafpaktos), fought near the mouth of the Gulf of Corinth, at the hands of the Holy League, a coalition of Catholic Mediterranean states. Despite this reversal, the Turks were still able to take Rhodes and the Dodecanese Islands from the Knights of St. John (1522), and Cyprus (1570–1) and Crete (1669) from Venice. While the fortunes of its possessions in the Morea continued to go back and forth, Venice stubbornly held on to the Ionian Islands and its strategic outposts in Epirus. The flowering of culture and enterprise that followed in the wake of Suleyman came to an end again at Vienna in 1683 when the invading Ottoman forces were defeated by a combined army of the Holy Roman Empire and the Polish-Lithuanian League. The aftermath was not only a retreat from Hungary but also the slow decline of Ottoman power over 200 years until the Empire finally broke up after the First World War. In contrast the West embarked on a period of empire building, technological innovation and revolution. The immediate result however, was that the Ottoman's enemies were joined by Venice and Russia (under Peter the Great) to form another Holy League. For Venice this meant that when peace was signed at the Treaty of Karlowitz (1699) it gained much of the Dalmatian coast, and the Peloponnese. From hence on, Ottoman endeavours were no longer expansionist but focused on regaining lost territories.

The peace was short-lived. The Ottomans retook the Morea (1715), but despite this success, lost the ports of Preveza and Parga in Epirus to Venice and were still unable to take the Ionian Islands from them. But by now even Venice's star was beginning to fade. An era of exploration had opened up the world and the scramble for new opportunities for wealth and empire building led to a struggle by the Atlantic facing states for control of the trade routes to the Orient. While on land much of central Europe was dominated by Habsburg and Russian imperial ambitions and Eastern Europe, North Africa and the Middle East remained under Ottoman influence, the conflicts of the Atlantic maritime powers demanded an ever-larger canvas on which to be played out. France and Britain, the increasingly dominant forces, were not content to confine their rivalry to North America or India but sought to spread their influence into the Mediterranean. Naval supremacy here depended on the control of bases from which to maintain a fleet and islands such as Gibraltar, Malta and Cyprus that formed a chain from west to east became key strategic locations. The Venetian Ionian Islands, which included both Corfu off the Albanian coast and Kythera at the southernmost tip of the Peloponnese, and their other small land bases on the Greek coast were now not only a thorn in the side of the Ottomans but of great interest to any power with expansionist ideas towards the Levant. Russia too increasingly had designs on the Mediterranean. The creation of its Black Sea Fleet by Catherine the Great's favourite, Prince Grigory Potemkin, meant that it was inevitably going to resist being hemmed-in in its base at Sebastopol in the Crimea. By the end of the century the eastern Mediterranean was a backwater no more but a major region of interest to what were to become known as the Great Powers, the powers who would attempt to partition the world over the course of the next two centuries.[2]

---

[2] The term 'Great Power' was first used by Lord Castlereagh, the British Foreign Secretary, in 1814, in reference to the Austrian Empire, France, Prussia, Russia and the United Kingdom. It was hoped the five could establish a formula for peace after the Napoleonic Wars based on the 'Balance of Power'.

The State of Play during Ali Pasha's Life

For Ali Pasha, born in the midst of the eighteenth century, his career was to be defined by the struggles and shifting alliances of the European powers and the internal divisions within the Ottoman Empire. His rise from obscurity to a despot courted by the Great Powers and dangerous to the Sultan was intimately woven into the story of Ottoman decline. Warfare was an almost constant state of affairs, interspersed by numerous short-term peace treaties during which the belligerents could take a breather, like boxers, and count their territorial gains and losses. Two major wars, the War of the Austrian Succession (1740–48) and the Seven Years War (1754–63) created two counter blocs. During the first conflict, Britain, allied to Austria, sought to pursue its war against France and Spain in the colonies (the Americas and India), while its enemies, allied to Prussia, fought a European war. Although in the second war allegiances changed, Prussia with Britain, Austria with France, Spain and Russia, the outcome for Britain was the same, an expansion of its empire and increase in the power of its navy.

The Ottoman Empire was not directly involved in these wars, but its fragile European borders were threatened along the Danube. Both Habsburg Austria and the Romanov Tsars of Russia took advantage of the periods of peace from the larger European conflicts to pursue an aggressive policy towards Turkey. Austria's endeavours however mainly benefited the Romanovs who bolstered their ambitions with a claim to a dynastic and religious right to authority within the territories of the former Byzantium. Sophia, the daughter of Thomas Palaiologos, the despot of the Morea and younger brother of the last emperor, had married Grand Prince Ivan III of Moscow. Her grandson was the first tsar of Russia, Ivan the Terrible. Citing this distant connection, the Romanov tsar, Peter the Great, inserted 'King of Greece' amongst his titles. The Russians also claimed leadership of the Orthodox Church. Catherine the Great, who inherited the throne by marriage, was an admirer of Peter and an Orthodox convert. She took seriously the notion that Russia should rule over her fellow believers in occupied Turkey and harboured notions of taking Constantinople, the spiritual centre of Orthodoxy and the seat of the patriarch of the Greek Church.

Turkey's problem was not only maintaining its borders, but also its internal peace. The Porte, the Ottoman government in Constantinople, was caught between efforts to reform and modernize while it struggled to maintain its grip on its volatile regions. Despite indecisive engagements with Austria or Venice, it had become evident that the Ottoman Army was no match for the new infantry and artillery of the West. The Empire sought aid from France on a number of occasions but military reform met with strong resistance. The janissary corps openly revolted with the consequence that Sultan Ahmed III was deposed in 1730. In 1799 Sir William Eton published *A Survey of the Turkish Empire*, his findings on the state of the Ottoman Empire. A former diplomat in Russia and Turkey he had gathered information as to the intentions of Catherine and the internal situation in the

Fig. 5: *Suliotes in traditional costume* (1824–1825) by Eugène Delacroix.

Balkans. His report underlined Ottoman decline, with the army in particular disarray, being seditious and mutinous and refusing all reform:

> their armies are encumbered with immense baggage, and their camp has all the conveniences of a town, with shops etc. for such was their ancient custom when they wandered with their hordes. The cavalry is as much afraid of their own infantry as of the enemy; for in a defeat they fire at them to get their horses to escape more quickly. In short, it is a mob assembled rather than an army levied.

As for the artillery, it was chiefly brass, and although with 'many fine pieces of cannon' they were ignorant of how to use it 'notwithstanding the reiterated instruction of so many French engineers'. Other munitions were old. Musket-barrels were 'too heavy' not being made of the latest soft iron and the art of making sabres forgotten with the only good blades being 'ancient'. The Turkish Grand Fleet 'consisted of not more than seventeen or eighteen sail of the line in the last war [Russo-Turkish war of 1787–92], and those not in very good condition; at present their number is lessened'.

Sultan Selim III's attempt to introduce European discipline into the Turkish Army by abolishing the janissaries managed to incite mutiny, which he was only able to appease by consenting to continue their pay during their lifetimes. He ordered however that there would be no more recruitment into the janissaries. Selim ultimately failed and like Ahmed he was overthrown and assassinated by order of his successor, Mustafa IV, in 1808. Mustafa came to his own abrupt end almost immediately, ousted and executed by another reformer, Mahmud II. This chaos and weakness at the centre allowed strong regional leaders to set themselves up in opposition to the Sultan, while smaller bands, such as the Suliotes of Epirus, were able to remain a law unto themselves in their mountain strongholds. Catherine saw in these internal weaknesses and the numerous ethnic and religious divisions an opportunity to be exploited.

The Janissaries

The Ottomans were the first power to maintain a standing army. Although their military success had relied heavily on their cavalry they also had a long-established method of using captured prisoners as mercenaries. To maintain an infantry force young boys were recruited from the conquered in the form of a tax, the *Devshirme*; a percentage of male children. Taken initially from mainly Christian youths in the Balkans, particularly Greece and Albania, the recruits were instilled with religious devotion to Islam and loyalty to the Sultan. The more able were then enrolled into the palace to be trained as administrators and officials in the state bureaucracy, while the remainder became soldiers or maintained order. The most famous of these conscripts were the janissaries. An elite corps formed in the mid fourteenth century they became recognized as the best-trained and most effective soldiers in Europe. The janissaries operated as a close-knit brotherhood associated with the religious order of the Bektashi Dervishes and subject to strict rules including celibacy. In the late sixteenth century such restrictions were relaxed and by the early eighteenth century the original method of recruitment was abandoned. By then they had become a powerful political force within the state and the growing weakness of the Sultans resulted in granting them increased privileges. Despite the rank and file frequently being left without pay when the government was in financial difficulties, the opportunities for the officers to enrich themselves made enrolment into their ranks desirable. Growing corruption and meddling in government administration, the engineering of palace coups and their resistance to the adoption of European methods meant they eventually became a liability. Their end (the Auspicious Incident) came in June 1826 when they again rebelled against modernization. On their refusal to surrender, Mahmud II finally crushed them by having cannon fired into their barracks in the capital. Most of the mutineers were killed, and those who were taken prisoner were executed. The remaining janissaries were imprisoned or fled into exile.

Ein Janitſchar.

Fig. 6: Janissary musketeer (1703) by Caspar Luken.

Fig. 7: Janissary from Ioannina (1828) by Otto Magnus von Stackelberg.

As central authority weakened, regional leaders saw their opportunity to take advantage of local circumstances. Muhammad (Mehmet) Ali Pasha, the Albanian commander of the Ottoman Army in Egypt, rose to power after the retreat of Napoleon in 1801, finally declaring himself Khedive of Egypt and the Sudan with the reluctant acknowledgement of the Porte; an action that led to the founding of modern Egypt. The Balkans too was fertile ground for provincial governors to stake a claim for independent rule. The Bushatli family created a semi-autonomous pashalik in Scutari (Shkodra) in northern Albania, Osman Pazvantoğlu, a Bosnian mercenary, took control of Vidin on the Danube (Bulgaria) and set up a rebel state and Ismail Pasha ruled a semi-autonomous personal domain around Serres in northern Greece. Pazvantoğlu was a friend of the Greek poet and political thinker Rigas Feraios, who was an intellectual inspiration behind Greek unrest. Wealthy Greek families associated with the Phanar district of Constantinople, hence Phanariotes, had attained such a significant role within the Empire and in the Danube provinces of Wallachia and Moldavia, today's Romania, that the Ottoman government was obliged to create two principalities with local Phanariotes appointed as princes of autonomous vassal states. Russia, with its borders on the principalities, was ready to exploit any discord between them and the Porte. Russia had had agents working in Greece since the time of Peter the Great, stoking the fires of discontent and promising that Russia would defeat the Turks and liberate the Greek Christians, who hoped this would lead to the restoration of the Byzantine Empire. Catherine developed a strategy to take Constantinople by the back door by exploiting unrest in the Morea. Conditions here had been generally good during the early eighteenth century, and the Greeks were even willing to help the Turks retake their territory lost to the Venetians in 1715, but by the 1760s things had deteriorated, with land tenure being increasingly unequally distributed between the Greeks and their masters.

At this time, Georgios Papazolis, a Greek officer in the Russian Army, was friendly with Count Grigori Orlov, one of Catherine's favourites at court. He persuaded Orlov that the Greeks were ready to rise up, and a plan was hatched to back Russia's fellow Orthodox followers against Turkey. Papazolis was the author of *Teaching and Interpretation of the Order of War*, a manual he managed to circulate in Greece, and about 1765, he and his agents began to prepare the ground for rebellion. When Russia again went to war with Turkey in 1769 Catherine agreed to the creation of another front, and Papazolis' brother Theodore was put in command of a small Russian force heading for the Mani Peninsula. The Mani Peninsula had never been fully subdued by the Turks and was seen as a favourable starting point to ignite a revolt. The Russian Baltic Fleet under Orlov's brother, Alexi, reached Mani with British connivance, refitting and taking on supplies at Portsmouth. Unfortunately for Catherine and her advisors they over-estimated the Greeks' willingness to fight in another Russo-Turkish war. Both sides expected greater support from each other. The Rebels, a small force of around 1,400 men mustered by the Greeks augmented by a few troops from the five ships supplied by the Russians, were soon defeated by the Sultan's Albanian irregulars who proceeded to run amok among the population even after peace was signed. They were only finally removed ten years later by the Sultan's forces in combination with the Greek chieftains. Though the uprising was a failure the Russian Fleet defeated the Ottoman Fleet at the Battle of Chesme off Chios. The failure of the revolt damaged Russian prestige amongst the Greeks who would look to other allies to achieve liberation.

At the end of hostilities between Russia and Turkey, the subsequent Treaty of Kutchuk Kainardji (Küçük Kaynarca) in 1774, which did nothing for the Greeks, granted Catherine a vague protectorate over all Orthodox subjects in the Ottoman Empire, giving her a further excuse to champion the cause of the Serbs and Greeks in the Balkans ultimately for her own ends. So when her grandson was born in 1779, inspired by Potemkin she named him Constantine, with the intention that he was to be brought up as a Greek prince destined to rule Constantinople. Her 'Greek Plan' was to partition the Ottoman Empire between the Russian and Hapsburg empires followed by the resurrection of the Byzantine Empire centred in Constantinople. Her provocations incited a new war with Turkey in 1787. With the Morea still suffering under the depredations of the Albanians and an increase in brigandage, her renewed invitation to the Greeks of the Morea to take part fell on deaf ears. The Suliotes of Epirus were to be more responsive, but by now it would be Ali Pasha who had to be reckoned with.

The impetus given by the Revolution to French ambitions meant that their most successful general, Napoleon Bonaparte, too would have his eyes on former Venetian territories and ultimately the Ottoman's important Eyalet of Egypt. As a result of Napoleon's successful campaigns against the Austrian forces in Italy, Venice fell into French hands. Although the Hapsburgs lost significant territories in the subsequent Treaty of Campo Formio, the Austrians gained Venice, while the Ionian Islands and Preveza were transferred to French rule, becoming the French Departments of Greece. Napoleon informed the French Directory, the committee that ruled Revolutionary France, that the islands 'are more important to us than all Italy put together' and the French foreign minister, Charles Maurice de Talleyrand, that they would 'make us masters of the Adriatic and the Levant'. Napoleon believed he would see the collapse of the Ottoman Empire in his lifetime and the occupation of the islands was a major stake in securing a 'share of it for ourselves'. Napoleon wanted to ruin Britain by cutting it off from its sources of wealth in the East. To this end his plan was to strike at Egypt, cut a canal at Suez through to the Red Sea, and create a new sea route to India. In 1798 he set out for Egypt taking Malta from the Knights of St John on the way. Although Napoleon's land army was successful his navy came up against Nelson, who defeated it at the Battle of the Nile. With their forces overstretched the French abandoned Egypt in 1801. Napoleon's failure created the opportunity for Muhammad Ali Pasha who, seen as a liberator, had the support to loosen Ottoman authority and set up a semi-autonomous region.

French eastward expansionism forced Sultan Selim III to reconsider his foreign policy. France, that had hitherto been an ally, was now a threat, whereas Russia, so long an enemy was now a potential ally. After Catherine's death (1796) her successor Paul was eager for rapprochement with Turkey to offset French ambitions. Britain also became concerned to preserve Ottoman integrity as a buffer between France and its Asian territories. Franco-Russian relations would veer dramatically from hostility to friendship and back again but initially Russia and Turkey, joined by the British, allied to throw Napoleon out of the Ionian Islands. The Turks allowed the Russians right of transit through the Turkish Straits and a joint Russo-Turkish Fleet under Admirals Fyodor Ushakov and Cadhirbey (Kadir bey),

Fig. 8: 'The plumb-pudding in danger: or state epicures taking un petit souper' (1805) by cartoonist James Gillray: William Pitt, the British Prime Minister and Napoleon Bonaparte carve up the world.

blessed by the patriarch of Constantinople, took first Kythira, then Corfu in 1799. They established the Septinsular Republic comprising the islands, while the mainland ports, Preveza, Vonitza, and Butrint, became vassals of the Sultan under the protection of the tsar. A 'Byzantine Constitution' was drawn up which gave the Greeks a limited amount of self-government.

Napoleon set to work to try and split the allies over the islands while encouraging discord in the Sultan's Christian provinces, especially in janissary-dominated Serbia, Moldavia and Wallachia. In 1807, the French, who were now friends with Russia after the Treaty of Tilsit, succeeded in having the islands ceded back, but despite their efforts they could not hold on to them. The British chipped away at them one by one between 1809 and 1814. In 1815 they became the United States of the Ionian Islands under British protection until 1864, when they were handed over to the kingdom of Greece. The battle for the islands and the old Venetian ports would play a major role in the story of Ali Pasha.

For the Ottomans the Napoleonic Wars upset the balance of power in the Mediterranean, the manoeuvrings for strategic advantage between Britain and France eventually leading to Britain emerging as the leading nation. Egypt continued to be difficult to control and remained semi-autonomous and in the Balkans, Serbia and the Danube provinces remained vulnerable in the north. Turkey in Europe was beset with instability and power struggles.

The growth of ideas of nationalism as a consequence of the European Enlightenment and the French Revolution fermented revolt in Serbia and in the southern Balkans; in the meantime, lawlessness and brigandry were a way of life.

Life in Albania and Greece

The disruption of the Ottoman invasion had a significant effect on the local population, the repercussions of which continued to be felt in Ali's lifetime. Maintaining the early dynamism of invaders while transforming into a government of occupation and then into a harmonious state for all its population proved to be a problem the Turks never solved. Originally the Sultan held supreme power both as head of state and also as the caliph, the leader and protector of the Muslim world. Although people of 'the Book', followers of those religions that were founded on the Bible, were not persecuted, conditions became less favourable towards them. In certain regions this led to wholesale conversion to Islam. The Greek heartlands remained staunchly Orthodox Christian but further north into Albania the people saw it as more expedient to change faith. Deforestation and over-farming made life increasingly difficult. Those who could not stomach the new regime and had the means fled abroad, mainly to Italy, but many Greeks found a welcoming refuge with their fellow Orthodox in Russia. The Ottomans recognized the rights of other faiths to retain their religious practices and laws. This meant that minorities formed their own *millets* across the Empire to look after their affairs. In Europe the *Rum Millet* (Roman nation) comprised a variety of ethnic groups and languages all united by their Orthodox faith, with its religious and political head the Ecumenical Patriarch in Constantinople and dominated by Greeks.

By the time of Ali, the Sultans had become victims of a system that fostered court intrigue and isolation within the Topkapi palace complex at Constantinople, where political power was in the hands of the grand vizier and the council known as the Sublime Porte. Local power was delegated to local governors who exercised varying degrees of autonomy. The Empire was divided into eyalets or pashaliks, areas ruled over by a pasha of the three tails whose ceremonial staff was decorated with feathers. The Eyalet of Rumeli or Rumelia took in most of the Balkans and was governed from Monastir, modern Bitola, in the Former Republic of Macedonia. The Morea formed its own eyalet with its capital at Tripolitza. Eyalets were further divided into sanjaks, ruled by a bey, and then *timars* (fiefs). Throughout the century the complicated administrative areas of Greece and Albania were constantly shifting. Control of Ioannina moved from the Sanjak of Thessaly, ruled by a pasha at Tirhala (Trikkala), to its own direct government appointee, Mehmet 'Kalo' Pasha, in the latter half of the century. Military organization and law and order operated on a number of levels, from the elite janissaries to local policing.

Central control was hindered by the lack of technical advances. Communications in many areas had not been improved for years, neither had modes of transport. Piracy at sea meant merchants were unwilling to risk their goods to shipping while land transport was still medieval in practice. The mountainous terrain of the Balkans inhibited movement and banditry added a further impediment. The main artery into Albania from the capital was still the old Roman road, the Via Egnatia, which ran from Constantinople via Thessalonika, Monastir, Ochrid, Elbasan and Tirana to Durazzo (modern Durrës) on the Adriatic, and on to Rome. To reach Ioannina from Thessaly involved crossing the wild mountain passes of the high Pindus range. These routes were still treacherous 100 years later as Edward Lear witnessed when he crossed back and forth in 1848–9. Passing through a narrow defile on the road from Ochrid to Elbasan he records:

> Beyond this… the road was perhaps more dangerous, and our progress still slower; at the narrowest point we encountered some fifty laden mules, and a long time was consumed in arranging the coming and going trains, lest either should jostle and pitch into the abyss beneath. At another sharp turning lay a dead ox skinned, filling up half the track (the edge of that track a sheer precipice of sixty or eighty feet in depth), and by no measures could we cause our horses to pass the alarming object; nor till our united strength had dragged the defunct to a niche in the rock, could we progress one foot's length. At a third *cattivo passo* [bad pass] a projecting rock interfered with the sumpter horses' idea of a straight line; and, lo! down went all the baggage, happily to no great distance, but far enough to occasion a half hour's delay in readjusting it.

To the south the best land route from Epirus to Athens, and the one taken by Lord Byron in 1809, was to cross into the Peloponnese and follow the coast to Corinth, and then into Attica.

Under Ottoman rule land could still be held in private, particularly smallholdings and land in more marginal areas; land given to religious foundations or put aside for charitable purposes, whether Muslim or Christian, was also respected. But newly conquered territory was seen as a potentially valuable resource for the Empire and a source of revenue. Land in Europe taken during Ottoman expansion, usually from those who had resisted invasion, was redistributed and given to key members of the military, particularly non-salaried cavalrymen (*Sipahis*) and janissaries, as compensation for military service, and to high-ranking slaves (*kuls*) of the Sultan to be managed as personal fiefdoms. This land reverted back to the Sultan when the occupier moved on or died, to be distributed anew. Taxes were gathered by the proprietor and a few days' labour a year was required from the peasants. Once the Empire ceased expanding, from the sixteenth century onwards, this relatively benign system fell into decline as the military class began to turn inwards on the Empire carving it up into private, hereditary landholdings, which a weakened administration was forced to recognize. By the time of Ali, most land was held under this new *chiflik* system, with the peasants reduced to serfs, no longer free to work for their own monetary gain, but labouring under the rule of a feudal lord for many days a week while a larger percentage of their harvest was seized. This oppressive rule caused many peasants to migrate from *chiflik* controlled areas, which in Greece meant into the mountains where Ottoman authority was tenuous.

Armatoli and Klephts

The armatoli were the Greek militia given the responsibility of keeping order in inhospitable regions plagued by banditry. Their opponents were known as klephts, from the Greek for thief. Originally the klephts were merely brigands who tormented travellers and raided villages, but after the Ottoman invasion many of those who retreated to the mountains to retain their independence took on the klephtic life. The numbers grew over the centuries so that they were able to maintain a warlike lifestyle that included raiding and highway robbery, blurring the line between resistance to Ottoman authority and plain lawlessness.

Fig. 9: *Warrior of Sellaida* (1825) by Louis Dupré.

In charge of the armatoli was a captain assisted by a second in command, usually a relative, and a number of section leaders. The captain often succeeded to or inherited his territories, which he was then allowed to run as a personal fiefdom with the effect that self-aggrandize-ment often led to a regime of extortion and violence being foisted on the local peasantry. This was perhaps hardly surprising as the captains were often drawn from individuals that had already achieved notoriety as a klepht, their reputation obliging the authorities to give them amnesty and then turning their talents to attempting to control the brigand groups operating in the region. As the links between the armatoli and the klephts were therefore close, this had mixed results. There was in fact little difference in organization between the armatoli and the klephts. The rank-and-file soldiers, the *palikaria* trained daily with their weapons, particularly developing skills of marksmanship with their prized weapon, the *kariofili*, a long musket. Like their enemies, the klephts, the armatoli had to match them for physical endurance and resil-ience to hunger and thirst. They also used similar guerrilla tactics, employing swift mobility and the ambush, often under cover of darkness. When under attack however the armatoli could throw up improvised forts, and if need be resort to swordplay. The more the authorities were unable to contain the activities of the klephts so their mystique grew, creating a heroic model of freedom that would be romanticized and have important consequences in the Greek War of Independence. The existence of so many armed and experienced fighters would also enable the Greeks to become a more formidable fighting force when the time came.

In areas where the Muslim population was small, particularly in the Peloponnese, Christians were able to hold on to or even eventually acquire property rights. This could be achieved by circumventing Ottoman legal proceedings or in lieu of services rendered in keeping the mountain passes safe. The system of communal administration of the Greek provinces was less successful in the north of the Peloponnese. The redistribution of popula-tion, with mountain areas being reoccupied, meant that certain districts maintained a form of independence from the Ottoman administration, developing their own social organization based around family and clan ties. In Thesprotia in western Epirus two tribes of Albanian origin stubbornly held on to their semi-autonomous way of life, the Muslim Tsamides or Chams, a south Albanian sub-group, and particularly the inhabitants of the mountainous area of Suli. The historic core of Suli consisted of four villages and their linked families, the heads of which formed a council. Renowned for their fighting prowess, the Suliotes ranks were swelled during the eighteenth century by disaffected Greeks drawn to the remoteness of their wild refuge, and a further seven villages were added lower down the mountain, form-ing a frontier zone from which the inhabitants would retreat in times of trouble. The code of these independently minded and warlike people was summed up by George Finlay as: 'Depredation they honoured with the name of war, and war they considered to be the only honourable occupation for a true Suliot.' Classified by the Turks as Greeks, they spoke both Albanian and Greek. The mountain regions enjoyed their degree of autonomy at a price. It was a harsh environment, and the communities, who relied heavily on sheep husbandry for their survival, were obliged to protect themselves and their flocks from raids and the arbi-trary acts of the Ottoman provincial governors by going well-armed. With the addition of marginalized Greeks, the constant surplus of able-bodied men meant it that was a small step to the formation of a warrior society. Amongst the Albanians this long-standing expediency of resorting to warfare as a way of life encouraged them to take up arms for a living. They became the most renowned mercenaries within the Empire, offering their services to pashas or Sultan alike, and increasingly taking power from the janissaries. For others in Albania and Greece banditry was an expedient alternative.

At the local level, elements of the pre-existing Byzantine military system had been retained by the Ottomans. In areas that had high levels of brigandage or in regions that were difficult for the Ottoman authorities to govern due to the inaccessible terrain, some Greeks were allowed to keep their privileges of self-policing and a degree of autonomy as a condition of accepting Ottoman rule. Banditry became the scourge throughout the Balkans and partic- ularly in the mountainous regions of Macedonia, Epirus and Thessaly. The bandits, known as klephts, by all accounts terrorized the countryside in time-honoured fashion; murdering, raping and pillaging. As the Christian klepht targeted the wealthy, which meant the Turk or Ottoman foreigner, the tax collector, the well-living primate or priest and the successful merchant, they came to be idolized, unlike their Muslim counterparts, as an expression of protest by the poor Christian peasantry. Given their inability to impose law and order, the Turks found it expedient to continue the local irregular militias requiring them to guard the roads and passes and allowing them to collect taxes. These Christian armatoli were organized in administrative districts known as armatolikia within the Ottoman system and responsible to local governors. During the eighteenth century there were around seventeen armatolikia. Ten of them were located in Thessaly and the eastern regions of central Greece, four of them in Epirus, Acarnania, and Aetolia, and three in Macedonia. The increase in numbers of dispossessed and warlike Albanians throughout Rumeli after the invasion was a challenge to the armatoli and to the military authority of the Ottomans where the use of their supreme weapon, their cavalry, was restricted.

The local governors often found it to their advantage to employ a thief to catch a thief, but as there was a high turnover of governors, the one-time armatoli could find himself next day a klepht and vice versa, blurring the distinction between them. Roles and allegiances reversed as the situation demanded while all the while the delicate status quo was maintained, with the Ottoman authorities progressively finding it more difficult to distinguish peacekeeper from lawbreaker. As both groups began to bond under a common Greek identity and mutual antipathy to their foreign conquerors, the abuses and independence of the armatoli lead to the Ottomans increasingly seeing them as a threat to their authority. In consequence, in order to decrease their power and numbers, the Turks took direct control, appointing a government official, the dervendji-pasha, authorized to protect the mountain passes and supplied with his own troops. This policy was successful in reducing numbers and, according to Finlay, local communities even preferred to pay for exemption from such obligations. This paved the way for Albanian mercenaries to be employed and, in areas with a large Muslim population, it was possible to give command to Albanians rather than Greeks. In 1740 Suleyman of Argyrocastro was appointed as pasha of Ioannina and dervendji-pasha with strict orders not only to curb the power of the armatoli, but to watch over the Greeks who were suspected of intriguing with the Russians. Suleyman achieved this by exploiting the greed, internal jealousies and feuds

Fig. 10: Separated by a narrow strip of water the people of Corfu inhabit a different Italianate world: Carnival in the early nineteenth century with onlookers from the mainland in *fustanellas*.

of the armatoli captains, aided by the people who suffered at their hands, and introducing Muslims into Christian districts to weaken their organization. This policy was continued by Kurt Pasha who succeeded him for fifteen years as pasha of Ioannina and dervendji-pasha, and then around the time the Russians invaded the Morea, as pasha of Berat and dervendji-pasha. The powers of dervendji-pasha gave him the pretext to reduce pay as well as numbers. When Russia was given the right to protect Christians within the Ottoman Empire after the peace of 1774, these measures were increased. The post of dervendji-pasha was one Ali would succeed to in 1787 with the same obligations.

Dervendji-pasha (*derbendler basbugu*)

The dervendji-pasha, or governor of the passes, was a highly influential position within the Ottoman administration in Greece and Albania. From the beginning of the eighteenth century the Porte had made various efforts to deal with the problem of banditry in the mountains, particularly by the klephts, and the growing insubordination of the armatoli. Eventually, in an effort to bring the Greek and Albanian paramilitaries into the system of government the post of dervendji-pasha was created in 1761 with jurisdiction over all law enforcement and with the intention of neutralizing both the bandits and the armatoli. The dervendji-pasha was given power to maintain his own small official army. First under Kurt Pasha and then Ali Pasha, the post's potential for wielding both military and political power was realized. Ali's holding of the office from 1787 to 1820 was an important step in his road to power.

Fig. 11: *The Abduction of a Herzegovenian Woman* (1861), a typically overwrought depiction of Turkish/European relations as depicted by Czech artist Jaroslav Čermák, simultaneously giving its audience the required amount of disgust and titillation.

Epirus and the Wider World

Although Epirus was regarded by foreigners as an unknown and exotic backwater, it was not cut off from outside influences or the world. Outside the Ottoman Empire there had long been trade links through Italy and into Europe and the ties of emigration went as far afield as Paris, Moscow or the Crimea. Increasing contact meant that the Western fascination with

"Tirailleur Francais, et Chevau-Leger de l'Armée du Pacha de Rhodes." ___ *Evolutions of French Mounted Riflemen.*

Fig. 12: James Gilray's view of Napoleon's Egyptian campaign as the French cavalry, on a donkey, engage with the heroic-looking Pasha of Rhodes in 1799.

the Orient was matched by a yearning for Western ideas and goods within the Empire, particularly by its European subjects. The end of the eighteenth century was dominated by the fallout from three defining events in European and World history: the American colonies' successful achievement of independence from Britain (1783), the French Revolution (1789) and the rise of Napoleon. These were significant not only for their political outcomes but also as embodiments of the ideas engendered by the intellectual and cultural movements of the time. The ideas of liberty that were the driving force behind these events had a profound influence on Turkey's disenchanted communities that were becoming more aware of their ethnic identities and nascent nationalism. The realities of life were complex but the propaganda and media of the day, as now, dealt in stereotypes. In the West the Turk was often viewed with a mix of terror and admiration. The Oriental was seen as capricious, lazy and cruel, but also as chivalrous, brave and noble, and untainted with the base dealings of money and gain; these latter dirty necessities being in the hands of the Turks' non-Muslim subjects, mainly the Greeks, Jews and Armenians, who were tainted by such activities.

The Enlightenment thinking that underscored these revolutionary movements did not go unheeded in Greece. Rigas Feraios was a political thinker and writer from Thessaly, heavily influenced by French ideas, who was prepared to take action to back his radical views. In 1793 he went to Vienna where he published pamphlets setting out his views on human rights and government. In an effort to seek aid from Napoleon in support of a pan-Balkan uprising against the Ottomans he was betrayed and captured in Trieste on his way to Venice by the Austrian authorities, then allied to Turkey, and handed over to the Ottomans, who had him tortured and executed. As a consequence he became a Greek national hero. Adamantios Korais, a humanist scholar and educator from Smyrna who lived for many years in exile in Paris was also highly influential in spreading Enlightenment ideals in Greece. The Italian and then French occupied Ionian Islands and westward facing Epirus were well-placed to absorb such influences and the contemporary accounts attest to the ideas of Rigas and Korais being circulated.

A further aspect of the Enlightenment for the Westerner spurred on by the desire for individual experience was foreign travel. For the aristocracy and those of sufficient means from northern Europe, and particularly Britain, this meant embarking on the Grand Tour. It was deemed edifying for the young to be exposed to the culture of the classical world and the Renaissance first-hand. From the late seventeenth century young men, often accompanied by a tutor and following planned itineraries, headed south to France and Italy to study history and art, and take in the latest in fashionable society. The outbreak of the French and Napoleonic wars in Europe put an abrupt halt to such undertakings. With the tour that usually culminated in the cultural delights (and otherwise) of Italy now being off limits, new itineraries were needed and Portugal and Corsica became destinations for a few. Fortuitously, when Napoleon invaded Egypt and the Ottomans warmed towards Britain new horizons were opened up. This had particular appeal for those educated within a system that laid such great emphasis on the Classics (Latin and Greek) for the superior civilization of ancient Greece, not only on the Greek mainland but in Turkey itself, could now be observed first-hand.

From the late eighteenth to the middle of the nineteenth century an influx of dilettantes, academics, artists, writers, travellers and eccentrics descended unto the barren plains of Greece to pick over the marble bones of the past in the hope of finding some meaningful connection with Homer and Thucydides. The Levantine Lunatics, as Lord Byron termed them, many of them British, but also Germans, French and other Westerners, went on to paint, record and loot the past. Marbles, such as those made famous by Lord Elgin, pilfered or otherwise from classical sites, made their way into the country houses and museums of Europe. Byron, although critical of his contemporaries, was in many ways one of them, the difference being that he made a point of appreciating the here and now, the reality of the Oriental present as opposed to the classical past, and embracing the people who lived there even if they were regarded as debased specimens by his fellow travellers. Byron was in the forefront of Greek travel and his writings brought the Oriental and revolutionary Greece to the public's notice. Many of his fellows were more ostentatiously philhellene, or lovers of everything Greek, but few were to achieve martyrdom like Byron in the cause of Greek freedom. Those that trod the same paths also left memoirs and journals, in fact there was an outpouring, for as well as the valuable academic works and new discoveries, everyone thought their own experience worth sharing, until the 'Greek travels' as an idiom became played out.

Although Enlightenment thinking was crucial to the spread of notions of political and personal liberty it created a reaction that expressed itself through what has been termed the Romantic Movement and romanticism. Though many of the so-called Romantics were loathed to attach themselves to any kind of label the European public was ready to idolize artists and thinkers, as well as politicians and soldiers, who expressed the often-conflicting emotions associated with the movement. The two greatest artistic heroes of the age, Beethoven and Byron, began as supporters of revolution, but their politics became ambiguous as idealism turned sour with the Reign of Terror (1793–4) and the French Republic's greatest general, Napoleon Bonaparte, crowning himself as Emperor in 1804. Both Byron and Beethoven were early admirers of Napoleon. On learning of Napoleon's elevation to the laurel crown, Beethoven famously scratched out his name from the title page of his just completed *Eroica* (3rd) Symphony, and rededicated it to his long-standing patron in Vienna, the Bohemian aristocrat Joseph Franz Maximilian von Lobkowitz. As France exported the revolution outside its borders, threatening the old regimes and monarchies of Europe, Beethoven remained true to the ideals of liberty, but under Napoleon these French ambitions had turned from liberating the people of Europe to empire building. Byron, an aristocrat himself, mirrored the opposing forces in his own personality. As much as he advocated freedom, especially personal freedom, he was prone to hero worship and to idolizing individuals and types, eager to find similar Napoleonic qualities in others. Napoleon and Byron, remote from one another in distance but linked by fame, were to play a major role in Ali Pasha's life. When Byron set sail for Epirus he was bringing with him a complex of attitudes and misconceptions that would begin the shaping of Ali's legend.

Chapter 2

The Creation of a Legend

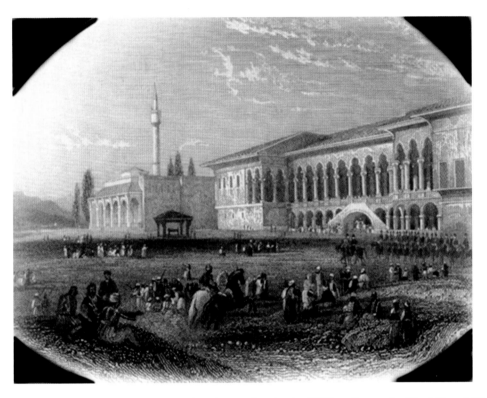

Fig. 13: Engraving by Edward Finden taken from a drawing by William Purser for *The Life and Works of Lord Byron* (1833).

> The sun had sunk behind vast Tomerit,[1]
> And Laos[2] wide and fierce came roaring by;
> The shades of wonted night were gathering yet,
> When, down the steep banks winding warily,
> Childe Harolde saw, like meteors in the sky,
> The glittering minarets of Tepalen,[3]

---

[1] Mt Tomorr; the highest peak in Southern Albania (2,416m/7,927ft) and a highly visible landmark.

[2] Aoös (Greek), Vjosë, Vjosa (Albanian) flows from Greece into Albania where it is joined by the Drino near Tepelenë.

[3] Tepelenë, the site of Ali Pasha's palace.

Whose walls o'erlook the stream; and drawing nigh,
He heard the busy hum of warrior-men
Swelling the breeze that sigh'd along the lengthening glen.

LVI   He pass'd the sacred Haram's[4] silent tower,
And underneath the wide o'er-arching gate
Survey'd the dwelling of this chief of power,
Where all around proclaim'd his high estate.
Amidst no common pomp the despot sate,   500
While busy preparation shook the court,
Slaves, eunuchs, soldiers, guests, and santons[5] wait;
Within, a palace, and without, a fort:
Here men of every clime appear to make resort.

LVII   Richly caparison'd, a ready row
Of armed horse, and many a warlike store,
Circled the wide extending court below;
Above, strange groups adorn'd the corridore;
And oft-times through the Area's echoing door,
Some high-capp'd Tartar spurr'd his steed away: 510
The Turk, the Greek, the Albanian, and the Moor,
Here mingled in their many-hued array,
While the deep war-drum's sound announced the close of day.

LXII   In marble-paved pavilion, where a spring
Of living water from the centre rose,   550
Whose bubbling did a genial freshness fling,
And soft voluptuous couches breathed repose,
ALI[6] reclined, a man of war and woes:
Yet in his lineaments ye cannot trace,
While Gentleness her milder radiance throws
Along that aged venerable face,
The deeds that lurk beneath, and stain him with disgrace.

LXIII It is not that yon hoary lengthening beard
Ill suits the passions which belong to youth;   560

---

[4] *Harem*, the women's quarters in the palace reserved for wives, concubines and slaves.
[5] Muslim monk or hermit often regarded as a saint; in Albania specifically a dervish, usually a Sufi who has taken vows of poverty and austerity, and particularly of the Mevlevi order known for their 'whirling' dance.
[6] Ali Pasha.

Fig. 14: *Ali Pasha hears the pleas of a supplicant* (1813) by Charles Robert Cockerell.

> Love conquers age -- so Hafiz[7] hath averr'd,
> So sings the Teian,[8] and he sings in sooth --
> But crimes that scorn the tender voice of truth,

---

[7] Fourteenth century Persian poet whose verses celebrating love, wine and nature are traditionally treated as allegoric by Sufis.

[8] Anacreon, a Greek lyric poet (*c.*582–*c.*485BC) from Teos in Asia Minor, famous for his drinking and love songs and poems.

Beseeming all men ill, but most the man
In years, have mark'd him with a tiger's tooth;
Blood follows blood, and, through their mortal span,
In bloodier acts conclude those who with blood began.

From *Childe Harold's Pilgrimage*, Canto II, published in 1812.

On the publication of *Childe Harold's Pilgrimage* in 1812, Byron later remarked, 'I woke up to find myself famous'. The poem's overnight success made the young Lord George Gordon an instant celebrity, and as a consequence of its international fame promoted the mystique of a hitherto obscure Albanian warlord, Ali Pasha. Its narrative follows the journey of a dissolute and disenchanted youth who seeks escape through exotic travel, a theme that was perfectly timed to tap into the growing Continental tastes for romanticism and Orientalism. It was not a work of pure fiction though, but an imaginative retelling of the author's own adventures, interspersed with meditations arising from his new experiences. One such key moment, the dramatic and evocative description of Byron's alter ego Childe Harold's arrival at Ali's court, gave the European reading public a tantalizing glimpse into a hidden world, and forever linked Ali with Byron both in life and the imagination. This fanciful version of the real-life, and at the time unlikely, meeting of the rising star of the Romantic Movement and a Balkan petty despot is conjured up in dreamlike language reminiscent of Samuel Taylor Coleridge's *Kubla Khan*, with its vivid portrayal of the Mongol emperor's paradise palace.[9] It was at Tepelene that Ali had built his own version of paradise, a lavish palace or seraglio, and it was here that Byron and his old Cambridge friend 'Cam' Hobhouse were invited to meet him, in 1809. Hobhouse kept his own diary of the journey and his account, with its description of Ali, was published a year later, filling out the prosaic details.[10]

When Byron and Hobhouse met Ali Pasha he was by then an established potentate in the Oriental fashion, and as a pasha of three tails, the highest rank, commonly given the title of vizier. Although Byron relished the notion of being a pioneer in travelling to such a remote region as Albania, and it is true that Ali's court would be relatively inundated with Western visitors following in his footsteps, he and Hobhouse were not the first Westerners to pay Ali court. Ali's growing clout and reputation had made him of great interest to the 'powers' (Britain, France, Austria and Russia) as well as of concern to the Sultan. The French had established diplomatic relations since 1797, and François Pouqueville, who would have a profound influence on French writers and politics, was their ambassador there from 1806 to 1815. Britain, concerned with this French influence, responded by making its own representations, and from 1801 onwards had formal relations. Captain William Leake was their man

---

[9] Completed in 1797 but not published till 1816.

[10] Apart from unauthorized English editions becoming widely available, within ten years extracts from *Childe Harold* were translated into Portuguese (1812), then Spanish, German, French, Dutch, Italian, Russian, Polish and Hungarian; Hobhouse's *Travels in Albania and other provinces of Turkey in 1809 and 1810* went through a number of revisions and editions.

in Ioannina, Ali's capital. Leake was well travelled and knowledgeable with a military man's interest in topography and ancient history. His own meticulous accounts of his experiences, *Travels in Northern Greece*, were not published until 1835, by which time Ali's name was well known. Leake's description of Tepelene, on a bluff above the River Vjosë (Aoos) with its palace 'one of the most romantic and delightful country-houses that can be imagined', while accurate, would not linger in the imagination to challenge Byron. Reality and romance would be in continuous tension in the recording of all that surrounded Ali. In his diary, Hobhouse records his first impression of Tepelene as 'ill-looking and small'.

Byron's poetic antennae were sensitive to a different reality and alert to the making of a legend, one growing in the telling there and then. Ali's life had already been committed to verse in the *Alipashiad* by his court poet, Haxhi Shehreti (Hatzi-Secharis, Hatzi-Sechris or Hadji Seret), a work Leake analysed in his *Travels*, and visitors were honoured in Ali's presence with war-songs about his victories over the Suliotes. Through Byron's eyes this inflated heroic vision of Ali, Albania and Greece became the raw material for an Oriental dream. Byron was also sympathetic to other resonances. His descriptions and meditations chimed in with universal, grass roots notions of liberty and nationalism that were taking hold all over Europe. In Britain, memories of the Jacobite Rebellions of 1715 and 1745 were still fresh. Rob Roy McGregor, whose exploits were fictionalized by Sir Walter Scott in 1817, was a prototype of the Romantic outlaw and freedom fighting folk hero. A legend too in his lifetime, he was moulded into a cultural icon of the nineteenth century. The tragically heroic defeat of Bonnie Prince Charlie and the Scottish clans at Culloden, which finally put an end to rival claimants to the British crown, only added to this myth-making. The stories around Ali, ambiguous and malleable, provided new source material for the outlaw turned hero, or tyrant turned freedom fighter, and Byron was particularly sensitive to the Romantic appeal of these contradictions.

Because of his turbulent family background Byron had spent his early childhood growing up in relatively humble circumstances in Aberdeenshire. As a Radical, he would have had little sympathy with the absolutism of the Stuart pretenders to the British throne, but he was descended on his mother's side from King James I of Scotland, and the history of his 'Ill starr'd, though brave' ancestors who were 'destined to die at Culloden', was all around him. His poem *Lachin y Gair* (1807) recalls the mountains of his youth where:

> my young footsteps in infancy, wander'd:
> My cap was the bonnet, my cloak was the plaid;
> On chieftains, long perish'd, my memory ponder'd,
> As daily I strode through the pine-cover'd glade;

With such thoughts in mind he found in Albania a second home. The rugged Epirote Mountains immediately struck a chord, being 'Caledonian, with a kinder climate', and the independence and feuding of the Albanian families reminded him of the humbled Scottish clans. The right to wear their highland dress, the kilt, had only been restored to them six years before his birth, so when he wrote, 'The Albanese struck me forcibly by their resemblance to the Highlanders of Scotland, in dress, figure and manner of living', there was an added poignancy. These foreign highlanders inhabiting their 'glens' dressed in warlike attire that consisted of a 'kilt', or *fustanella*, recalled the lost highland glory. Even the Bristol born Hobhouse succumbed to this Caledonian nostalgia; the Gulf of Arta, reminding him of Loch Lomond. A few years later, Sir Henry Holland (from Cheshire), who went on to study medicine at Edinburgh University, also made the connection. He visited Albania between 1812 and 1813 and in his subsequent account put the size of population at less than 2 million with 'the superficial extent of Ali Pasha's dominions not differing greatly from that of the sister kingdom' of Scotland.

Ali already had a ferocious reputation. Byron and Hobhouse were not totally ignorant of this before they set off for his territories, but they were young; Byron was only 21, and somewhat politically naive. They had decided to visit Ali seemingly as the result of a last-minute whim while on a stopover in Malta, a port of call on their Grand Tour. As the usual itinerary for such an enterprise was no longer available due to Napoleon's occupation of Italy, they had taken a circuitous route via Portugal and Spain, with the intention of making for Constantinople and the Levant instead; wanderings that would provide the raw material for *Childe Harold*. Britain's treaty with the Ottomans in 1799 had opened up the option of visiting the Balkans on the way, and in particular Greece, the authentic birthplace of classical civilization. Albania was a further detour.

Malta, liberated from the French in 1800, was quickly becoming key to British interests and shipping in the Mediterranean. Here they met Spyridon and George Foresti, father and son, Greeks from Zante, one of the Ionian Islands, and both in the service of the British Government. Spyridon had acquired a dashing reputation when, as Assistant to the English Consul at Zante, he had single-handedly boarded *The Grand Duchess of Tuscany*, shot and overpowered the pirate who had captured her and salvaged £80,000 worth of cargo. With the islands back in the hands of the French, he was now the exiled English resident in Corfu, apparently with time on his hands. Idling on Malta as yet undecided as to their next move, it was Spyridon who seems to have been largely responsible for Byron and Hobhouse visiting Albania and Ali.

Foresti showed them the sights, all the while beguiling them with stories of Ali, who was at this time friendly towards Britain. Napoleon had apparently sent Ali a snuffbox with his picture on it. Byron wrote to his mother that Ali thought 'the snuffbox was very well, but the picture he could excuse, as he neither liked *it* nor the *original*'. Hobhouse's diary records that Foresti told them of 'some curious passages from the wars of the Suliotes written in Modern Greek' in which,

> Three hundred women flung themselves over a cliff. The son of the chief Suliote being taken before the son of Ali Pacha in Ioannina, the young Pacha addressed him with, 'Well, we have got you and we will now burn you alive' – 'I know it,' replied the prisoner, 'and when my father catches you he will serve you in the same manner.'

Within six days, in late September, Byron and Hobhouse were aboard *The Spider* and under sail bound for Preveza, with letters of introduction to 'Captain Leake' at Ioannina and to Ali's court. The exact motives and circumstances of Foresti in diverting Byron towards Ali are murky and will be examined later.

On arrival at a newly built barrack at Salora, the tiny port and custom depot of Arta, Byron was regaled by songs from the Albanian guards. One song eulogized the taking of the nearby port of Preveza from the French (and its Greek defenders), while extolling the name of Ali. Hobhouse tells us that when Ali's name came round in a song it was dwelt on and roared out with particular energy. This event had taken place eleven years earlier, but the material found its way into *Childe Harold*, where Byron paraphrased the war-songs sung by the victorious dancing Suliotes:

Remember the moment when Previsa fell,
The shrieks of the conquered, the conqueror's yell;
The roofs that we fired, and the plunder we shared,
The wealthy we slaughtered, the lovely we spared.

I talk not of mercy, I talk not of fear;
He neither must know who would serve the Vizier;
Since the days of our prophet, the crescent ne'er saw
A chief ever glorious like Ali Pasha.

These were the very same Suliotes he had heard about killing themselves rather than surrender to Ali. The song goes on to glorify Ali's eldest son, 'Dark Muchtar' in Byron's phrase, who with his horsemen was at this time distinguishing himself campaigning on the Danube against the Russians.

Thomas Hughes who travelled through Greece between 1813 and 1814 with the architect and archaeologist Charles Cockerell records in his own *Travels* that songs of Ali Pasha's exploits were commonplace. As he sailed through the Gulf of Corinth toward Epirus, he was introduced to Ali in song by the sailors on his boat who 'struck up one of those wild national airs… [which] turn generally upon the exploits and adventures of Ali Pasha or some other modern hero'. Byron's telling of the taking of Preveza avoids the ferocity of Ali's attack and the mutilation of the executed prisoners. These dark deeds had been reported to Napoleon and published by Captain JP Bellaire in 1805, but he judiciously does not mention the beheading of the Greeks in front of Ali or the pyramid of skulls. Byron was receiving a swift education in the shifting alliances of Albanian politics. As he noted 'some daring mountain-band' would challenge Ali's power and 'from their rocky hold / Hurl their defiance', but they would not yield; they could always be bought for gold however. Indeed, adaptability was a necessary virtue of survival. As Edward Lear noted of his host when lodging in Himara many years later (1848); a Greek 'palikar', he had had an adventurous history as 'one of the Khimariotes taken by Ali Pasha as hostages, and was long imprisoned at Ioannina; he was also in the French-Neapolitan service, and more lately, one of Lord Byron's suite at Missolonghi' during the Greek War of Independence.

Despite any doubts, Byron delighted in the novelty of Albania, liked the Albanians and in a letter to his mother is full of admiration for the Albanian troops, the 'best in the Turkish service' and much taken with everything Turkish. Byron's attitude to things foreign was open. He made a point of not being biased towards Britain, taking everything on merit, and was disappointed with his servant Fletcher for complaining about everything, from the accommodation,

Fig. 15: The Palace of Ali Pasha at Ioannina from *The Life and Works of Lord Byron* illustrated by JD Harding, 1835.

the modes of transport, the food and drink, to the lack of tea! Hobhouse did not share Byron's wholehearted enthusiasm. In his diary he relates that foreigners were not welcome in Epirus, noted the subservience of the local Greeks and the arrogant behaviour of the Turks who happily let off their guns at whoever displeased them. At the same time he introduces his audience to what became the familiar tropes of Orientalist art and literature: the luxury and colour, the chaos and the squalor, the secretive latticed windows of the houses, the bustle of the bazaar.

Their first encounter with the ferocity of Ali's rule was on entering his seat of power at Ioannina, where they were sickened by the sight of an arm and part of the right side of a body hanging from a tree. A reminder that Ali's

> dread command
> Is lawless law; for with a bloody hand
> He sways a nation, turbulent and bold: 420

Their first impression was that these were the remains of a robber. Although in his *Diary* Hobhouse says the sight made he and Byron 'a little sick', in his *Travels* he shows a certain amount of restraint in condemning this spectacle of Eastern barbarity by commenting that it was only fifty years previously that such a sight would have been common within Temple Bar in London. Only later were they made aware it was a part of the unfortunate Euthemos Blacavas, an insurrectionist Greek priest beheaded five days earlier. If it was Blacavas, who had led a nationalist revolt in Thessaly in the spring of the previous year, it had been some

Fig. 16: *The house of Nicolo Argyris in Janina* (1813) by Charles Cockerell, where most of the notable British visitors lodged. Hughes refers to the plate that illustrates his book as a 'beautiful and accurate view'.

time since he was captured, tortured and then executed. Anyone who had read Pouqueville's rather gloomily gothic account of his own first audience with Ali would have been prepared for such macabre sights. On his second meeting, Pouqueville passed two freshly severed heads stuck on poles adorning the courtyard of the audience chamber. These had not been there the day before, but went unremarked by the mingling clients and petitioners awaiting their turn. Byron's poetic account is more impressionistic and circumspect, hinting that such dark deeds 'lurk beneath', and prophetically that through the stain of Ali's 'bloody hand', 'bloodier acts conclude those who with blood began'.

Byron's likening of Albania with Scotland recognizes perhaps more than a superficial similarity of topography and clan structure, but of poverty and disadvantage well away from the effete world of the court of George III and the Regency. Byron the outsider, not entirely welcome in his own land, was happy to embrace fellow outsiders in a way that other well-bred travellers were not. The examples of Ali's cruelty were another matter. From the reports these acts would appear as though they were something unique to the East. By twenty-first century standards Ali's behaviour was appalling, and seemed shocking to many of his visitors, but the superiority of the Westerners towards what they saw as Oriental despotism would give the impression that they were coming from a world that was totally unused to such things. Yet, in Britain 'Butcher' Cumberland, George III's uncle, had not got his nickname for nothing in the aftermath of Culloden (1745–7), it had not been long since the French revolutionaries had displayed their own taste for bloodletting

Fig. 17: Lord Byron in Albanian dress (1813) from a painting by Robert Philips.

in the dark days of the Terror (1793–4), or the atrocities committed by both sides in the Dos de Mayo Uprising and the Peninsular War (1808–14), so unflinchingly depicted by Francisco Goya in his series of prints *The Disasters of War* (undertaken between 1810 and 1820).

Ali was not in Ioannina but away on campaign in 'Illyricum', as Byron put it, besieging his brother-in-law, Ibrahim Pasha, in the well-fortified town of Berat. The rather put out Leake, whose plans had been inconvenienced by Byron's arrival, had informed Ali of their visit, paving the way for an audience by telling him that his visitor was a man of great family. In response, Ali had left instructions for Byron to be treated as befitted an 'Englishman of rank'; everything provided gratis. The guests were put up in the house of Nicolo Argyri Vrettos, a Greek merchant and patient put upon default host for Ali's foreign guests. Cockerell and Hughes also stayed with Agryri three years later. Hughes found the ingratitude of Ali towards the Vrettos family, which he had reduced to such poverty that they could hardly cope with the upkeep of their house, worthy of comment whereas Byron was much less questioning in his observations.

Once installed in the house of Nicolo Argyri, Byron fell under the spell of the vizier's generosity and luxury and he and Hobhouse were soon trying on Albanian costume. Byron's may have been the one he was to wear in his famous portrait by Thomas Phillips, painted in 1813. They were treated royally, shown round Mukhtar's palace by Hussein, his 10 years old, but very grave, son, who entered into a courteous conversation about the British parliament. He asked the two noblemen whether they were in the Lords or the Commons, thus impressing them with his knowledge of external affairs. Mahomet, Ali's other grandson, also around 10 or 12 years old, showed them round Ali's palace, which was said to have 300 chambers. The son of Ali's second son, Veli, pasha of the Morea, was living in the palace and already had a pashalik of his own.

In contrast to Byron's fulsome verse, the prose accounts of Hobhouse and Leake dwell on the often shabby appearance of Ali's retinue and the quaint juxtapositions of Oriental opulence, silks and furnishings, harems and slaves, with haphazard and misjudged attempts at Western taste. All this existed, it was noted, within a region of backwardness and squalor, with the exception of those areas with proximity to Italy and a history of interaction with the outside world. Complaints of the poverty and dirt of the accommodation with its resident vermin are frequent; even if for the seasoned traveller through Italy, the fleas were not necessarily any worse. The population too was often unwashed and the fleas could even be spotted jumping in the divans of Ali's palace, brought in by the visiting public. Ali, 'so accustomed to the rudest Albanian life in his youth', showed no disgust when receiving petitions from the lowest of his subjects, whose dirtiness Leake obviously found hard to bear. Ali treated them with familiarity and allowed them

> to approach him, to kiss the hem of his garment, to touch his hand, and to stand near him while they converse with him, his dress is often covered with vermin, and there is no small danger of acquiring these companions by sitting on his sofa, where they are often seen crawling amidst embroidered velvet and cloth of gold.

At the same time, in 1804, Ali had just completed a magnificent audience chamber in the seraglio of the castle that was

> not surpassed by those of the Sultan himself. It is covered with a Gobelin carpet, which has the cypher of the King of France on it, and was purchased by the pasha's agent at Corfu.

Fifteen years later an anonymous American contributor to *The North American Review and Miscellaneous Journal* (1820), described the palace as being in 'the Chinese taste', with small pillars and points on the roof, painted red and white and decorated with large pictures of battles, hunts and 'wild beasts devouring each other, the work of poor Italian artists'. Indeed this 'taste' apparently stretched to opera. This was the young Edward Everett, the first American to visit Ioannina, who had received an introduction to Ali through Byron. On the same visit was a young Venetian opera dancer joining a troupe of Italians to entertain at the wedding of one of Ali's grandchildren. Such culture clashes appear more frequently than would be imagined in such a remote area. Everett was greeted by a German band playing 'God save the King' in Ali's court at Tyrnavos in Thessaly; Americans were usually taken to be English. Ali's eclecticism is endorsed by Hughes, who records that the new seraglio at Preveza was adorned with Persian carpets and Venetian mirrors. This was not so uncommon in a changing world. The reforming Sultan Selim III, who was keen to absorb Western influences, decorated his palaces in the Italian style while European fashions were imitated in the capital. Of course the acquisitive owners of the finest European houses and palaces had long been stylistic plunderers. There was an irony in the snobbish criticism of the travellers to Ali's court, coming as they did from lands with a penchant for chinoiserie and where the Prince Regent himself indulged his own fantasies for Chinese-Islamic pastiche in the Royal Pavilion at Brighton. Eager to counteract what he saw as the naive myopic classicism with which his contemporaries viewed modern Greece, often only to be disappointed with the present reality, Byron plays up the Ottoman in his verse and the acceptance of things as they are, emphasizing the Orientalist vision.

The harem; something of undying fascination to Western writers, and Everett gives it due attention. Nothing, except religion, defined the Oriental more than the harem and the hamam (bath). Ali was said to have anything from 200 to 400 women in his harem (and perhaps 300 boys, called Ganymedes, in the seraglio), depending on whom to believe. Some were slaves from Constantinople, others native Greeks or Albanians, generally volunteers (or had been volunteered) that could be married off at the right moment to the officers of the court, some had been taken by force. According to Everett, Ali at this time had one wife, 25 years old; he was around 70 by this time. Nubian eunuch guards would stand at the door and attend the women on visits to the bath or out in a covered wagon. In the Ottoman court it was common for black eunuchs to guard the harem, as they had been rendered completely sexless as opposed to their white counterparts who served in the administration. As well as his palace in Ioannina, Ali had two summer residences, one at the north of the lake

Fig. 18: Ali's grandsons, Ismail and Mehmet (1825) by Louis Dupré.

and one in the town. Here he could retire with the 'most favoured ladies of his harem'. The town retreat, a marble-floored pavilion surrounded by a wild garden, citrus groves, figs and pomegranate, with roaming deer and antelope, contained a central octagonal 'saloon' with a marble fountain and an Italian 'organ' playing Italian tunes. Hobhouse's diary adds that the gardens were in disarray and the organ was a water-organ. Typical of the strange amalgam of East and West, the pavilion was said to be the handiwork of a Frenchman, perhaps a onetime prisoner. Hughes comments on the use of foreign designers, obtained by whatever means. The extensive gardens of the Tepelene seraglio were the creation of two Italian gardeners, 'somewhat in the style of their own country'. Deserters from the French Army in Corfu whom Ali had taken in, he provided them with houses, a good salary, and wives from his own harem. The exotic picture at Ioannina was completed by the scenes, which Hobhouse did not witness but eagerly imagined, of Ali cavorting with members of his harem, some of whom would dance to an Albanian lute as he reclined on a sofa, to indulge in 'the enjoyment of whatever accomplishments these fair-ones can display for his gratification'.

Ali's exploits were not only being told in song but stories about him were widely circulated. Hobhouse records that hardly had his party stepped ashore before they learnt from a Greek teacher in Arta that Ali, 'having made the most of his youth' suffered from an incurable disorder with the symptoms of secondary syphilis. Rumours of his lurid exploits were common currency: the debaucheries of his court, the oriental splendour, the gold, silks, jewels, the activities of the concubines and scores of pages, the young orphaned sons of parents he had murdered and attached to him like puppies; Ali, bored with his courtiers, roaming the streets of Ioannina in the night disguised as a merchant, in search of adventure. One of the most notorious stories doing the rounds concerned the drowning of twelve young maidens in the Lake at Ioannina on the orders of Ali. This incident took on a life of its own, reaching a large

Fig. 19: Ioannina with Ali's citadel by Finden.

international audience by its mention in *The Gaiour* (infidel), published in 1813, in which a Venetian Christian extracts revenge for the drowning of his lover Leila, a slave and member of the harem, by the Emir Hassan. Byron set the narrative in the recent past, the abortive Russian-backed rising of the Greeks in the Morea of 1770 which was put down by Hasan Pasha. A note at the end however acknowledges the inspiration of the Ioannina lake drowning. Byron claims factual credence by recounting Ali's use of drowning as a punishment, the details of which he heard in part from Vassily, his guide supplied by Ali, who claimed to have been an eyewitness to events. In essence the wife of Mukhtar Pasha complained to Ali that her husband had been unfaithful. She supplied a list of his supposed twelve beautiful lovers, who were then seized, tied in a sack and drowned in the lake the same night without a cry. Phrosyne, in Byron's account, the fairest of the twelve, then became the subject of many a local ballad and coffeehouse story that had spread throughout the region.

The numbers of the victims vary. Cockerell heard the tale from Psalidas, the schoolteacher of Ioannina, who also told him of Ali's massacre of the villagers of Gardiki in 1799. By then it had more details and a new twist. Phrosyne, now Euphrosyne, was a celebrity who attracted a host of admirers due to her wit and beauty. The dissolute Mukhtar became her lover, but his wife was the daughter of the pasha of Berat whose friendship Ali was at that time especially anxious to cultivate. Ali burst in on Euphrosyne with his guard at midnight and after calling her the seducer of his son and other names, he forced her to give up whatever presents he had made her, and had her led off to prison with her maid. Next day, in order to make a terrifying example to check the immorality of the town in general and his son in particular, he had nine other women of known bad character arrested, and they and Euphrosyne were led to the brink of the precipice over the lake on which the fortress stands. Her faithful maid refused to desert her, and with echoes of the Suliote women, she and Euphrosyne, linked in each other's arms, leapt together down the fatal rock followed by the others. Another version had it that Mukhtar had refused to give his wife an emerald ring, but had given it to Euphrosyne, whose husband was away in Venice. It was rumoured she had also turned down the advances of Ali. Ali arranged a dinner inviting Euphrosyne, and a selection of the most charming and elegant ladies and some prostitutes. His policemen then burst in, tied them up and shut them in a church all day by the lakeshore, telling them they were condemned to death. The women supposed that Ali was expecting them to be ransomed. That night Euphrosyne and sixteen other girls were drowned in the lake.

George Finlay, who fought with Byron during the Greek War of Independence, told the tale in his *History of the Greek Revolution* (1861) some years later by which time it had become even more colourful. Euphrosyne was the beautiful 28 years old niece of Gabriel, the archbishop of Ioannina, who spent too much time reading 'naughty' episodes in classical literature rather than studying the saints, which led her to revive the customs of the hetairai, the educated courtesans of ancient Greece. While her husband was away in Venice, hoping to keep away from Ali's designs on his wealth, Euphrosyne was entertaining the wealthy young men of the city and enticing the attention of Mukhtar who showered her with gifts. Her behaviour caused scandal and encouraged imitators, to the outrage of the pious, both Christian and Muslim. After the complaints of Mukhtar's wife and under a veil of public duty, or even out of rejected jealousy, Ali decided that such activities had to be stopped and punished. Following their arrest, Euphrosyne and her accomplices were held in the Church of Saint Nicholas, until the next night when they were rowed across the stormy lake in small boats and summarily thrown overboard, without being tied up in sacks as was the custom, to drown with solemn dignity. Again Finlay attests to the eyewitness account of one of the guards. The Christian population was indignant and the funerals of the women drew large crowds, but Ali, apologizing for the severity of his justice, justified his actions by saying he would have pardoned them but no one had stood up to intercede for them.

Such incidents and the notoriety of Ali's propensity for acts of cruelty as reported in the West only seemed to add to his mystery and romance. In fact many of his punishments were part of the Ottoman culture. The drowning of women in sacks was the result of a Turkish taboo against the shedding of female blood; a common punishment for the prostitutes of Constantinople was to end up in the Bosphorus. The extreme case was when the Sultan Ibrahim I (1640–1648) was rumoured, in a fit of madness, to have ordered his complete harem of 280 to be drowned. Suffering was used particularly to deter brigandry, rebellion or political offences. Thus impalement, sometimes using the stake as a spit so that the victim could also be roasted alive, was not uncommon. Hughes reported that despite initially disbelieving the stories he was told on good authority that criminals were roasted alive over a slow fire, impaled, and skinned alive. Sometimes they had their extremities chopped off or the skin of their face stripped over their necks. While still alive the victims were able to plead for water to no avail, as the populace was too afraid to help. Leake saw a Greek priest, the leader of a gang of robbers, nailed alive to the outer wall of the palace at Ioannina in sight of the whole city. On his own death Ali's head was sent to the Sultan in Constantinople. This was a recognized end for offenders where heads were displayed outside the palace.

On setting out for Ali's palace at Tepelene, Byron, who seemed determined to see everything in terms of a great new adventure, proudly asserted that he was the first Englishman, with the exception of Leake, to venture 'beyond the capital into the interior'. The Frenchman, Pouqueville, of course had also travelled extensively throughout Albania and Leake admonished Hobhouse for relying with too much credence for background information from Pouqueville, 'who is always out'. In reality, neither Hobhouse nor Byron, nor any of the other English writers had much to say in his favour, often criticizing him for his inaccuracies and anti-British bias, but happy to plunder his writings when it suited them. When they arrived at Tepelene on a baking late afternoon, Byron was typically reminded of Scott's description of Branksome Castle in his *Lay of the Last Minstrel* (1805) and, allowing for the difference in dress, its feudal customs. The pomp, ceremony and colour of the court made a deep impression. Byron was more taken by the show of military activity than the reality that Ali, inconveniently, was actually at war. Ali had around 5,000 men actively besieging Berat, so the palace was obviously on a war footing, with messengers coming and going from the front line. While Byron shows little interest in the wider military picture, the warlike nature of the Albanians, whom he believed all to be brave, rigidly honest and faithful, capture his imagination. He wrote to his mother describing the pomp of the court:

> The Albanians in their dresses (the most magnificent in the world, consisting of a
> long white kilt, gold worked cloak, crimson velvet gold laced jacket and waistcoat,

silver mounted pistols & daggers), the Tartars with their high caps, the Turks in their vast pelisses[11] & turbans, the soldiers & black slaves with the horses… in an immense open gallery in front of the palace, the latter placed in a kind of clois-ter below it, two hundred steeds ready caparisoned to move in a moment, couriers entering or passing out with the despatches, the kettle drums beating, boys calling the hour from the minaret of the mosque.

Again Hobhouse is less awestruck than Byron. As the visitors followed 'an officer of the palace, with a white wand', they approached their audience with Ali by proceeding 'along the gallery, now crowded with soldiers, to the other wing of the building, and… over some rubbish where a room had fallen in, and through some shabby apartments… into the chamber in which was Ali himself… a large room, very handsomely furnished, and having a marble cistern and fountain in the middle, ornamented with painted tiles, of the kind which we call Dutch tile'.

  When finally ushered into the presence of the vizier, visitors were confronted with a decidedly portly man of medium height, around 60 years old, with a long white beard and deceptively benign aura, and sharp light blue eyes. Ali received Byron with respect and hos-pitality, standing up to greet him and flattering him by saying he could see he was a 'man of birth' because he had 'small ears, curling hair and little white hands'. He was not magnifi-cently dressed, but wore a high turban of fine gold muslin and his waist was adorned with a yataghan, or short sabre, studded with diamonds. Though he knew Ali cruel, Byron was impressed by his courtesy and military reputation:

> his manner is very kind & at the same time possess that dignity I find universal amongst the Turks. - -
> He has the appearance of anything but his real character, for he is a remorseless tyrant, guilty of the most horrible cruelties, very brave & so good a general, they call him the Mahometan Buonaparte. Napoleon has twice offered to make him King of Epirus, but he prefers the English interest & abhors the French as he told me. He is of so much consequence he is courted by both, the Albanians being the most warlike subjects of the Sultan, though Ali is only nominally dependent on the Porte.[12] He has been a mighty warrior, but is as barbarous as he is successful, roasting rebels etc., etc.

Rather than being confronted with a lion in his prime Byron had met more of a wily old fox, to whom age had bestowed the air of an almost otherworldly fatherly humility and wisdom. On his way to Tepelene, Byron had experienced first-hand the brutal acts of repression and petty disregard for the ordinary people, turfed out of their homes to give Byron's party lodgings, but this experience of the arbitrary and avaricious nature of Ali's government contrasted with the courtly display only seemed to give an added frisson to their audience. The comparison of Ali with Napoleon was enough of an accepted fact by this time to go unquestioned, though after his death,

---

[11] Short fur-lined jacket like those worn by the Hussars.

[12] Refers to the Sublime Porte, the central government of the Ottoman Empire.

in the Introduction to 'Les Orientales' (*Oeuvres Complètes de Victor Hugo*, 1829), Victor Hugo made the comparison with reservations. Ali was 'the only colossus of this century who can be compared to Bonaparte… and is to Napoleon as the tiger to the lion, or the vulture to the eagle'.

Pouqueville had been less impressed. He found that Ali did not measure up to what he had imagined from the stories he had heard. In his *Voyage en Grèce* (1826–7), he elaborates slightly on his previous accounts, perhaps with the flourishes of hindsight that emphasize Ali's 60-odd years of age. Ali again greeted them standing:

> He saluted us, embraced M. Bessières, and drawing himself back in a tottering attitude; he let himself fall backward on the corner of a sofa, apparently without having perceived me. A spectre, with a white beard, accoutred in black, who was present, honoured me with a slight movement of the head to intimate that I was welcome.

Despite the doddery appearance of the corpulent and wrinkled Ali, his Greek secretary lies prostrate on the floor in a state of fear. Pouqueville was excited to see the man who styled himself as a second Pyrrhus, 'a new Theseus – an aged warrior covered with wounds', but what he found was someone whose 'suppleness of the motions of his countenance; the fire of his little blue eyes; impressed on me the alarming idea of deep cunning, united with ferocity'.

Byron in a note to *Childe Harold*, called Pouqueville's account in his *Travels* of the 'celebrated Ali' incorrect. Byron, however, was lavished with attention. Ali entertained Byron and Hobhouse with refreshments and pipes, showed them a mountain howitzer in his apartment, while boasting he also possessed several large cannon, and an English telescope, through which Hobhouse tells us, Ali laughingly explained that the man 'they saw on the road is the chief minister of my enemy, Ibrahim Pasha, and he is now coming over to me, having deserted his master to take the stronger side'. His genial manner impressed them, while giving little away. He did say, though, that the British Navy had taken Zante (Zakynthos), Cephalonia, Ithaca, and Cerigo (Kythera). Congratulating them upon the news, which had arrived a fortnight before, he said he was happy to have the English as allies, believing they would not undermine his authority like the Russians and French by protecting runaway robbers, for which read insurgents. He went on to profess that he had always been a friend of Britain 'even during our war with Turkey, and had been instrumental in bringing about a Peace'.

Despite the opulence of Ali's court, Cockerell describes Ali, in contrast to his son Mukhtar, as displaying an austere sobriety. Mukhtar had turned from a happy and open youth to a gloomy and ferocious adult, while still leading a dissolute life. Everett paints a picture of the mainly Muslim elite living a life of luxury and depravity while the peasants struggled in abject poverty. Ali was calculated in the image he projected to his Western visitors, playing up the venerable old man, with a manner that Cockerell found 'so mild and paternal and so charming in its air of kindness and perfect openness' that the contrast with his reputation is the more chilling. Ushered into his presence Cockerell, 'remembering the blood-curdling stories told of him, could hardly believe [his] eyes'. Accompanied by George Foresti, who had replaced Leake, they were confronted with Ali, 'a truly Oriental figure', seated on a crimson sofa trimmed with gold.

He had a velvet cap, a prodigious fine cloak; he was smoking a long Persian pipe, and held a book in his hand. Foresti says he did this on purpose to show us he could read. Hanging beside him was a small gun magnificently set with diamonds, and a powder-horn; on his right hand also was a feather fan. To his left was a window looking into the courtyard, in which they were playing at the *djerid*,[13] and in which nine horses stood tethered in their saddles and bridles, as though ready for instant use.

Later Cockerell visited Mukhtar, who, although he was also in good-humour, was:

without any of the inimitable grace of his father, which makes everything Ali says agreeable… Mukhtar's talk was flat… very civil and rather dull. He smoked a Persian pipe brought him by a beautiful boy very richly dressed, with his hair carefully combed, and another brought him coffee; while coffee and pipes were brought to us by particularly ugly ones. On the sofa beside him were laid out a number of snuff-boxes, mechanical singing birds, and things of that sort. The serai itself was handsome in point of expense, but in the miserable taste now in vogue in Constantinople. The decoration represented painted battle-pieces, sieges, fights between Turks and Cossacks, wild men, and abominations of that sort; while in the centre of the pediment is a pasha surrounded by his guard, and in front of them a couple of Greeks just hanged, as a suitable ornament for the palace of a despot.

All visitors to Ali were intrigued by how he had attained his position, and where he had come from, and various accounts of his life were a common feature of the travel books, often repeating the same tales. In essence it was a story of a climb from disinherited obscurity to power by way of banditry and cunning. Hughes was told of the days when Ali had 'not where to lay his head' and how his mother possessed 'all the martial qualities of an Amazon'. Once enough power was amassed, Ali was able militarily to take on increasingly larger opponents, while always appearing to serve his ultimate master, the Sultan; whether distinguishing himself against the Austrians and Russians, or the Bosnian rebel Osman Pazvantoğlu (Paswan Oglou), but at arm's length from the seat of power in Constantinople. As Byron put it in a nutshell:

Ali inherited 6 dram and a musket after the death of his father … collected a few followers from among the retainers of his father, made himself master, first of one village, then of another, amassed money, increased his power, and at last found himself at the head of a considerable body of Albanians.

The truth was of course more complex, but a rags-to-riches tale was the pleasingly more satisfying. There was even a rumour that he had overcome his destitute state by discovering a pot of gold hidden under a tree, which enabled him to hire his first followers. The story, attested by Guillaume de Vaudoncourt but doubted by Pouqueville who says it was invented by the Greek scholar Psalidas, was too good to leave alone, and it became part of the repertoire of Ali tales.

---

[13] A combat game involving a horseman throwing a blunted spear at an opponent.

Fig. 20: Ali's second son Veli (1825) by Louis Dupré.

Ali told Byron to consider him as a father whilst he was in Turkey, while he looked on him as a son. Byron and Hobhouse stayed four nights. The scent of the forbidden lurks in their accounts. Byron was open about his homosexual desires in letters to friends and homosexuality was a further mysterious element in the mix of Ali's personality. Byron had intimated that one of his reasons for undertaking his tour was to inquire into the praiseworthy nature of sodomy from ancient times onwards and he made no secret of his affairs with local boys while in Greece. Hobhouse notes in his *Diary* that Ali looked 'a little leeringly' at Byron. He then showered Byron with gifts of sweets as for a child and requested that he visit 'often, and at night when he was more at leisure' and by implication, on his own. Peter Cochran suggests that the discrepancy between the number of meetings recorded by Byron and Hobhouse raise the possibility that Byron indeed saw Ali on his own and was probably entertained by his Ganymedes. At Tepelene, one of Ali's doctors, a Frank and native of Alsace,[14] the son of an

---

[14] Peter Cochran suggests this was Ibrahim Manzour, but there is no evidence he was in Epirus until 1814.

eminent physician from Vienna, informed them that Ali's body was unscathed and that within groups with a lack of females 'pederasty… was openly practised'.

In contrast to Ibrahim Manzour, who stressed the dangers of travel amidst the savage inhabitants of Albania along 'bad roads that are both dangerous and disagreeable', the hospitality of Ali and his son Veli impressed Byron enough for him to write in his notes on *Childe Harold* that the difficulties of travelling in Turkey had been greatly exaggerated. In fact Byron preferred Turkey, as he calls it, to Spain and Portugal. It should be remembered that he had special treatment, always being looked after with guards and his every requirement being catered for. Ali gave him a bodyguard of forty men to escort him through the dangerous passes. Byron then went on to stay with Veli Pasha in the Peloponnese on his way to Athens and was treated even more generously as a brother. In a letter to Hobhouse from Patras on his way to Athens and to Francis Hodgson from Athens, he boasts of having received a stallion from 'the Pacha of the Morea', Veli, who 'received him with great pomp, standing, conducted me to the door with his arm around my waist, and a variety of civilities, invited me to meet him in Larissa [in Thessaly] and see his army'. Other travellers agreed with Manzour, attesting to dangers and discomforts real enough.

In retrospect it seems strange that it was not until Byron and Hobhouse had left Ali and returned to Vostitsa, on the Gulf of Corinth, that they realized to their surprise the enmity between the Greeks and Turks. Hobhouse wrote in his journal, 'We have observed the professed hatred for their masters to be universal among the Greeks.' Until then, under the spell of Ali, they had thought Albania and Greece to be tranquil provinces of the Empire. It too dawned on them that their visit, oiled as it was by the wheels of British diplomacy, was not as innocent as they thought. Perhaps they had been used; unaware of British imperialist designs they were only too eager to go as supplicants to Ali's court. The Romantic Ali would be the image that Byron would portray in verse, even if in reality he knew more.

An ambiguity remains in Byron's vision of Albania and Greece. When he realized that he and his alter ego, Harold, were travelling through an enslaved culture under Turkish will, he was already indebted to the hospitality of the masters. The revulsion and admiration he feels for Ali and the brutality of bandit law are never resolved. In *Childe Harold* (1812) on the one hand he wallows in Ali's bloody deeds, only then to remember, 'Fair Greece! sad relic of departed worth!' and the 'Spirit of Freedom!', and 'the scourge of Turkish hand' that holds the populace enslaved.

Though Byron's sympathies shifted, he never totally gave up his feeling for the Turks, even during the Greek War of Independence. For Hobhouse too, the situation was complex; the Suliotes are bandits not freedom fighters, whose songs commemorated robbing exploits (Byron's song beginning 'Tambourgi, tambourgi' is punctuated by 'Robbers all at Parga!'). Again, it was only when the Suliotes came in on the Greek cause of liberty that perceptions changed.

In Byron's view he had been an explorer, almost another Columbus, bringing back riches from an exotic and faraway land. As he wrote to Henry Drury in 1810:

> Albania indeed I have seen more than any Englishman (but a Mr. Leake) for it is
> a country rarely visited from the savage character of the natives, though abound-
> ing in more natural beauties than the classical regions of Greece… where places

without name, and rivers not laid on maps, may one day when more known be justly esteemed subjects for the pencil and pen.

When not in poetic mode, Byron was an accurate observer, as later travellers attest. Edward Lear backs up Byron's account of Albanian singing and is more outraged by the use of women as pack animals and general drudges by their menfolk, set to employment ploughing, digging, sowing and repairing the highways. Byron's description of Albania in the *notes* to *Childe Harold* impressed the mountaineer Bill Tilman, who served with the partisans in the Second World War and wrote *When Men and Mountains Meet* (1946). Paddy Leigh Fermor commented on Byron's accurate eye for women's costume in *Roumeli: Travels in Northern Greece* (1966), when he found little changed. But it was the poetic Byron that was the one that mattered, and had the more profound influence.

Although the Europeans at Ali's court reported their personal experience, they were drawn to reinforcing the Westerner's stereotypical view of the East. From Pouqueville onwards, who despite his position was more concerned with Ali's appetites, atrocities and scheming than his administration and place within the international context, they played up the otherness, with the result that Ali becomes an all purpose caricature of the Oriental despot, with all the expected vices and contradictions. Byron took Pouqueville's Ali and sprinkled magic dust on him, with the result that, despite his basis of authenticity, his Albanian excursion in *Childe Harold* had more in common with the fictitious writings of Chateaubriand, something he was loath to concede. François-Auguste-René, Vicomte de Chateaubriand, his political opposite, diplomat and founding figure in French romanticism, had visited America and the East; he only got as far as Corfu before heading south to Greece and the Levant in 1806–7. His subsequent travel writings were fanciful and his two works of literature *Atala* (1801) and *René* (1802) about the Native Americans, although purporting to have the air of veracity were not based on actual experience. *Atala* and *Childe Harold* are both works of exile and disillusion, the events of which explore the exotic, taking place on the edge of civilization. In *Atala* it was commonly believed that Chateaubriand was extolling the virtues of the 'noble savage', although he denied this, and Byron's Albanians too have the same primitive qualities. Byron's visit to Ali was a pivotal moment in his life; he began *Childe Harold* only a week after. And he had read Chateaubriand, a debt Chateaubriand felt Byron never acknowledged. The result is that the Ali episode gives off the air of exotic adventure despite its basis in fact. Because of the fame of *Childe Harold*, in European eyes Ali becomes a character inhabiting another world, rather than a real person, something which later narratives did little to dispel.

To assess whether Thomas Hughes was correct in his statement that 'the three greatest men produced in Turkey during the present age, have all derived their origin from Albania… the late celebrated Vizir Mustafa Bairactar,[15] Muhammad Ali Pasha of Egypt, and, the greatest of them all…' Ali Pasha, we shall have to look behind the myth.

---

[15] Alemdar Mustafa Pasha, grand vizier of the Ottoman Empire (d.1808) who overthrew Mustafa IV and instated Mahmud II against the will of the janissaries.

Chapter 3

Ali Pasha's Life: The Rise

I n his *Travels*, Thomas Smart Hughes summarized the problems of attempting a coherent biography of Ali Pasha:

> The earlier parts of this wild romantic history never can be very accurately and authentically described, since they rest almost entirely upon oral traditions, or accounts which have been compiled from those traditions after a long intervening time: and though I have perused probably fifty of such records, yet I never met with two that agreed with each other, either in the relation of facts or the development of motives.

Hughes was astute enough to acknowledge the difficulty of making sense of a mass of exaggerated and half-remembered tales without external evidence, but this did not deter many of his contemporaries. The wider range of sources available today, including official archives, has provided alternative scenarios and some firmer background detail to set against the traditional accounts. Modern scholarship has accessed Venetian and Ottoman records that help in hazarding a chronological reconstruction of Ali's life and the workings of his court. The inability of the early biographers to disentangle fact from fiction and their reliance on the sensational and the lurid may have diminished their value, but they did have the advantage of meeting Ali in person, so their first-hand experience cannot be dismissed out of hand.

Ali's life was certainly one of extremes. He had lived on the edge, yet could be beguiling and full of good humour in person during his latter years. His guests were as much enthralled by the fairytale nature of his court and the frisson of being in the presence of a capricious despot as by his exhibitions of cruelty. A dreamlike quality appears to hang over Ali and his court, even when reality burst through with a jolt, and it was easy to fall back on the melodramatic stereotype; the tyrant flaunting his power and wealth, made the more intriguing by his colourful rise from barbaric obscurity to bandit king. Despite their air of studied objectivity, his Western observers could not help but be seduced into fitting him into an already accepted mould, unable to rationalize his contrary nature. That he was a wily old fox they all agreed but were apparently naive enough not to imagine that Ali might be manipulating his image for his own ends. The philhellenic Pouqueville was no admirer and happy to emphasize Ali's misdemeanours for his audience, others may have been more cautious but the stories were too good and the Oriental veneer too enticing to be completely let go.

That these outsiders were drawn to Ali's court was a testament to the perception of him as a ruler. At the height of his power around 1812, when he received most of his influential visitors, he ruled over an area with a population of 1.5 million, including Albania as far north as Durazzo (which he never took), Tirana and Elbassan, and southern Macedonia and Greece

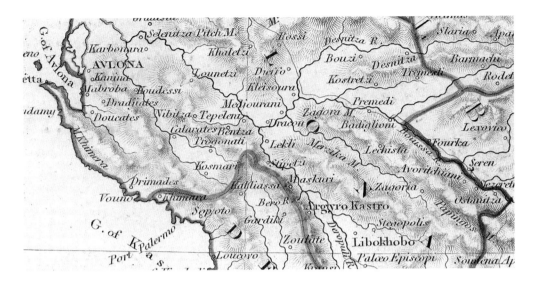

Fig. 21: The region around Tepelene.

from Thessalonika southwards with the exception of Attica and the islands. It was this territorial clout, testing of the Sultan's authority, that added fascination to the flamboyant tales about him, but Ali wanted to be taken seriously as a player on the international stage. With the European powers eager to seize any opportunity that would give them advantage in the Mediterranean, Greece ripe for revolt and the Sultan fearful of inroads into this vulnerable and difficult region, Ali was nicely placed. Though Ali Pasha of Ioannina was no petty warlord only of interest to the outside world through the entertaining romance of his lifestyle, the rapid growth of his legend would soon obscure the hard realpolitik of his life.

This storytelling and myth-making was so pervasive that even the date of Ali Pasha's birth remains obscure. Pouqueville and Ibrahim Manzur give it as 1740 (the date followed by most early biographies) whereas other sources, including diplomatic correspondence, give it as late as 1752, with a number of dates occurring in between. Hughes favours around 1750, saying Ali was reluctant to talk about his date of birth, always affecting to be younger than he really was. His place of birth is more certain: Beçisht, a hamlet high on a mountain slope on the opposite bank of the River Vjosë to Tepelene, close by a Tekke or convent for dervishes. Tepelene was then a small town lying in the shadow of Mt Trebushín, surrounded by vineyards, which according to Leake produced 'a poor red wine', and on the higher land, wheat and barley, while 'kalambókki'[1] were grown on the banks of the river. The local agas[2] enjoyed a degree of independence, but despite some municipal organization there was little communal harmony and a general lack of social order. Frequent quarrels broke out, requiring its wealthy landed proprietors to live in a cluster of fortified houses. In Leake's opinion it was a mere 'village' consisting of 'not more than eighty or ninety Musulman families, with a small detached suburb of Christians' and of 'no great embellishment to the scene'.

---

[1] Modern Greek *kalaboki*, a general term for maize or dhurra (Egyptian corn).

[2] *Aga*: an honorific title for a civilian or military officer or elder.

Ali's lineage is as hazy as his birth. It is generally agreed that his forebears were Christians who embraced Islam, but when is uncertain. Finlay says that to Osmanlis (Ottoman Turks) and strangers he claimed he was descended from a Turk from Brusa[3] who had received a grant of land or revenue (*ziamet*) in compensation for services rendered, probably military, from Sultan Bayazid I (1389– 1402) and his family converted not long after. Such claims were common practice, a way of claiming legitimacy to landholdings by incumbent beys[4] who attested they had received their sanjaks or fiefdoms as rewards, rather than the more likely case that their conversion was merely a matter of expediency. Ali's biographer, Ahmet Moufit, great-grandson of his sister, Shainitza (Siachnisa), produces an alternative earliest known ancestor, Nazif, a Mevlevi dervish[5] from Kütahya in western Asia Minor who settled in Tepelene in the early 1600s. An unlikely later date for conversion has been put at 1716, when Ali's paternal grandfather, Mukhtar Bey, took part in the siege of Corfu during the seventh Ottoman-Venetian War (1714–18). Mukhtar's father already had a Muslim name, Mustafa Yussuf. Mustafa, or Mutza (Moutzo) Housso from the region of Argyrocastro twenty-five miles to the south of Tepelene, had achieved enough fame as a brigand, warrior and clan chief to receive the accolade of being remembered in a folk ballad, and the clan took the name Moutzohoussates after him. He then gained respectability by obtaining the title of bey and possibly official recognition as deputy governor of Tepelene, a sub-district of the sanjak of Avlona.

Mukhtar continued in his father's footsteps, treading the well-worn fine line between loyal subject and outlaw, fighting both for and against the Turks; it was during a loyal moment that he lost his life fighting for the Sultan. The Venetians were losing the war in the Morea but under the inspired leadership of their German commander at Corfu, Count Johann Matthias von der Schulenburg, they were holding the Ionian Islands. If Muktar did convert to Islam at this moment it did not protect him. Praised for his bravery, he also earned himself the title 'martyr of the faith' in Turkish sources. Whether Mukhtar gave his life for Allah or not, Ali's religious leanings would be a matter of continued debate. His laxness in religious observance and tolerance in dealing with his Christian subjects was, paradoxically, seen as a stick to beat him with by Western observers. Leake has a general dig at Islam through Ali with a comment on the lacklustre adherence of the Albanian Muslims to ritual and doctrine. In contrast the Orthodox Christians were seen as lost in rounds of pointless fasting and primitive superstition. Ali's faith may not have been fervent (he was happy to partake in drinking wine), but he kept alive his ancestral connection to the Mevlevi and Bektashi orders of dervishes. If this was a tactic it was astute, the dervishes were popular amongst the Albanians, the janissaries and within the Imperial Court.

The Bektashi Order took a more liberal approach to Islam, which Leake thought suited Ali. He made endowments to tekkes and for visiting dervishes whom he made particularly welcome at Ioannina. Ali's adherence to Bektashism is further borne out by the image of the *zulfiqar* on his personal banner. This device was the legendary scissor-like cleft sword given by Muhammad to his cousin Ali ibn Abi Talib, the fourth caliph. This warrior caliph became particularly revered by Shia and Sufi Muslims and Ali Pasha's seal also bore the inscription

---

[3] Modern Bursa in north-west Anatolia, the Ottoman capital before Erdine.

[4] *Bey*: title of nobility.

[5] A Sufi order of Islam from central Anatolia, also known as 'Whirling Dervishes'.

in Persian 'let there be hope for Ali-Asker', another reference to him. Wandering holy men, usually Bektashis, were said to be gifted with the ability to tell the future and Manzour states that in later life Ali kept a Persian mystic, Cheik Ali, at court to whom he became devoted. His dabbling in Sufism may have been criticized as naive but as with much in his life, expediency was seen his uppermost concern. Manzour tells of a strange instance in 1818 when Ali coerced or persuaded a whole Christian village within his home region to convert to Islam. The likelihood is that this was in some way a mutually acceptable arrangement whereby the village avoided the *haraç* or capitation tax that non-Muslims were forced to pay and Ali would have gained some loyal followers from the boys taken to Ioannina to be educated within prominent Muslim families. Such actions would enhance his reputation within Muslim circles and the Turkish sources play up his actions as a defender of Islam in his fight against the Suliotes, but he was not particularly anti-Christian or self-consciously Muslim. When Ali came to wield power, he showed no favouritism to either community, being equally harsh to both.

If religion was of secondary importance, brigandage plays a central role in Ali's story, but it was not a way of life unique to the Balkans. The Scottish borders had supplied the difficult terrain for the cross-border activities of the reivers up until the seventeenth century, and similarly Italy was renowned for its *banditi* who exploited the borders between the rival states,

Fig. 22: Wandering Bektashi dervish (1809, anon).

but in Greece, and Albania in particular, brigandage had become endemic. The harsh land-scape afforded little profit from maintaining flocks, but gave ample opportunity and security for raiding one's neighbours. In such a landscape, the methods of the brigands where akin to those used by irregular or partisan soldiers. Raids, ambush, pillage and plunder, the capture and ransom of prisoners and extortion, were tactics that could prove useful under different circumstances. Tribal chiefs maintained their own locally recruited fighting bands through the success of such enterprises. Hughes observed that fighters could disband at a moment's notice if they felt like it, so a steady supply of booty was essential to maintain loyalty. Becoming a bey was, as in Mukhtar's case, the recognition of the hereditary leadership of a tribe or clan and its fighters. On his death, some of his followers and his title went to Ali's father, Veli Bey, who, as a testament to the state of constant instability that prevailed, then had to ruthlessly impose his own authority as clan leader. Despite contradictory accounts, it is clear that rivalry had broken out between Veli and his cousin Islam Bey over the division of the inheritance which included exacting feudal control over a number of wealthy and well-manned Albanian Christian villages.

According to the Greek *Chronicle of Epirus* (1864) and Turkish archive sources it was Islam that achieved initial success. As was customary by this time, de facto assumption of power was officially recognized retrospectively by the Porte and he was given the title of pasha of the two tails and made governor of the sanjak of Delvino, only to be dismissed after proving inefficient and unpopular, handing Veli his opportunity. In the summer of 1759, Veli attacked, murdering his cousin and destroying his residence. According to Hobhouse, as Veli was the third son he could only claim his inheritance in Tepelene by force, so he attacked the town with his klephts and burned his brothers alive. Three years later it was Veli's turn to be acknowledged by the Porte. He was given the title of *mir-i-miran*, bey of beys, and promoted to pasha of the two tails and *mutasarrif* (a governor directly appointed by the Porte) of Delvino, and probably holding the sanjak of Avlona as well. Hughes interestingly puts Veli's appointment down to his good relations with the Greeks and the intercession on his behalf by the influential Greeks of the Phanar district of Constantinople. But he was another who did not enjoy his success for long; his actions also made enemies and he was driven out of Tepelene and died soon after. Finlay, perhaps citing a more colourful account, has Veli murdered by his rival chiefs after he had poi-soned his two elder brothers to take over the position as local governor. The use of poison is a recurring theme in the disposal of rivals and it was even said he accidentally poisoned himself. However he died, he died young, and when Ali was something between 10 and 15 years old.

It is disputed as to whether Ali's forebears ever achieved the status of pasha. Ismail Kemal Bey, Albanian nationalist and founder of independent Albania, claims in his memoirs (1920) that Ali came from an obscure family, whereas in the opinion of Denis Skiotis, Ali was born into the highest rank of Muslim Albanian society. Contrary to the picture painted of him as being a barely educated ruffian he was given a formal schooling in Islam and the art of gov-ernment. Pouqueville quotes Jerome de la Lance, an Italian doctor who sought refuge at Ali's court, as saying he was a poor pupil who preferred outdoor activities with musket or sabre and Sir William Eton, a resident authority on matters Ottoman, claimed he had no Turkish. That he learnt both Turkish and Greek as corroborated by Leake is the more likely reality. The scribes at Ali's court were to use Turkish to write to central government, and Greek to communicate with the local populace. Ali may well have been, as the Greek primate of Argyrocastro told the Habsburg court, the descendant of the noblest family across the region, but by the time he succeeded his father, his rivals had already stripped the family of much of its land and wealth. Less flatteringly Peter Oluf Brønsted described Veli as a pasha of 'the third rank' who left Ali little finance or influence. But he did at least leave two wives and three children, two boys and a girl. Their exact relationships are again obscure.

Ali's life was thrown into turmoil following his father's death. His mother, Esmihan Hanim, showing commendable grit, was forced to take control of his father's band to retain their position. Her ruthless spirit was seen as unnatural by commentators and she was demonized in contemporary accounts in consequence. That such decisive action may have been necessary was marred by the detail that she was said to have ruthlessly poisoned Ali's rival half-brother and his mother to ensure Ali's inheritance. Esmihan, or Hamko in Albanian, was without question a doughty woman. Her lack of femininity was further compromised by her willingness to throw off the veil and fearlessly lead her followers into battle. Hamko's 'tigerish' behaviour was thought by Ali's biographers to be a source of his own streak of cruelty and his great respect for her was perceived as weakness. Ali said she had made him 'a man and a Vizier', and given his youth and the adversity of his fatherless situation he must have relied on her strength and guidance. Ali had to adapt quickly to revive the fortunes of his clan, and this could not be achieved by force alone. Hamko, who was the daughter of the Bey of Konitsa,[6] was shrewd enough to arrange a political marriage between her son and Ümmügülsüm (Um Giulsum Hanum), usually rendered as Emine, the daughter of the powerful Kaplan Pasha of Argyrocastro. Argyrocastro was then the seat of the sanjak of Delvino and Kaplan had succeeded Ali's father, Veli, as *mutassarif*. Emine would be the mother of two of Ali's sons, Mukhtar and Veli; their younger brother Selim would be born much later, in 1802, to a slave. The date of Ali's marriage is uncertain, and to a degree is influenced by his date of birth; it has been put between 1764 and the early 1770s. Part of the problem is whether Ali's father-in-law was alive to see his daughter married. Kaplan Pasha fell foul of the Porte authorities for the usual charges of corruption, murdering rivals and stealing tax revenue and he was beheaded at Monastir in 1766. It was suggested that Ali was in some way responsible for having Kaplan being brought to book for treason, but if the later date for Ali's birth is accepted and the lack of evidence, it is more likely Kaplan was dead already.

Attempting a coherent chronology for the next twenty years of Ali's life has been ignored by or vexed his biographers for the reasons Hughes observed, and in consequence this mysterious period supplied much of the material for the romance that fed into the myth. It was a time of almost constant warfare, and the tales recount how Ali fought by whatever means, whether as feudal bey or bandit chief, to regain his birthright at Tepelene. To begin with, Ali and Hamko strove to reinstate the Moutzohoussates by eliminating all opposition, including challenges to the clan leadership. There was obviously little room for sentiment as his stepbrothers were summarily dispatched and the family feud with Islam Pasha concluded by the murder of his widow and children. Any increase in their power had to be at the expense of their neighbours,

---

[6] Today in Greece near the Albanian border.

a course certain to create enemies, and their rivals were not prepared to be easily subjugated; they had plans of their own. The surrounding towns and villages formed a confederacy against Ali and Hamko and they were forced out of Tepelene. At some point, as the story goes, Hamko was ambushed and beaten by bands from the villages of Hormovo and Gardiki near Tepelene. Although the villagers were Christians and Muslims respectively, the two communities were allies. Hamko and Ali's sister, Shainitza, were imprisoned and gravely humiliated, most probably sexually assaulted, although the accounts are euphemistic on this point, an incident made much of in all the versions. According to Hughes they were ransomed after a month, perhaps by a Greek merchant, but Hamko is also more heroically said to have escaped. Whatever the details the event was traumatic enough for Hamko to want severe retribution and her ordeal instilled in Ali a merciless desire for revenge that would fester for many years. From how he satiated his lust on Gardiki, Ali gained his reputation for never forgetting a grudge and being willing to wait however long until he could find a way to pay it back with disproportionate cruelty.

His mother's abduction must have been when Ali was at his weakest ebb and helpless to act. This low point, with Ali resorting to a life of itinerant banditry in the mountains, has been given as the time of his capture by Ahmed Kurt Pasha of Berat. When this happened is uncertain. Pouqueville puts it as early as 1764, too early if Ali was born in the 1750s. The confusion is further muddied by the exact status of Kurt at the time. Kurt was a member of the Mutzaka family, a noble family from Avlona. He did not become the first pasha of Berat and dervendji-pasha (guardian of the passes) until 1774, after previously attaining the position of sanjakbey (administrative and military governor) of Delvino (1771) and Avlona (1772). Berat was the administrative centre of the sanjak of Avlona and the pashalik of Berat was created as a reward for his service to the Porte against the troublesome Mehmed Pasha Bushati of Scutari on the northern border of Albania. This has led to the theory that Ali was taken by Kurt twice, or at least definitely in 1775 when it is known that he was in Kurt's service. One reason proposed for the hostility of Ali towards Kurt was the latter's rejection of his proposal to marry Kurt's daughter, Miriem. Miriem was handed in marriage instead to the more established Ibrahim Bey of Avlona in 1765, forming a useful alliance between the two families. Ibrahim went on to become pasha of Avlona and Berat, and the rivalry with Ali would continue until his death. Hughes hints that Ali's reputation as a robber disrupting the passage of merchants and caravans was such that the government was required to take steps, authorizing Kurt as dervendji-pasha to apprehend him. Between the possible dates of his capture Venetian dispatches give what may be the first tantalizing documented reference to Ali.

War had broken out between Russia and Turkey in 1768 and the Suliotes, along with other inhabitants of Epirus, had responded in support of Russia, encouraged by Catherine the Great's Orlov rising in the Morea, which gave hope for a widespread revolt against the Empire. Despite the Venetians' difficulties with Albanian names, Skiotis suggests the records show that Ali and his cousin Islam Bey of Klisura, between Tepelene and Berat, were part of a force of 9,000 Muslim Albanians under Suleyman Tsaparis, Aga of Margariti, that took on the Christian Suliotes in 1772. The Suliotes had been raiding the villages of the local agas, depriving them of income. Further, they were supported financially and with provisions by the Venetians, who found them useful allies in their endeavours to protect their territories at

Preveza and Parga. Margariti borders the Suli Mountains to the west, so in addition the powerful Tsapari family had ambitions of gaining influence over the maritime trade of Thesprotia and Acarnania as well as controlling the villages of the plain. Many previous attempts to subdue Suli had failed, the most recent in 1759 and 1762, and this effort fared no better. Suleyman attacked Preveza as part of the same campaign with no result. Ali and Islam may also have been involved in a threat against Ioannina and Arta the following year. If we take the second date as the date of Ali's capture then Ali's involvement in these military offensives show that he had already achieved some kind of status as a warrior. When Kurt had another go at Suli in 1775, which achieved no more than the previous attempts, Ali could well have been called into action against the Suliotes once more in his service. Ali's first unequivocally documented action took place the following year when Kurt was once more at war with Mehmed Pasha Bushati. Now recognized as a force in his own right, Kurt had been entrusted by the Porte with the exploitation of Albanian lands belonging to the Sultan's sister, lands previously held by Mehmed. Mehmed was understandably not pleased with the alteration in the balance of power and resorted to force. In the subsequent engagements around Kavaje and Tirana, Ali and Islam distinguished themselves, turning the tide of battle. Things turned sour when Ali and Kurt fell out over the division of the spoils and Ali resumed his itinerant lifestyle, but with his reputation as a *palikar*, or warrior, greatly enhanced.

The relationship between Ali and Kurt Pasha is complex and confused. Leake suggests a family tie between Kurt and Ali's mother. As a result it has been claimed that Kurt provided security for Hamko and that Ali, when he was captured by an injured neighbour, was only saved from death through Kurt's intervention. Finlay and others make much of this supposed relationship, suggesting that Kurt may have been his uncle, or even, in Holland's account, that Hamko was Kurt's daughter. Depending on how close the relationship was this would impact on the motives of the parties, but it seems from the Turkish sources, Ali was not under Kurt's protection nor did he owe his advancement to him, in fact the opposite. The version of events Ali himself preferred are those told in the *Alipashiad*, where Kurt is cast as the villain of the piece, being Ali's adversary during his early years, akin to the rivalry of the Sheriff of Nottingham and Robin Hood. Ali's capture was by deception when he came to Berat in a show of feudal fealty, and once he manages to escape Kurt's clutches, Kurt organizes the tribes and villages against him. It must have suited Ali's purpose to promote his youthful rise as a heroic battle against the devious and powerful pasha of Berat. In the *Alipashiad* Ali succeeds at the death of Kurt, but fortunes were reversed in reality during a slow war of attrition. In 1778, Kurt's first setback was when he was disgraced and dismissed from his position due to the intrigues of Mehmed 'Kalo' Pasha of Ioannina, who took over the sanjak of Avlona. The guardianship of the passes then went to a Turk from Thessaly, Catalcali Haci Ali Pasha. As a newcomer to the region and held in contempt by the Albanian *palikars*, the Turkish Pasha turned to the young Ali Bey for help, appointing him as his deputy with the task of asserting order over the unruly brigands while he remained in comfort and security at home in his fortress in faraway Chalkis on the Island of Euboea.

Around this time local tradition has it that Ali met with Saint Kosmas who is remembered for his gift of prophesy. Kosmas was on a mission to counter conversion to Islam amongst

Christian villagers. Travelling through Epirus establishing schools and preaching he made a prophecy that one day Ali would become great. Perhaps he saw in Ali the mixture of personal charisma and courage mixed with ruthless determination and cunning that must have kept him going in adversity. Ali could only have induced men to follow him if he had these qualities and the ability to ensure that he could reward their services. Finlay acknowledged he was 'brave and active, restless in mind and body' but what may have been a Machiavellian aptitude for seizing opportunities, in the circumstances a must if he was to be successful, he condemns as a lack 'of all moral and religious feeling' and a willingness to exploit clan, ethnic and religious rivalries to suit his purpose. For Westerners such opinions were coloured by their attitude to the East. Ali was the embodiment of many of the less desirable Oriental traits that they found in the Albanians, and even the Greeks, where mendacity and double-dealing were second nature and cunning the height of human achievement. In a culture that believed truth was to be avoided and morality was a weakness to be exploited, Ali could proudly proclaim he could deceive anybody and nobody could outwit him. By the time he was holding court for foreigners he had become a puzzle, full of contradictions and quixotic moods, the qualities of his youth perhaps twisted with age and the need to hold on to power. His displays of good humour, which made him popular amongst his companions, and his affection for his family and loyalty to his friends, would have been vital in his rise, but later shows of affection and tolerance were interpreted as danger signals that he was plotting something. In hindsight, Finlay summed him up as audacious, wary, affectionate and cruel, tolerant and tyrannical, his potential for brilliance undermined by his passions and greed, which limited his vision, with men ultimately serving him as an act of self-preservation. This was in the future, but that there was some connection between Ali and Saint Kosmas is borne out by the church Ali built in his honour in Kolkondas in Albania, within the jurisdiction of Kurt Pasha. Kosmas had fallen foul of both the Venetians and the Turks and even aroused the suspicion of Greek village elders and it was here that he was executed in 1779. Accused of being a Russian agent he was hung without formal charges. Forever ambiguous, Ali's veneration of Kosmas was not appreciated by some of his fellow Muslims.

Catalcali Haci gave Ali a free hand as his deputy, Ali's first recognition by the Ottoman state. Although the control of the passes would put him at direct odds with Kurt, it gave Ali great power with authority over much of Rumeli. First he eliminated the military and civil officials appointed by Kurt, replacing them with his own men drawn on merit and with no regard to religion or ethnic group; the only stipulation was their avowal of personal undying loyalty to Ali. As a counter to Finlay, this could be seen as a form of equal opportunities. To be successful he also needed the cooperation of the paramilitaries, both Albanian and Greek, but there was little love lost between the two. Using his new position he was able to build up a network of contacts amongst the leaders of the Albanian bands and the captains of the armatoli. Those Albanian fighters unwilling to bend to his authority he relocated (in contravention of Ottoman policy and for a fee) to the Morea where they could continue their occupation of plunder unmolested, giving the Greek armatoli a welcome respite. Success also depended on wealth. Without restriction by a superior authority he now had the safety to operate both legitimate and illegitimate protection rackets giving him the resources to recruit mercenaries and put money aside for bribes for when the need might arise.

One of Ali's enemies and a source of information on Ali for the Sultan, Demetrius Palaiopoulos, the primate of Karpenisi in the southern Pindus Mountains, summed up the situation of his rise to power in a letter to the Porte in 1810 saying that Ali established peace and order by keeping his ulterior motives hidden under a cloak of wheedling cajolery in his dealings with the local officials. Typical of such underhand methods were his dealings with the people of Missolonghi. In order to collect a debt owed by a sea captain, Michaeles Avronites, first he arrived in the town with his Albanians in a show of force. Avronites was from Cephalonia and therefore a Venetian subject and when, conveniently for him, he could not be found, Ali seized some other Venetian subjects, including the consul, Barozzi, who made the mistake of protesting. To obtain the release of the prisoners, the leading men of Missolonghi declared that they would honour the debt themselves after a thirty-day period. Ali freed the prisoners, but only after he sequestered 500 barrels of merchandise bound for the Ionian Islands as a guarantee. Despite the further protests of Barozzi, the mayor and Ali's superior, Catalcali Haci, the good men of Missolonghi never saw their goods again. After years of intimidation the docile inhabitants of Epirus were faced with the unenviable choice of an officially recognized tyranny or indiscriminate violent anarchy; it was easier to accept the former. Initially Ali only held the post for five months, but it was a turning point. He had managed to impose unity and order, a systematic and heavy tax regime, concentrated and centralized power and amassed an enormous sum of money in a short space of time.

In 1779 Kurt was back, having used the well-tested methods of intrigue and bribery at the Porte. Ali's good use of his own time during Kurt's sabbatical meant he was not intimidated but in a position to wage a counteroffensive. Ali's best way to expose Kurt's lack of authority was by mounting a challenge to pressurize the Porte into accepting him back on the basis that he had the more established powerbase. As a show of force Ali took an army of 2,000 to 3,000 Albanians on a march through Thessaly, dispersing them on the way to intimidate the towns and villages and extract money as they went. At Trikkala he led his own detachment of 300 disciplined and well-turned out, well-ordered troops, including cavalry, into the near deserted town; many of the inhabitants had fled in advance, and the rest locked themselves away. It was in his interest that discipline was maintained so he proceeded to billet his troops without harm, showing the people that he could be trusted to keep the peace. Once the correct amount of protection money had been received, Ali and his men left the town in peace. The Swedish scholar and collector of Islamic and Biblical manuscripts, Jakob Jonas Björnståhl, who was journeying to the Holy Land, witnessed the incident. Björnståhl is the first Westerner to give an account of Ali. The Ali Bey, the 'young but powerful man' at the head of the column who carried great respect amongst the Albanians and 'possessed great riches', can be identified by his banner with the *zulfiqar* emblazoned on it as the future Ali Pasha. Björnståhl did not reach his destination but died shortly after in Thessalonika.

When Ali reached Farsala, home of Catalcali Haci, together they set in motion a plan to dispose of Kurt Pasha. First Ali would take the district of Karli-Eli (Acarnania), the western region, and north of the Gulf of Corinth. His soldiers there had already paid another visit to Missolonghi and relieved its citizens of some more tribute. Ali followed with 4,000 men and occupied Vrachori (Agrinion) the regional capital, where he linked up with Albanians returning from their ravaging of the Morea. Kurt responded by moving his troops south into Epirus, calling for loyalty from the armatoli and putting pressure on the Venetians to withhold their ships from Ali, restricting any approach by sea. The situation had become so serious the Porte was impelled to intervene. Their admiral and general Kapudan Pasha Cezayirli Gazi Hasan, who had come out with honour from the defeat by the Russians at the Battle of Chesme, had already been despatched to suppress the Albanian irregulars causing havoc in the Morea in the aftermath of the Orlov Revolt. He was now ordered to divert through Macedonia and Thessaly to re-establish order there. Calling on the help of the local Turks, the armatoli and the Greeks peasants, who were allowed to arm themselves, he tried to drive out the Albanians, but without the success he achieved later in the Morea. There Hasan Pasha was significantly helped by local Greek contingents. Typical of the shifting loyalties of the time a veteran of the Orlov Revolt, Konstantinos Kolokotronis, made the mistake of leading his klephts in support of Hasan against the marauding Albanian irregulars. Part of a force of 3,000 under Hasan, he took part in the 'Massacre of the Albanians' when 12,000 Albanians were slaughtered. Once the Albanians were destroyed Hasan then turned on Kolokotronis, and after a struggle had him captured and killed. Konstantinos' son Theodore Kolokotronis would become the hero of the Greek War of Independence. Despite Hasan's efforts peace was only temporarily restored and after a while the Albanians continued to pour into the Morea.

The presence of the redoubtable Hasan persuaded Ali it was prudent to return to Tepelene. Ali was clever enough only to engage in military action when he thought it would be to his advantage. There was no point in taking on a high-ranking Ottoman commander when he was actively trying to negotiate a position within the Ottoman administration. Back in Tepelene he set about restoring his family's position and power base there. This proved a good move. When he learnt that his suit at the Porte had failed, he was in a position to call up his traditional tribal and feudal allies and turn on Kurt's nearby garrisons in force, proceeding to ravage the mountain districts between Tepelene and the outskirts of Ioannina for the next two years. Kurt Pasha had no desire to tackle Ali head-on but the Porte, who wanted Ali's disruption dealt with, forced his hand. Even though Kurt could muster a superior force of 10,000 men, including 100 cavalry, he could not defeat Ali in battle in the mountain passes, so he resorted to laying siege to Tepelene. For a moment Ali was on the back foot. Shortages of food and the lack of plunder, the sustenance of the *palikars*, whose loyalty depended on the amount of booty a leader could provide, meant that the expedient tactic was to slip through the blockade without resorting to open battle. That Ali was on the loose caused alarm throughout Greece, so much so that the Venetians, who were now referring to him as the 'famous Ali Bey' of Tepelene, and the Russians were alerted. The Albanians were hoping Ali would be their champion and heap revenge on their adversaries after their mauling under Hasan Pasha, so when Kurt Pasha was informed that Ali was making for Butrint, he too thought he was making for the Morea with that intention. Kurt sent a force of 6,000 to the Bay of Arta, distributing sums of money amongst the local chieftains as they went, to cut Ali off from his route south and trap him against the sea. Ali wasted no time in mustering the support of his allies, Islam Bey of Klisura, Hasan Tsaparis, son of Suleyman and Aga of Margariti, and Demoglou of Konispoli, on the coast south of Butrint. His friends kept the local forces of the pasha of

Delvino busy skirmishing while Ali slipped further south towards Arta and Preveza. Ali's manoeuvres alerted the Venetians and caused such a panic the pashas of Trikkala and Eubeoa were asked to send their armies to Kurt Pasha's aid. But Kurt had misread Ali's intentions. With his 6,000 men tied down protecting the coast, Ali changed direction and headed for Ioannina, taking and fortifying important villages on the way.

Kurt's troops under his son-in-law, Ibrahim Bey, were unable to dislodge Ali and a stalemate ensued. After failing to engage Ibrahim in a decisive encounter Ali again retreated to the safety of Tepelene. Kurt tried to impress the Porte by sending a number of severed heads as proof of Ali's demise, but order had not been restored and the unrest continued. Although Ali had not been able to defeat Kurt's forces outright, each step enhanced his prestige. Once more he had been able to defy Kurt and undermine his authority, moving and raiding at will and collecting considerable booty in the process. The Venetians too had taken notice and were ready to open up relations in order to use him as a counterweight for their own protection. The pasha of Delvino, Mustafa Kokka, had become a particular thorn in their side, threatening territory that they laid claim to near Butrint and Ali had become such an important player that he could be used to influence the Porte in who was appointed governor of the town. In 1783, acting on his own authority and risking the accusation of treason, Ali sent a formal deputation of friendship to the *Provvedentore de Mar* at Corfu. In return for offering to help the Venetians in their objectives, Ali, who expected any day to receive the title of pasha of two tails, asked them to intercede on his behalf at the Porte to speed up the process. The Venetians kept their side of the bargain, describing Ali in flattering terms, while he caused trouble for Mustafa Kokka to emphasize his military weakness. Furthermore the Porte had the problem of backpay still owed to the Albanians who had put down the Greek revolt in the Morea during 1769–70, which had reached astronomical sums. Ali's satisfactory solution of the Butrint problem that had soured Turkish-Venetian relations for some time and his high prestige among the Albanian fighters underlined that he was now the de facto force in the

Fig. 23: *Albanian palikars in pursuit of an enemy* (1820) by Charles Robert Cockerell.

region and it was time to bypass Kurt Pasha and Mehmed's rebellious son Kara Mahmud Pasha Bushati of Scutari. In 1784 Ali was made *mir-i-miran* on the condition that he led 1,000 troops on campaign, possibly as part of the response to the Russian annexation of the Crimea. He was then promoted to pasha and made governor of Delvino for over a year.

After a twenty-year struggle leading his Albanian followers on campaigns of widespread pillaging and extortion, Ali had demonstrated that he was more than a match for any of the government forces sent against him. His policy of exploiting small hostilities, personal vendettas and family feuds, in preference to open warfare, ate away at his competitors' authority until he achieved his aim of re-establishing his family. Having been accepted into the Ottoman elite, it appears he did not keep his promise to the Porte to go on campaign. This may have been because the Crimean crisis had been put to one side, but whatever the reason; instead he diverted his might against the inhabitants of Hormovo. Hughes attributes this move to part of a general imposition of his will on the towns and villages around Argyrocastro, his ultimate goal, which he hoped to take by exploiting internal divisions. He did not achieve that aim but his smaller targets fell to him. Hormovo had shown friendship to Argyrocastro in the past so it was an opportune moment to play out his grudge against them for the part they had played in the humiliation of his mother and sister and he came down on them without mercy for their persistent resistance to their feudal master. A further justification is hinted at by Leake who tells of their reputation for terrorizing the Pass of Tepelene by waylaying and robbing travellers; now the roles were reversed with Ali the law-enforcer. According to Hughes he had made approaches to the town under the pretence of friendship and to seal an alliance, but when it came to ratifying their agreement, instead of appearing with a few hundred followers he let loose over 1,000 men who razed the village to the ground. The men were killed, the women and children sold into slavery, and the headman, Cavus Prift, roasted alive on a spit over an open fire; or in the words of the *Alipashiad*, he 'became a kebab in the frying pan'. It was obviously something Ali was not ashamed of. The ferocity of his actions had the desired effect of frightening the neighbouring villages into submission and gaining him the governorship of Ioannina soon after.

The semi-autonomous coastal enclave of Himara had long been a source of trouble. They were steadfast old allies of the Suliotes and both sought refuge in each other's territories. With their close links to Italy, the Himariotes had a long history of resisting Ottoman occupation and professional soldiering, their young men finding employment in the rival armies of Venice and the Kingdom of Naples. The Venetians had their own *Reggimento Cimarrioto* which they had deployed in their wars in the Morea and used to garrison their Ionian possessions but with their decline the Himariotes were used on a more irregular basis. Good relations with Venice who controlled the straits was vital to their shipping and a boost to their income in times of privation and their collaboration had helped the Venetians maintain forts along the coast. The Russians too recruited sailors for their navy from the area and like the Suliotes, the Himariotes had supported the Russians in the failed Orlov Revolt. The Porte saw Himara as a weak link in its defences and, as nominal subjects of the Sultan, owing taxes and military service, their actions were highly questionable. As governor of Delvino, Ali could claim jurisdiction and in 1785 he moved against them. Rather than the open conflict with the Porte pursued by his rival pasha in Scutari who was courting the Austrians, Ali could subdue the Himariotes on behalf of the Sultan, strike a blow against Venice and consolidate his own power at the same time. Despite little assistance from their friends Russia and Venice, they even approached Austria for help, Himara held out. Ali had other matters on his mind.

His first attempt to rule in Ioannina had been a failure. He had made enemies of both the Greeks and the Turks and protestations were sent to the Porte. After his refusal to give up the post, he was ousted in favour of a resurgent Kurt Pasha. Before he could make any attempt to retake Ioannina, he was then called on to fulfil his duties to the Sultan. The alternative expansionist policies of Kara Mahmud Pasha of Scutari were trying the patience of the Porte. While Ali had been busy in Himara, Kara had been invading Montenegro in the hope of creating an independent state with the blessing of Austria and Russia. During the following campaign Ali may have acquitted himself well, but the general outcome was not a great success. The *Alipashiad* credits Ali with capturing the important town of Ochrid in Macedonia, taking 2,000 prisoners and sending 1,000 heads to Constantinople, much to the pleasure of the Sultan. Despite the poem's attempt to make Ali the hero of the hour who brings Mahmud to heel, Mahmud had managed to sow discord amongst his enemies, including defections from Ali's Albanians, forcing an accommodation with the Porte. There is a suggestion that these defections were due to a lack of commitment on Ali's part, but he showed enough loyalty to the Sultan against his insurrectionist rivals to enhance his position within the Porte. From the government's point of view at least it was useful to pit overreaching regional leaders against one another in the hope that they would be mutually weakened.

Ali was soon called away again to support the Turkish war effort led by the Grand Vizier Koca Yusuf Pasha after resumption of hostilities along the Danube. It was during this war with Russia and Austria (1787–1791) that he is said to have entered into secret correspondence with Prince Potemkin, by this time the ex-lover of Catherine the Great, promising his allegiance to Russia if Turkey lost the war. The story is that his favourite nephew Mahmud was taken prisoner by the Russians and during the negotiations for his release, Ali and Potemkin discussed matters

Fig. 24: The Turkish Army advances on Sofia in Bulgaria in 1788, by Lucas Hochenleitter.

to their mutual advantage. Ali was fully aware of Catherine's intentions regarding Greece and the revival of the Byzantine Empire. Under Potemkin's influence the first step was the creation of a new independent Orthodox princedom of 'Dacia' from the Ottomans' Danubian provinces with Potemkin as Prince. They exchanged gifts, and a regular correspondence between them was commenced, from which Ali entertained strong hopes of being acknowledged sovereign of Epirus once his friend had taken Constantinople and installed Catherine's grandson Constantine as Emperor. Richard Davenport claimed in his *Life of Ali Pasha* (1836) to have seen a watch 'set in diamonds' that Potemkin gave to Ali as a show of his 'esteem for his bravery and talents'. Despite the Russian success Potemkin's relations with Catherine had soured. Hughes asserts that this correspondence, along with other contacts that Potemkin had with Greek and Turkish chieftains, became known to Catherine and probably brought about his death, presumably alluding to the rumour that he had been poisoned at Jassy during the peace negotiations. For Ali, campaigns like these would have been a learning experience where he witnessed first-hand the discipline of the janissaries and the European troops on a large scale. Although the war did not go well for Turkey, they lost the Crimea to Russia, personally for Ali it was another step forward. Rather than the trail of bloody murders that Pouqueville delights in to account for his promotion, including that of the treacherous Selim Bey Kokka of Delvino whom he supposedly stabbed with his own hand on the orders of the Porte, it was as a reward for his services in war that he was awarded the pashalik of Trikkala in Thessaly.

In the meantime Kurt Pasha had died. Kurt was succeeded in Berat by his ally, Ibrahim Pasha, who would continue the rivalry with Ali for control of central Albania. Despite this there was a power vacuum left on Kurt's death and the Porte, as usual accepting the reality on the ground, gave back to Ali control of Ioannina, to the displeasure of some of the inhabitants who fled the city for the remote areas. Threatened by Ali's surrounding of the city in a show

Fig. 25: Ioannina (1820) by Charles Robert Cockerell.

of strength with forces raised from his new domains in Thessaly and a fake document of authority from the Sultan, the colourful account has it that the inhabitants of Ioannina were hoodwinked into letting him in before the Porte could do anything about it. Other traditions suggest that Ali had garnered enough support from the notable families of Ioannina and the important surrounding villages willing to petition the Sultan for his appointment. For instance, through their commercial activities the wealthy families of Kapesovo in Zagori had connections in Constantinople and by cultivating such alliances Ali was able to create a network with links to the capital. The *Alipashiad* makes much of Ali's connection with Zagori, suggesting it was part of his inheritance bequeathed by his father. Most accounts of Ali attribute him with influence in high places at the capital and a willingness to use bribery as well as persuasion to achieve his ends, and Hughes credits his advancement to more than a little financial coercion through his friends. That some of the inhabitants would welcome Ali as a liberator was due to the state of near anarchy that prevailed within the town walls, with feuding families taking potshots at one another from the windows of their fortified houses; a situation of lawlessness reminiscent of that between Montagues and Capulets in fourteenth century Verona. Hughes' theory was that his petitions failed, so acting before news could arrive he inveigled his way in before any action could be taken. Ali's own court archives give the earliest known reference to him as 'pasha of Giannena' as 15 March 1788, a date probably close enough to his seizure of power, a moment that made him the de facto autonomous ruler of the area for the next thirty-four years. The formal recognition of Ali's position by Abdul Hamid was one of the last acts of his reign; a post confirmed by Selim III on his succession.

Once installed Ali made sure of his situation by looking after the right people, courting those who needed his favours and recompensing his supporters with positions and rewards. The pashalik of Ioannina was followed by his appointment to the long coveted post of der-vendji-pasha with the responsibility of keeping communication with the Porte open. With these formal titles to back up his authority it was now time to consolidate his power within Epirus by other means. Like his mother before him, Ali realized that advantage could be attained and sustained through alliances cemented by marriage and with Ibrahim installed in Berat, this was a good moment to shore up his north-eastern flank while he dealt with mat-ters in southern Epirus. The marriages of his sons, like his own, would be made for strategic advantage. Hughes tells us that Mukhtar and Veli and his nephew Mahmud Bey were duly married to daughters of Ibrahim Pasha of Berat and Avlona, who having previously shunned his advances, was now obliged to acquiesce; this is independently confirmed by Ismail Kemal Bey, Ibrahim's great-nephew. Ali's sister, Shainitza, likewise was a commodity and she was married off to Suleyman of Argyrocastro, the town Ali had long had his eyes on. Suleyman's family came from nearby Libokovo in the Zagori region, where Ali built a fortified seraglio as his sister's dowry. According to Leake she had been married previously to Suleyman's brother Ali, but he had died, or was murdered by his brother with Ali Pasha's connivance. Shainitza's son Adem became governor of Libokovo and her daughter by her first husband was in turn married to Veli Bey of Klisura. With Ioaninna and his network of alliances in place, he could now turn to the vexing problems to the south and the coast, where Venetian authority had undermined the efforts of previous governors.

Chapter 4

Ali Pasha's Life: The Fall

Ali's early life gives no indication that he was seeking kingly power at the outset. With hindsight the chroniclers played up or invented moments of good fortune to mark out Ali as a fated man and rather like Macbeth and the witches, the idea of ascending to the 'throne' was nurtured by mystics and fortune-tellers. In the same manner, much is made of him cynically removing rivals one by one by murder and intrigue. If Ali had a moment when it became clear the path was opening for him to be more than a provincial ruler it was with the acquisition of the pashalik of Ioannina and the control of the mountain passes. His fortunes were enhanced by the fact that he achieved this at a time when there was a momentous shift in the international political situation that put Epirus at the centre of diplomatic intrigue. The likelihood is that Ali, like any opportunist, took each step as it came, taking advantage of the new realities to play one party off against another and as his power increased his ambition merely increased with it until the realization dawned that he could carve out a little empire for himself, chipping away a bit at a time without directly threatening the Sultan. A priority was the neutralization of the various disruptive factions competing with one another, the klephts, the armatoli, the Albanian beys and agas, the Christian notables, so as to bring the whole region under a centralized government system. He could achieve this with the apparent blessing of the Sultan on the pretext that he was weakening the arbitrary actions of the armatoli and the ayans (powerful Muslim landowners) that caused distress amongst the peasant population. Ali was the master of utilizing petty rivalries and the art of divide and rule. Under the cloak of bringing justice to all he could attack the rich and powerful, earning a reputation amongst the poor farmers of being, in Finlay's words, 'a hard man but a just pasha' while lining his own pockets. Rather than the random acts of previous Muslims defending the Empire he would be systematic and justified, seen as doing his duty as the Sultan's vassal.

An extreme example of Ali's ruthless opportunism and exploitation of a situation was how he dealt with Moscopole in modern Albania, a once wealthy mountain city near Konitza. Said to be the largest town in the Balkans, it was a leading Aromanian (Vlach) and Greek intellectual centre, well endowed with schools, a hospital, an orphanage and numerous churches. It was such an important centre of culture that it possessed the first printing press in the region outside Constantinople from which progressive, and to the authorities dangerous, ideas were disseminated. When the inhabitants learnt of the Russian intention to aid a Greek uprising in the Morea they made the mistake of letting their support for the Orlov Revolt be known, and in consequence they were raided by Albanian irregulars in 1769. After a series of attacks at the hands of brigands, the town was already in a reduced state when Ali delivered the *coup de grâce* in 1788. Given their past sympathies and with Turkey at war with Russia it was perhaps a convenient time to deliver such a destructive blow to the town that it could never regain its former position. Referred to as Bossigrad in many of the sources, the reason for Ali's attack, carried out with his usual trickery and with the aid of the armatoli, Palaiopoulos and Kanavos, was that he was ridding the passes of bandits. Kir Petros, a native of Konitza, informed Leake that Moscopole and Konitza previously contained 5,000 to 6,000 houses, but after the 'tyranny of the pashas' they were reduced to 800. Petros, who worked in the service of Ali, put much of the present distress of the local Christian population down to the avarice of the Bishop of Ioannina. Whether this was a factor or not, with their town destroyed the population of Moscopole moved elsewhere, many of the elite fleeing to Thessaly and Macedonia, or even further afield to Vienna, Budapest and on to Transylvania where they were influential in awakening the national consciousness of the Romanians. Berat and Konitza were the main beneficiaries from Moscopole's commercial collapse. The presence of many disposed artisans and merchants from Epirus in towns out of Ali's reach indicates that these actions were part of a policy to ruin economic rivals in order to enrich his capital at Ioannina. One beneficiary was Monastir, along with its neighbouring villages. Monastir was enriched to such an extent by fleeing Christian Aromanian craftsmen and tradesmen that it would eventually supersede Ioannina as the regional centre after Ali's fall.

Fig. 26: Ioannina and Corfu.

The pashalik of Ioannina included Thesprotia, which was home to the semi-autonomous Muslim Tsamides and the Christian Suliotes, a situation Ali would not be prepared to endure. Theoretically the Suliotes paid their dues to an official based in Ioannina, the spahi, at this time Bekir Bey. Leake tells us that Ali wanted to take this directly into his own hands, and when Bekir refused he was promptly put in prison. Up till then the Suliotes had been dutiful subjects paying their taxes. This seems rather at odds with the fact that various pashas and armies had made several attempts to subdue them over the course of the century and they were renowned terrorizers of the surrounding villages. Their recourse to armed resistance appears something of a chicken and egg situation, Leake apologizing for their behaviour as their only recourse to Turkish intimidation. To shore up their position the Suliotes had formed a confederacy that dominated a large number of neighbouring villages. Only thirty miles south-west of Ali's capital at Ioannina Suli posed a constant threat, because within its romantic and precipitous mountain stronghold it was so remote that even in the Second World War the British were able to set up an airbase there from where they could operate virtually undisturbed by the Germans. With a population of no more than 450 families divided into 19 clans, it could muster a fighting force of 1,500 men. With Turkey engaged in its war against Russia and Austria on the Danubian border their lawless activities, which were again causing disquiet amongst the locals, were more than an irritant. A diplomatic success scored by Russia in the Treaty of Kutchuk Kainardji (1774) that concluded the previous war was the acknowledgement by the Ottomans of Catherine as protector of the Orthodox Christians within the Empire. This gave her an excuse to interfere over the border with her agents fanning the flame of discontent. Once again she invited the Greeks to throw in their lot with Russia in order to divert Turkish forces. This time her pleas fell largely on deaf ears; the Peloponnesians were no longer enthusiastic, still suffering as they were from the reprisals of the Albanian irregulars for their part in the Orlov rebellion.

The ever-eager Suliotes were another matter and they responded positively to Catherine, thus providing Ali with an ideal opportunity, to move against them as a loyal supporter of the Sultan. Contemporary accounts also implicate Ibrahim Pasha and his allies in inciting the Suliotes against Ali; but the fact that, in March of 1789, the chieftains of Suli wrote to Louitzis Sotiris, the primate of Vostitsa (modern Aigio) in the Morea and a Russian agent, declaring that they had gathered 2,200 men ready to take up arms against Ali as the Sultan's representative in Epirus, confirms Russian involvement. Forewarned of the Suliotes' intentions Ali immediately mobilized his forces. He attacked Suli with his old allies the Tsapari family and the agas of Paramythia and a force of 3,000 men. Luckily for Ali, the Russians having encouraged them once again their support fleet failed to materialize. Ali's first assault was beaten back with considerable losses, and spurred on by their success, the Suliotes turned rogue and joined forces with klephtic bands from the Pindus, ravaging both Greek and Albanian villages in Acarnania as far as Arta and up to Ioannina itself. The failure of the Russians scuppered any plan of the Suliotes joining forces with the sea captain Lambro Kanzani (Lambros Katzonis) who was fighting with the Russian navy in the Aegean. They were said, however, to have supplied men to Kanzani when he, having also been abandoned by the Russians, turned pirate and began harrying Turkish shipping. Kanzani, who dined with Byron in Constantinople in 1809, achieved further fame by making an appearance in *Don Juan* and *The Bride of Abydos*.

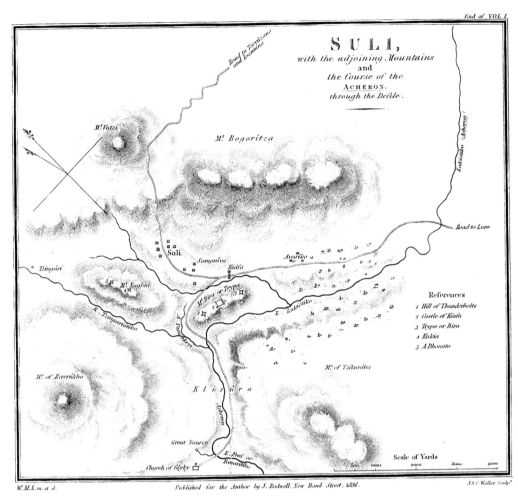

SULI,
with the adjoining Mountains
and
the Course of the
ACHERON,
through the Defile.

References
1 Hill of Thunderbolts
2 Castle of Kiafa
3 Trypa or Bira
4 Kukia
5 A Dhonato

Published for the Author by J. Rodwell, New Bond Street, 1836.

Fig. 27: Map of Suli by William M Leake, *Travels in Northern Greece*, Vol. 1 (1835).

The actions of the Suliotes had lost them friends amongst the armatoli, and if Ibrahim was involved he may have had a change of heart, the arrangements for Veli's marriage to one of his daughters have been put to around 1792. Having failed in his direct assault on Suli, Ali turned to another tactic, guile, and an art with which he would be popularly associated. In the klephtic song known as 'Katsoudas', his ruse to capture an adversary is to dupe him with an offer of friendship. Katsoudas is invited to Ioannina to join Ali's service. At first Katsoudas is warmly entertained by Ali, inducing him to lower his guard, confess his misdemeanours and hand over his booty; then as he bows his head in submission in comes the executioner and 'off went his head'. This reputation for double-dealing and deception became a major component of the various versions of Ali's dealings with the Suliotes. Their fame for uncompromising resistance and Ali's attempts to crush them ensured that their confrontations would take on mythical proportions almost from the outset. All the chroniclers dwell on the same details. In 1792 Ali was mustering an army said to have numbered up to

10,000 men to attack Argyrocastro in response to the town's lack of enthusiasm in accepting his imposition of a Bey. This was apparently merely an elaborate feint to lure the Suliotes out from their mountain stronghold. Ali wrote in Greek to the Suliote captains Georgios Botsaris and Lambros Tzavelas asking for their assistance. Several translations of the letter are given in the accounts; the one quoted below was made by Sir William Eton from a copy given to him by a dragoman who was in Ioannina at the time:

> My friends, Captain Bogia [Botsaris] and Captain Giavella [Tzavelas], I, Ali Pasha, salute you, and kiss your eyes, because I well know your courage and heroic minds.
>
> It appears to me that I have great need of you, therefore I entreat you immediately, when you receive my letter, to assemble all your heroes, and come to meet me, that I may go to fight my enemies. This is the hour and the time that I have need of you. I expect to see your friendship, and the love which you have for me. Your pay will be double that which I give to the Albanians, because I know that your courage is greater than theirs; therefore I will not go to fight before you come, and I expect that you will come soon.
>
> This only, and I salute you.

The captains cautiously took the bait, perhaps only to test Ali's intentions. Botsaris replied saying he could not muster enough followers but that Tzavelas would join his army with seventy men as a sign of friendship. After at first being put in the frontline, their suspicions were confirmed when Tzavelas and his men were surprised and seized, some killed on the spot and the rest put in chains and sent to Ioannina. Ali then marched on Suli. Botsaris was already waiting for him. Following the usual Suliote stratagem he had retreated and was dug in with provisions on Mount Tripia, the four villages abandoned and the wells soured. Ali took personal charge aided by Mukhtar, by then pasha of the two tails, and a number of vassal chiefs; and in his train, Tzavelas. Various means were then tried, including the threat of death by flaying alive, to persuade Tzavelas to betray his kinsmen, but to no avail. Tzavelas was then offered his freedom and overlordship of Suli if he could get the Suliotes to submit. Tzavelas agreed, but he was required to hand over his 12 years old son, Fotos, in exchange as surety. Once safe in the mountains Tzavelas sent Ali a letter:

> Ali Pasha, I am glad I have deceived a traitor; I am here to defend my country against a thief. My son will be put to death, but I will desperately revenge him before I fall myself. Some men, like you Turks, will say I am a cruel father to sacrifice my son for my own safety. I answer, if you take the mountain, my son would have been killed, with all the rest of my family and my countrymen; then I could not have revenged his death. If we are victorious, I may have other children, my wife is young. If my son, young as he is, is not willing to be sacrificed for his country, he is not worthy to live, or to be owned by me as my son.
>
> Advance, traitor, I am impatient to be revenged. I am your sworn enemy. Captain Giavella.

Fotos was taken to Ioannina. Eton's dragoman claimed he was a witness when the boy answered Veli Bey's assertion that he was waiting orders from his father to roast him alive by saying, in true playground manner, that he was unafraid because his father would do the same to Veli's father if he got hold of him. The Suliotes continued the struggle undeterred and in time-honoured fashion the women joined the fight under the command of Moscho, Tzavelas' wife. After making no headway in penetrating the high strongholds and some of his support beginning to waiver Ali was forced to cut his losses. He released Fotos and his other hostages, paid a ransom for the liberty of his own prisoners and signed a truce. Yet another campaign into Suliote territory had proved futile and costly, his troops driven back near to the outskirts of Ioannina by the Suliotes and their allies and the number of his Albanian troops killed counted in the thousands as to the less than 100 Suliotes. Eton was a well-connected and well-travelled observer resident at the time in Moscow and Constantinople. His account of the war is the earliest published and written soon after the events; its stories embellished on by later writers to become part of the Suliotes folklore. Eton's quotations from letters give it the air of veracity but his mistaken and colourful account of the death of Ali's son Mukhtar in

Fig. 28: 'Suli', *Journals of a Landscape Painter in Albania…* by Edward Lear.

one engagement throws an element of doubt on the details. If the exact details are in doubt, the result was not. For Ali it was a humiliation he would not forget.

Correspondence from Ali's archive places Veli's wedding in around August of 1794. One of Ali's patrons, Spyridon Golemis, could not attend, so he wrote in apology to Ali in July sending two boxes 'of a few sweets' as a wedding gift. He expressed great joy at the news, implying a relationship of genuine affection between Ali and Veli. The sources reveal that Ali's relationship with Mukhtar was less cordial. Soon after or on his wedding Veli was given the title of pasha. Assuming Veli was not taking another wife, and there is no indication he did so, this was the marriage made to cement good relations between Ali and Ibrahim of Berat.

Despite Ali's setback in Suli, his standing at Constantinople was significant. In response to a plea from the pasha of Negroponte (Euboea) Ali was able to use his influence to effect a reversal of the death penalty imposed on him. Ali's position of strength had been attained by force within an environment of lawlessness but it now was vital to maintain the peace in order to keep his coffers filled. Villagers complained to him of raids by klephts, often from neighbouring villages, and Suliotes stealing sheep. By offering protection to towns and villages in return for declarations of loyalty he could increase his network of control over an ever-expanding area, planting his representatives and negotiating terms and tax arrangements as need be. Typically letters addressed to Ali from his supplicants are full of obsequious and flattering phrases reflecting the power relationship between them. The people of Kokosi in Thessaly wrote to Ali in 1794 on behalf of 'Platini, Scourpi, Koffi, and the rest of the villages', beginning, 'Your most glorious, sublime, prosperous pasha, our lord, we your servants… kneel in front of your highness, and we kiss your noble hand, and footprints…'. They go on to request the prolonged stay of one of Ali's *boluk-bashis* (officers) with his men to protect them from bandits. In response his letters are terse and factual. Similarly on his becoming pasha of Ioannina, the villagers of Kato Soudena asked to be put under his protection in return for payment, and pointedly everyone signed the letter with a promise. Protection was not only from bandits. Although he was officially a representative of the government, Ali offered protection from the Sultan's tax collectors too, diverting funds that otherwise would have gone to the state for modernization, particularly to the army, or from other persons in authority. By ceding their village to Ali communities could put themselves under his jurisdiction. As Kostas Mitsou, a notable of Dervenditsa (Anthochorion near Metsovo) in the Pindus wrote in his diary, 'In the year 1795… Ali Pasha made us slaves and took our village as a *cifi-lic*', and for this plus a yearly tribute he undertook to pay their local taxes to Trikkala, but not those to the Porte. Ali further interfered with the collection and disposal of government tax revenue through the bribery of officials or the allocation of tax collecting duties to his family and followers. According to Finlay the higher ranks of the Orthodox Church colluded with Ali in as much as the bishops were willing to act as his tax collectors, hence the comment by Kir Petros to Leake about the Bishop of Ioannina.

Not all communities were cowed. Sometimes roles were reversed and Ali would pay to bring a community into his realm or villages would threaten to breakaway, as in 1802 when the villagers of Chebelovo complained that Ali was showing favouritism to their neighbours. If a community was discontented with Ali's rule it could seek recourse in the Ottoman kadi courts and in neighbouring imperial authorities, or even directly in Constantinople itself. The political intrigues of the Imperial Court meant that his position as dervendji–pasha could never be totally assured and so he kept the wheels oiled at central government through his connections at the capital. In 1797 Stefanos Misiou, one of his lobbyists in the Phanariot elite, informed him that there was a rival bid for the control of the passes. Misiou advised him to make a higher offer to the Treasury and to seek better relations with the local communities who paid him tax, as complaints would give the authorities the excuse to give the post to his rival. In 1798 Ali's power was felt as far as Veroia, a regional centre in Macedonia, and in 1799 he was formally granted the governorship of Thessaly to rid the region of bandits, followed by all of Rumeli. The area that Ali controlled and that which was formally recognized as his were not exactly coterminous, but by shows of force he was able to exert pressure to extract taxes beyond the strict confines of his borders. By 1803 several villages in the district of Florina, also in western Macedonia were concluding agreements regarding taxes and dues to be collected. From correspondence with the Divan Efendi at Constantinople it is known that his tax-collecting powers eventually stretched as far north as Prilep, in the centre of the modern Republic of Macedonia, through the ruse of using false identities as a tax-farmer.[1]

In 1796 Kara Mahmud Bushati of Scutari invaded Montenegro once more, but this time with the approval of the Porte so as to bring the fractious tribes under control. When he was killed in battle at Krusi, one of his territories, the sanjak of Ochrid, temporarily passed to Mukhtar, formalizing the spread of Ali's influence in the north. The extension of Ali's territory north and eastwards did not tempt him to move his centre of operations. Ali was relatively secure within his own mountain homeland and with his acquisition of the natural regional centre of Ioannina, he became part of an international network. The stability he brought helped the town become more cosmopolitan and his increased importance attracted a growing number of foreigners to his court. The French already had consuls at Arta and Preveza when, according to Vaudoncourt, Ali tried to approach Louis XVI as a precautionary counter to protect him against his enemies at Constantinople, with no success. Once he was firmly established though, he was strategically well placed to take advantage of the forthcoming political manoeuvrings of Britain, France and Russia. By 1794, according to the Russian Consul General at Ragusa (Dubrovnik), Cezzar Pasha of Damascus (who later helped in the defeat of Napoleon in Egypt), Mahmud Bushati Pasha of Scutari and Ali Pasha of Tepelene were regional governors who had usurped authority and the Porte could do little about it. Ali's weakness was his inherited problem of the Venetians who hemmed in Epirus from the sea, controlling the ports and the Ionian straits. They had obtained an agreement from the Porte in 1788 that allowed no Turkish vessels access and no gun emplacements within a mile of the coast. These constraints were a hindrance to the trade of Epirus as well as to Ali's military ambitions. But Venice's star was on the wane. The Treaty of Jassy, concluded between Russia and Turkey in 1792, allowed Greeks to sail under the Russian flag, laying the foundation of Greek shipping and opening up trade with the Crimea. Events then changed even

---

[1] Tax farming was tax collecting through a third party who would perform the function for a fee, a common perk in the Ottoman system.

more dramatically to the west in Europe. Revolution in France was followed by the arrival of the French on Ali's doorstep as the dominant force. Eton's dragoman informant of the events in Suli was an interpreter sent on business to Ali Pasha in Ioannina by the French consul of Salonika, Esprit-Marie Cousinéry, a philhellene and supporter of Greek independence. Here he met de Lassale, the consul of Preveza, or as Davenport calls him 'a shipwright', and the discussions turned understandably to developments in France and the revolution. Lassale's mission was to obtain timber from Epirus for the French Navy, and in the words of the drag-oman, 'revolutionizing that country'. The policy of the French was to turn Ali against the Porte and make him the 'successor of Pyrrhus'. Lassale offered French assistance with arms and ammunition if Ali could subdue Suli and Himara. Lasalle's further involvement was short; he met an unhappy end, shot by one of Lambros' captains on the streets of Preveza.

From 1792 the French Republic was at war with much of Europe, and by 1794 their forces were making ground in Italy under their dynamic young general, Napoleon Bonaparte. The Republic of Venice fell to Napoleon in 1797 and by the Treaty of Campo Formio the pos-session of the Ionian Islands and the neighbouring ports of Arta, Preveza, Vonitsa, Parga, Igoumenitsa and Butrint were transferred to France. French eyes were then turned to the mainland. These outposts, and the islands beyond, for so long a thorn in the flesh of the Ottomans, were prizes that Ali coveted to consolidate his own position, and he was prepared to manoeuvre in whichever way necessary to get them. Panagiotis Aravantinos, the nine-teenth century historian of Epirus, claimed that Ali had already surreptitiously obtained the governorship of Arta under the false name of 'Mustafa', a person who never existed, holding it from 1796 until his death. In the meantime the French established garrisons under the command of General Antoine Gentili and a small naval force at Corfu. When General La

Fig. 29: 'Kimara', *Journals of a Landscape Painter in Albania…* by Edward Lear.

Salchette and 280 grenadiers marched into Preveza with the aura of liberators the people gave the troops a warm welcome. The British may have derided Napoleon as that 'Corsican upstart' but his famous victories meant that he became an idol to many who saw him as a potential liberator, a notion he was happy to encourage. His charisma was such that even German intellectuals imagined him as an almost Christlike figure riding at the head of his army, a man of destiny, or as Friedrich Hegel put it, 'the world-spirit on horseback', an idea that travelled to the uncowed clans of the Mani Peninsula in the Peloponnese who took to praying to his portrait alongside that of the Virgin Mary, while the klephts of Epirus flocked to the banner of his Ionian regiments. The advance of the French armies was seen by many of the subjugated people of Europe as a march of freedom. In Vienna, inspired by the ideal-ism of the French Revolution, Rigas Feraios was agitating for a pan-Balkan revolution and printing pamphlets on political reform and 'the Rights of Man'. Caught up in the euphoria of the moment the townsfolk of Preveza called their transfer to France as the 'First Year of Liberation'. Rigas was on his way to Venice to ask for support from Napoleon when he was apprehended by the Austrian authorities. Napoleon in turn was more interested in Egypt and ultimately the route to India. Although the Ionian Islands were merely stepping stones within this grand plan, Greek liberation would help dismember the Ottoman Empire. So as Napoleon fantasized about becoming liberator of Greece, French agents set to work stirring up revolutionary sentiment.

Rather than the policy of the Venetians, who fostered good relations with the pashas of Delvino and had supported local independently minded groups such as the Suliotes and Himariotes as buffers to protect their coastal enclaves, the French sought to make friendly advances towards the rival pashas to sow discord within the Empire. Ali saw an opportunity in this new situation. Professing a mutual hatred of the Venetian aristocracy that had ruled the Ionian Islands he immediately opened secret communication with Napoleon, then still in northern Italy. As relations between France and Turkey were verging on open war, this was tantamount to treason. The French proved so anxious to appease him in order to facilitate their own agenda against Turkey, that Ali was able to persuade them to help him put an end to the independence of the Himariotes once and for all. Gentili reported back that Ali was full of admiration for Napoleon and the French. Ali made a fuss of the deputation to Ioannina, even bestowing a wife on a member of the party, the young adjutant general Rose, and in exchange for a tricolour cockade and promises of friendship agreed to dispatch supplies in return. Rose's marriage was a grand affair during which a *ballon aerostatique* was released from a fairground and if the girl was Ali's illegitimate daughter as was suggested, their friendship was more than formal. In a secret meeting with Gentili, Ali was more forthright, asking for armaments, military technical assistance and access for warships in the waters around Corfu. As a result of his charm offensive, in the spring of 1798 Gentili agreed to connive with Ali in ferrying a body of his Albanians from Arta through the straits by night in contravention of the treaty that had stood between the Venetians and the Porte to launch a surprise attack on Nivitza (Nivice), the most prosperous town on the coastal littoral between Butrint and Avlona. The fact that men from Himara were employed in the Neapolitan Army that fought against Napoleon may have influenced Gentili's decision. Landing Ali's troops in the bay at Lukova to the north they outflanked the town which commands the entrance to the narrow valley routeway into Himara from the landward side. His force attacked Nivitza and its neighbour Agios Vasili, a mile to the north, on Easter Sunday when the inhabitants were at prayer, taking the town and other villages, reducing them to ruins, and ravaging as far north as Himara itself. Six thousand unarmed civilians were said to have been slaughtered, some by roasting alive and impalement, and the rest of the population were sent to Ali's farms near Trikkala, their land then divided up to be cultivated by his planted population of Saranda. Ali left a small square fortress at Agios Vasili guarding the entrance to Himara and to keep an eye on the remaining population of Nivitza. With the Himariote league destroyed and the whole of Himara from the important fisheries of Saranda to the castle and harbour at Porto Palermo, he had possession of the coast as far as Avlona and a region encircling the pashalik of Delvino. Ever aware that his actions would be reported at court he made sure that his agents in Constantinople put a favourable spin on his conquest to reassure the Porte it was done to subjugate the infidels; and as a safeguard he duly paid a feudal tribute to the government.

Over the winter of 1797–8 duty called once again along the Danube. This time Osman Pazvantoğlu was the problem causing the Sultan grief. The rebel governor Pazvantoğlu was carving out his own state with its capital in Vidin, in modern Bulgaria, and an army variously estimated as from 50,000 to 100,000 men had been dispatched under the Grand Admiral Hüseyin Küçük to take the city and capture the renegade. Ali was reluctant to show himself to the French as subservient to the Sultan but his enemies at the capital would make the most of his non-compliance to an official decree. Ali tried to absent himself from having to take to the field in person by using his position of dervendji-pasha to require the people of Karpenisi in the southern Pindus to write to the patriarch of Constantinople informing him that they were in fear of bandits if Ali left them unprotected. This ruse evidently did not work. According to Pouqueville, Ali took 20,000[2] of his Albanians to the front, where it is suggested that he needed a show of force to protect himself from assassination. In the event, Ali distinguished himself in the conflict, but overall the campaign ended in failure, and as was the way of things, Pazvantoğlu was forgiven by Selim III and made a pasha; for his part Ali was rewarded with the title *Aslan*, the Lion, by the Porte. This seems a more likely scenario for his acquiring the title *Aslan* than the massacring of the Himariotes as is suggested in some sources. The campaign against Vidin took place in February 1798, so Ali may not have even been present in Epirus during the attack on Himara; Mukhtar had been left in charge at Ioannina. The French were angered by Ali's involvement against Pazvantoğlu, whom they were also grooming, and Ali in return was disappointed in their lack of financial and military support. They had even gone so far as to offer him the crown of Albania once they had taken the Morea, but it was soon evident this was not going to happen. With relations soured, both sides underwhelmed by each other's commitment, it was expedient that on his return home he now felt duty-bound to heed the Sultan's call to drive the French out of Epirus.

In June 1798 the French took Malta. The next step was their long-held objective of Egypt, precipitating war with the Ottomans. Two weeks later the army disembarked at Alexandria pushing

---

[2] Other figures are 10,000 or 16,000.

Epirus to the sidelines. The siege of Vidin lasted until August, so Ali was still on the Danube at this time. Mukhtar had been keeping Ali informed of subversive activities by the French, including the dispersal of leaflets and tricolour cockades designed to incite revolt, particularly amongst the Suliotes. Ali attained special dispensation from the Sultan to return home to deal with matters while still keeping the lines of communication open with the French. One version of events has it that he offered to throw in his lot with the French in return for the Island of Santa Maura (Lefkas), the ex-Venetian dependencies on the mainland and the right to place a garrison on Corfu. If true, the commander-in-chief of the French forces on Corfu, General Louis François Jean Chabot, unsurprisingly turned down his offer. His course of action was made clear with the declaration of war in September. The accounts of Hughes and Pouqueville suggest he gained a commission to deal with French aggression through his agents at Constantinople, implying some underhand lobbying, but it would obviously have been in the Porte's best interest for him to take authority in a time of war as the most powerful pasha in the region and guard the Empire's western border. The version of events given by Ali's hagiographer Haxhi Shehreti in the *Alipashiad* is that the Porte was so slow to react that he took it on himself without official sanction to mobilize over 20,000 troops against an impending French invasion.

Having assembled his forces, he did not wait for the French to make the first move. Encamped before Butrint and with little feeling for his previously professed friendship, he lured the unfortunate Rose, temporarily in charge at Corfu, to a meeting at Filates, near Igoumenitsa, where he was promptly taken prisoner, tortured and then sent to Ioannina in irons. That Rose fell into Ali's trap was in part due to his naive trust in Ali's loyalty. Ali evidently had given the impression that he had thrown in his hand with the French and his manoeuvres were to counter any approach by the Turks or Russians. Rose apparently gave little away as Ali adopted the same tactic on the French sub-lieutenant of Butrint. Whether Ali gained much from these methods, the lightly defended Butrint soon fell, and with Igoumenitsa, the main port of access to Corfu, in his hands he turned on Preveza. General Chabot, who was at Butrint, thought it more expedient to cut his losses and retreat to Corfu. Ali's approach was made easier by his old adversary Georgios Botsaris, who allowed his troops passage through Suliote territory in return for a payment. Many of the inhabitants had already fled to the nearby islands leaving the town to be defended by La Salchette's garrison and the townspeople's pro-French civic militia, some Ionian islanders and 60 Suliotes under Captain Christakis, numbering around 700 in all. The French decided to make their line of defence the narrow isthmus from which direction any landward approach has to be made rather than the town walls. They hastily built entrenchments and fortifications close by the ancient city of Nicopolis which overlooks the plain before the town, but to no avail. Ali's superior force, which included his own Greeks and Suliotes, outnumbered them ten to one. On 12 October, Ali watched the ensuing battle, during which Mukhtar led a cavalry charge, positioned on a hill above Nicopolis. Hughes records that he built a small serai there on the same spot on which the Emperor Augustus had watched his victory over Anthony and Cleopatra at the Battle of Actium fought out in the bay. Under the weight of such odds the town fell, a victory in part eased by the counter-propaganda of Metropolitan (Archbishop) Ignatios of Arta, an agent of Ali's, who undermined the resolve of the defending Greeks.

Fig. 30: Louis-Auguste Camus de Richemont directing the building of a trench at the Battle of Nicopolis (1894) by Felician Myrbach.

Over the next few days the French garrison and its Greek defenders were massacred, some of them it was said in Ali's presence as he entered the town. According to Pouqueville, Ali was unable to prevent this wholesale slaughter by his troops, which does not entirely square with subsequent events. The following day Ali had 300 Greeks killed in front of him. Some defenders who had escaped to the mountains foolishly returned on the promise of an amnesty; 170 of them were then summarily executed by the sword at the Salora customs. Those that survived were marched to Ioannina where Ali organized a grand reception for his victorious troops. Many of the prisoners died on the way but those that made it walked at the head of the procession holding the cut and salted heads of their companions while they were jeered at and pelted with stones by the city's pro-Ottoman residents. The women and young girls were, as the *Alipashiad* proudly attests, 'sold… at Ioannina like negro slaves'. Pouqueville put the surviving French total at 200, in other words most of the French force, undermining the notion that they were slaughtered along with the Greeks. Nine of the captured French grenadiers, La Salchette and two officers were then sent in chains to Constantinople for questioning, along with the heads of the executed prisoners for the acknowledgement of the Sultan in a job well done. One of the officers, the commander of the French engineers, Louis-Auguste Camus de Rhichemont, had been spared through the personal intervention of

Mukhtar, who had been impressed by his bravery. The surviving officers were joined by Rose, and sent to the Castle of the Seven Towers, the Yedikule fortress in Constantinople. There they met Pouqueville who had been taken prisoner by Barbary pirates as he was returning from Napoleon's campaign in Egypt after the Battle of the Nile. Rose's condition was too far gone and he died of his wounds despite Pouqueville's attempt to save him. Richemont did survive and wrote an account of the engagement. He was ransomed in 1801, possibly through the auspices of Napoleon's mother.

The massacre at Preveza became a notorious event, remembered in song as witnessed by Byron on his arrival at the Salora customs, and with repercussions that would influence

Fig. 31: Lieutenant Richemont taking down an Albanian horseman.

Fig. 32: Being shown the severed head of a French soldier by Ali's men by Felician Myrbach (1894).

Greek nationalism. Some Suliotes fought with Ali and Byron was more taken with their war-like braggadocio than that it was there that the 170 were executed. Preveza itself was left in ruins, the property of the Greeks seized by Ali and redistributed amongst his Albanians. The remaining population was dispersed into the surrounding countryside where they were set to work in the marshy land around the Ambracian Gulf. Hughes estimated that the population had fallen from 16,000 to 3,000 when he visited and that Ali, in contrary fashion, continued to despoil the town and oppress its inhabitants while at the same time making it his naval depot, the 'Portsmouth of Albania', and a favourite residence. Ali next turned to Vonitsa on the opposite shore of the Ambracian Gulf. This time the town fell without a fight, the inhabitants surrendering after the intervention of Archbishop Ignatios on Ali's behalf.

Parga, to the north of Preveza, had long been a place of refuge for fugitives from Turkish rule and was thus of particular annoyance to any ruler of Epirus. Backed by a steep mountain its territory formed a small enclave two or three miles round the city. With a population of up to 4,000, Parga was always considered an important military outpost for the Ionian Islands, and particularly in respect of Corfu for which it was termed 'the Ear and the Eye'. Immediately after the fall of Preveza, Ali wrote to the Pargians, 'Learn men of Parga, the victory of this day and the fate of Prevesa'. Offering an olive branch and a promise allowing them the form of government they desired 'as fellow subjects of my sovereign', he proposed a parley. Ali's first entreaty was ignored. He persisted, leaving out mention of subjugation to the Turks but urging the inhabitants to murder the French garrison. The Pargians replied on 16 October that Ali's tyrannical actions, their love of liberty and their sense of honour meant they had to turn down his offer. The strong defences of the town and the citizen's resolve made Parga a particularly vexing problem that would become another of Ali's fixations. In the meantime, since his harassment of Missolonghi in the late 1770s, Ali had had his eyes on the region of Aetolia-Acarnania lying to the southeast of Vonitsa. Having been unable to gain control through interference in its governance, he saw a chance to move his troops into the province, known as Karli-Eli in Turkish, while forcing the region's civil administrator and tax collector to seek refuge in the citadel at Vonitsa. This act of intimidation brought a reaction from the Ottoman government who pre-empted any further aggression by granting the entire sanjak of Karli-Eli minus the sub-district of Missolonghi as a private royal domain to Mihrişah Valide Sultan, the mother of Selim III and co-regent, forcing Ali to back down from a direct confrontation with the Porte. The province was administered on behalf of the Valide Sultan by Yusuf Agha, a cousin of her treasurer. Leake tells us that Ali made frequent presents to Mihrişah and Yusuf in order to keep on good terms.

Santa Maura, the closest of the Ionian Islands separated from the mainland by a narrow channel, became a more legitimate object of desire. But international events were to thwart Ali as he was on the brink of seizing the island. Napoleon's attempt on Egypt had forced Turkey to join the Second Coalition led by Britain and Austria into an alliance with Russia. Ali's actions had made the Porte anxious, and as a Russian-Turkish Fleet made its way to take the islands from the French it was made clear that Ali should be sidelined. Unsure of the welcome he might receive and of his objectives the government refused to send troops to Ali for any attack on island defences. Ali was on the point of negotiating another surrender with the local inhabitants who were ready to revolt against the French garrison when the Russian squadron arrived. Barely a month had passed since the fall of Preveza and Admiral Fyodor Ushakov[3] was laying siege to the island and citadel of Corfu; the Pargians decided this was a good time to put themselves under Russian protection, and the French garrison, vulnerable to attack from the sea by the Russians and by Ali on land, had decided it was better off in Corfu leaving the town undefended. Once the Russians had taken Zante they offered Parga

---

[3] Sometimes given as Oksakoff.

their protection, and the Russian admiral sent a Russo-Turkish force to take charge of the city. Napoleon, who was still in Egypt, must have been blissfully unaware of events as he was still writing to his officers in December urging them to cultivate good relations with Ali.

After a year of fighting the Russo-Turkish force took Corfu, ending the French occupation of the Ionian Islands. Ali, with his son Veli and Ibrahim Bey of Avlona were obliged to assemble a large land force to join the siege. Their part in the Siege of Corfu was largely of a diversionary nature but Ali's involvement increased his reputation to such an extent that it was widely reported that Rear Admiral Sir Horatio Nelson himself, only recently victorious over the French Fleet at the Battle of the Nile, sent his congratulations. In 1800, the seven islands were formed into the independent Septinsular Republic, a tributary state of the Ottoman Empire paying a triennial tribute but under the protection of both powers and with a 'Byzantine' Constitution acceptable to the Porte. It had been important to the Porte for Ali to gain the mainland dependencies before any intervention by Russia. As a result the former Venetian possessions were ceded to Turkey on condition that their religious freedom should be honoured, there should be no extra taxation, they continued to be governed by their own laws and customs and that no Muslim acquire property or settle amongst them, apart from the Turkish governor. Civil unrest on the islands after the change of rule, in the Turkish view stirred up by Russian agents, gave the Russians the excuse to increase their garrison putting the new Republic under their de facto military occupation. Despite the removal of foreign powers from the mainland, Ali was unable to exert direct influence over the ports. The situation as regards to Parga was ambiguous. The Pargians preferred to deal directly with the Porte than fall to Ali so with Suliote aid they resisted his menaces for a further six months while a deputation was sent to Constantinople where, through the minister for the Ionian Islands at the Divan, they procured a *Voivode* (governor) to be sent as protection. When Britain and France briefly made peace in 1802 this arrangement was endorsed in the Treaty of Amiens. Any designs Ali had for further conquest had to be put on hold and the governor of the mainland dependencies, Abdoulah Bey, refused to satisfy Ali's demands allowing him to take possession of Parga. Britain's peace with France was short-lived and on resumption of hostilities in 1803 Ali approached the British Embassy at the capital requesting that an emissary be sent from Britain to him at Ioannina to give advice on how he should proceed. When the first official British contact with Ali, William Hamilton, arrived he made his usual promises of assistance during the coming conflict.

From correspondence sent by Veli, who was in Adrianople at the time, to Ali, it is apparent that Veli thought Haxhi Shehreti was incapable of representing Ali's best interests at the Porte, referring to him as both a 'friend' and a 'fool'. In his *Alipashiad* Haxhi Shehreti suggests that Ali's actions against the towns in French hands were undertaken on behalf of the Sultan to put down Greek insurrection. As the towns were not under Turkish rule and that Turkey was at war with France this seems an unnecessary extra justification. The towns were though a source of increasing Greek nationalist sentiment encouraged through French interference. The Suliotes had received money, munitions and supplies from French ships through Parga. These activities were aimed at weakening the Ottoman Empire. Exchanging French influence on the Christian population of Epirus for Russian was no great improvement, but while they were allies supplies were cut off and the Porte seeing an opportunity obliged Ali to finally bring the Suliotes down. Learning from previous mistakes, Ali realised that a direct assault on Suli was impossible and he initiated a slow war of attrition. With his allies the Tsiparis family of Margariti he blockaded Suli with a ring of twelve fortresses, with one at Gliki guarding the only road in. This was slow and dangerous work as Suliote sharpshooters picked off his men. During construction an estimated third of Ali's troops deserted. While his investment of Suli was progressing Ali was keeping an eye on other matters. In 1802, another of his slow-burning campaigns finally paid off when he took Delvino after seven years of intermittent fighting that Leake said left the surrounding villages in ruins. Now he had Epirus under one control from Arta to Avlona and Tepelene. Suli was the only blemish in his complete mastery of the region.

The Suliotes themselves were in some state of disarray. Georgios Botsaris had been persuaded or bribed to join Ali's camp, taking with him some valuable munitions. Fotos Tzavelas, the son of his old comrade Lambros, was now the leader of the Suliotes. Georgios did not survive the war, he was said to have died of a broken heart when his son and 200 of his followers were cut to pieces by his erstwhile comrades in the mountains. While Ali received imperial supplies and could call on the support of his surrounding pashas, including that of the lukewarm Ibrahim of Berat, mustering an army of around 20,000 men, increasingly the Suliotes were becoming starved and exhausted. He finally attacked in autumn 1803 leaving nothing to chance. The main body of Suliotes were assembled at the stronghold of Kungi, just above Suli village, where with their situation becoming more desperate and short of food and ammunition it was decided that those who wanted to surrender could. Ali, realizing that his soldiers were also wearying of the fight, saw a chance to take the leaders alive as hostages and expel the Suliotes from their stronghold. Through the auspices of Veli an arrangement was made with Fotos Tzavelas for the Suliotes to surrender. A monk known as Last Judgement Samuel, who was in charge of the magazines, took control of the faction that preferred death to capitulation, and with the knowledge of Fotos, he waited with five companions until Ali's troops came to take the arsenal and then when all were inside he put a match to it. Once the Suliotes agreed to abandon their homeland, the four villages were destroyed, and the survivors numbering around 4,000, were packed off to find refuge in Parga and the Ionian Islands. A few put their trust in Veli and remained. That Ali and Veli were not always in accord is shown in an outspoken letter to his father: 'And regarding the arrival of your highness to these parts [Suli], I don't find it appropriate because you have a long shadow and they are afraid and don't come out; that is how I see it and may your years be long. Your slave, Velis'. Veli had shown himself to be more of the diplomat, seeking common ground rather than conflict. In Holland's assessment: '… His military reputation is below that of Mouctar Pasha, but in political sagacity, he is considered to be greatly his superior'.

The history of the Suli War has become the stuff of legend and partisan storytelling. The versions that portray Ali as the epitome of the cruel and duplicitous tyrant, especially those heavily reliant on Perraivos' *History of Suli and Parga*, portray all his actions as ones of betrayal. In these versions he cynically sets his men on the Suliote refugees as they make their way to Parga, the Suliotes only surviving because the soldiers have not got the stomach to kill them. The Suliotes who remained, under a promise of protection from Ali withdrew to the safety of the mountain of Zalongo. Whether this was all a ploy or a typical piece of Ali double-dealing, he reneged on his promise and ordered his troops to attack them. Many of the Suliote men were prepared to fight to the death, the women also preferred death rather than be taken and sent into slavery. In order to cheat fate over fifty women, holding their children in their arms, formed a circle dance on the cliff at Zalongo and then one by one, reaching the edge they threw themselves over. The dance became commemorated in folklore as the Dance of Zalongo and the news of the mass suicide of the Suliote women so well known that it spread throughout Europe. These events may have happened but another version makes Ali's motivation different. The *Alipashiad* does not gloss over that many Suliotes were made slaves but puts the emphasis on Fotos' desire for peace and Ali's honourable dealings with him, releasing his wife who had been made hostage, and giving him and several families safe passage to Parga. William Plate of the Royal Geographical Society, summarizing the evidence in *The Biographical Dictionary* (1842), infers that Ali was infuriated by the deception of the monk Samuel and sought to take revenge on the fugitive Suliotes, who were then forced to fight their way through to Parga. Some decided to double back and seek refuge at the convent at Zalongo. The convent was stormed and the defenders slaughtered. Those that could escape, mainly women and children, made their way to the mountain top where they performed their dance of death rather than dishonour before they could be reached. Of those Suliote men who survived in exile some went on to find service wherever they could, for the Russians or the French, in the Ionian Islands or the Turkish Army, or even with Ali. For those unfortunates that were captured the harem awaited the women and children, while for the men a slow death of torture, followed by impalement or burning.

The defeat of the Suliotes had an effect on the relationships among the neighbouring tribes and families. Treaties of friendship and non-aggression existed between Muslim and Christian families. Fotos Tzavelas was a blood brother of Isliam Pronios, the most powerful bey in Paramythia. Ali became aware that the Pronios family was only giving half-hearted support to his cause, even passing information to the other side. Ali was not prepared to turn a blind eye. At first he invested their castle at Galata with a token force as a gesture only to increase it at the first so-called provocation, a fabricated alliance with the pasha of Berat. The Pronio family were soon thrown off their land and the village of Paramythia destroyed. Using this technique he infiltrated the district bit by bit. The ascendancy of his one-time allies, the Tsaparis family, similarly came to an end. In 1807, like their neighbours the Proniates before them, they were forced by Ali to abandon their properties and seek refuge in the Ionian Islands. From there they went to join Muhammad Ali Pasha who had taken control in Egypt, only returning on the death of Ali to resume their positions as tax collectors and *chiflik* holders.

Ali's victory over the Suliotes was soured by the death of his wife, Emine, who according to the melodramatic account expired after her entreaties for Ali to show clemency towards the Suliotes fell on deaf ears, leaving him heartbroken and blaming himself for her murder. They had been married thirty years or more and Ali was now around 60 years old. It was towards the end of 1802 that his third son Selim was born to one of his slaves, perhaps an indication that domestic matters were a little more complex. She was then put in charge of the harem at

Tepelene. From a letter to Lord Elgin, British Ambassador to the Ottoman Empire, from his chaplain Philip Hunt who was in Corfu, we learn that on hearing the news he had a brother, Mukhtar shot the unfortunate Tartar messenger dead on the spot. It is usually attested that as a reward for his destruction of Suli, Ali was made *beylerbey* (lord of lords) or Valisi of Rumeli and his son Veli, the pasha of the Morea, a promotion that may also have caused some friction between the brothers. The *beylerbey* was a high rank equivalent to a viceroy with military authority for the province. There were probably other reasons. Constant war was having a disruptive effect on the stability of the Balkans. While Ali had his hands full subduing the Suliotes, the activities of the klephtic bands had not been curtailed. In a letter to Ali in March 1802, Ismail Pashabey informed him that he had mustered 200 men to go after the robber bands in Patraziki (Ypati) and Agrafa straddling the road to Lamia. This region in the southern Pindus was where the one-time shepherd turned klepht, Antonis Katsantonis, operated and his exploits were such that he was rapidly becoming a local hero.

At the same time in the north, Pazvantoğlu had resumed his raids along the Danube and the threats from both Muslim and Christian bandits (hayduks and klephts) were so intense that Selim III had been forced to issue a decree (10 July 1801) renewing the virtually dictatorial powers granted to the Valisi of Rumeli, Hadji Mehmed Pasha for a further two years. This appointment must have achieved little as, faced with the continued anarchy, the Sultan then gave the post to Ali on 28 January 1803, before he had subdued Suli in the winter of that year. Ali was not one to miss an opportunity to make the most of his new position and summoned the neighbouring pashas to contribute to an army that would make a show of strength in the troubled districts. Having amassed 80,000 troops Ali made a tour of inspection of the new territories in Macedonia that were now under his official authority, issuing advance orders for their provision with food and money, expenses that naturally fell on the local inhabitants, particularly the trade-guilds. By the spring of 1804 he was encamped outside the walls of Philoppopolis (now Plovdiv in southern Bulgaria) having left a trail of destruction and dispensing rough justice to those who had disturbed the peace. This exhibition of his power did not fail to raise alarm bells at the capital and unrest amongst Ali's tributary troops was put down to the connivance of his enemies. Ali prudently decided it was time to go home, laden with booty taken from the robbers. Back in Ioannina he met with the newly arrived British Consul-General John Philip Morier, to whom he expressed the possibility of Epirus becoming an independent state built from the ruins of the Ottoman Empire with British support. The Sultan was right to be worried.

The activities of the klephts closer to home continued, and those of a devious mind implicated Ali in encouraging the state of affairs to manipulate the Sultan into giving him more power. In 1806, probably due to the death of Mihrişah the year before, Ali achieved his wish to get control of Karli-Eli, so that his domains encircled the southern Pindus where Katsantonis operated. It is not clear whether the actions of klephts like Katsantonis were in support of the Suliotes, motivated as some would have it by their display of stubborn courage, or the exploitation of Ali's preoccupation in Suli and the diversions of Pazvantoğlu. Amongst some of the armatoli and klephts Russian propaganda was having its effect, turning their disaffection into a growing freedom movement, but ideas of national identity were not fully formulated, so the notion that Suliotes and klephts would join forces to create a new state rather than for their own personal version of liberty were perhaps still premature. Prominent amongst the band captains who later became acknowledged supporters of Greek liberty were Nikotsaras (Nikos Tsaras) from Olympus, Demitrios Palaeopolos from Karpenissi and the priest Euthemos Blakavas, names that would go on to be celebrated in klephtic and patriotic song. Blakavas was an example of a man turned outlaw through the outrage he felt at the injustices put on his people, whereas Nikotsaras and Palaeopolos were at various times armatoli in Ali's service. When Nikotsaras turned bandit after shooting a Turkish soldier he caused such havoc to the population of Thessaly that he had a price put on his head. After a suitable hiatus in his activities he made up with Ali and was reinstated as one of his armatoli, but the mood of the freebooters was changing. Nikotsaras' intentions became clearer when he joined the Serbian uprising.

The situation along Turkey's border had deteriorated once more. As a term of their cooperation with the Ottomans, the Russians had imposed the rule of two Phanariot Greeks with pro-Russian leanings as hospodars in Wallachia and Moldavia, Constantine Ypsilantis and Alexandru Marusi respectively, thereby drawing the provinces into their orbit. Previously Ypsilantis had been active in Vienna in 1799 in the nascent Greek independence movement and he was sympathetic towards the Serbian uprising. After the Austrians and their Russian allies were crushed by Napoleon at the Battle of Austerlitz in 1805, the fragile relationship between Turkey and Russia cooled with Selim, who had tried to pursue a course of neutrality between the competing powers, beginning to favour the French interest. Ypsilantis' loyalties were now too much for the Porte and the two hospodars were deposed. In retaliation Ypsilantis turned on his previous masters, returning the following year at the head of 20,000 Russian troops heading towards Bucharest to unite with the Serbs. To counter the Russian offensive a large army was mustered by Sultan Selim under the Grand Vizier Ibrahim Hilmi Pasha with regular troops and a core of janissaries drawn from Constantinople and the Balkans. Ali and Ismail Pasha of Serres were given responsibility for provisioning the army. With Russia back at war with Turkey, and its ally Britain, Ali saw another opportunity to show his loyalty to the Sultan by attacking the Ionian Islands, ostensibly to bring them 'back' under Turkish control, as dependencies, while at the same time resuming his claim on the coastal towns of Epirus directly controlled by the Porte. Under the pretext of defending the towns from Russian aggression, he got Veli to drive out the governor Abdulla Bey from Preveza and move his forces into Butrint, Igoumenitsa, and Vonitsa. Ignoring the treaty of 1800 he imposed his own arbitrary system of government, confiscating property and levying new taxes. Once again Parga stood out against his entreaties. Turning to the Russians for protection, the admiral commanding at Corfu responded by sending a garrison.

On his part Ali demanded that the Russians surrender up the Suliotes who had taken refuge in the islands. The Suliotes had been joined by klephts from the Morea fleeing Veli's attacks, including the most famous of all and future leader of the Greek revolt, Theodore Kolokotronis, making up a sizeable force. When Count Georgi Mocenigo, an Ionian Greek in Russian service, refused Ali's demands, Ali prepared to attack Santa Maura where many of the Greek captains and their men were exiled. After Austerlitz Ali had reopened diplomatic relations with France and Pouqueville was appointed ambassador to his court in November 1805 replacing Julien Bessières who had been resident in Ioannina for a year. Bessières and Pouqueville were already acquainted; they had been on the same ship taken by pirates in 1798. Napoleon's victory had forced the Habsburgs to leave the Third Coalition against France that included Britain and Russia and dissolve their Empire, and formally relinquish their claims in the Treaty of Pressburg to any territory in Italy and Dalmatia, making Epirus and France neighbours. According to Pouqueville it was through his efforts and the good auspices of French diplomacy at Constantinople that Veli had obtained the Morea and Mukhtar the sanjak of Lepanto, including Kari-Eli, although how he would have achieved this seems far-fetched as he was in Paris after his release by the Turks in 1801. Good relations with Napoleon meant Ali could count on French aid for his designs on Santa Maura. Ali's force of 5,000 men was augmented with two gunboats, French officers and artillery and Guillaume de Vaudoncourt, an artillery general from Napoleon's Italian service, was put to work on the siege emplacements and defences at Preveza. Since around 1800 Ali had embarked on an ambitious programme of castle building and public works and Vaudoncourt went on to refashion Ioannina on a grand scale. In response Moncenigo persuaded the Senate of the Septinsular Republic to send Count Ioannis Antonios Kapodistria, who had no military experience, to organize the defence of the island. Kapodistria, the former Inspector of Education, was given the title of Military Governor and Commissioner Extraordinary; he would go on to become the head of the Greek state.

Over the summer Kapodistria set about fortifying the narrow isthmus by which any attack on the island was likely to come. He was aided by Archbishop Ignatios who had grown sick of Ali's methods and escaped his agents to join the other Greek volunteers from Corfu, the other islands and the mainland, and Colonel Michaud, a French engineer in Russian service, and a force of Russian troops. The Russian troops included a regiment of Light Riflemen led by General Papadopoulos, a Russian Greek. This was an irregular force made up of 3,000 Himariotes, Suliotes, Greeks and Albanians who had fled from Ali and were now in Russian service, veterans of conflicts in Naples, Tenedos and Dalmatia. With Russian troops behind him and confronted by Ali with his French officers, Kapodistria prepared for a more 'European' battle. He built a regular system of defence along an extended and well-prepared line, while Bishop Ignatios hired a fleet of small boats against a sea attack. Meanwhile Ali proceeded with caution; in part waiting for reinforcements and restrained by his French advisors who were reluctant to fight their fellow countrymen on the opposing side in a matter of little concern to them. A stand-off ensued broken up by skirmishes during which Kapodistria's men took prisoners to gain information on Ali's movements. Kapodistria's cause was aided by the raids of Katsandonis and Kitso Botsaris, a son of the 'traitor' Georgios Botsaris, and their 700 armatole who attacked one of Ali's villages, burning much of his property and forcing him to retaliate. Kitsos too had changed sides, having served Ali as armatole of Radovizi near Zalongo and as a negotiator between Ali and the Suliotes. While the 'patriotism' and commitment of some of the other volunteers was questioned and complaints made against Kolokotronis for seizing ships indiscriminately, Ali's attempt to bring up five guns from Lepanto was seen off by a Greek ship manned by armatoli. Such efforts delayed the build-up

of his forces in Preveza including some Greeks and forty French artillerymen. As he waited
for more French reinforcements, a further interruption occurred when he had to return to
Ioannina with 1,600 men to meet with emissaries from the Sultan.

As Ali was poised to attack, and with nerves fraying on the opposing shore, he was thwarted
by events far away in East Prussia. Napoleon's decisive victory over the Russians at the Battle
of Friedland forced Tsar Alexander to make peace and the Treaty of Tilsit (July 1807) put
the Ionian Islands, Butrint, Parga, Preveza and Vonitsa back under the protection of France,
rather than as was implied by French promises, giving them to Turkey. By August, French
troops under General César Berthier were arriving in Corfu. When Kapodistria notified Ali
of the situation he replied that a truce between France and Russia had nothing to do with him,
but he would respect it as long as no armatoli remained on the mainland. Ali's interpretation
meant he held on to Butrint, Preveza and Vonitsa, but he was unable to influence events at
Parga where the Russian garrison handed over to the French as agreed. Kapodistria would
have preferred the exiled armatoli to remain in Russian service but he managed to convince
them to enrol under French command as an alternative to a life of continued outlawry. The
change of alliances did not dampen Ali's desire to acquire Parga, but now he tried the diplomatic tack through Berthier, who in turn notified Napoleon. Napoleon was not impressed
with Ali's demands and told the Pargians to defend their country. When Kapodistria learnt of
the death of an armatole during Katsantonis' defeat of Ali's troops at an engagement known
as the Battle of Mount Prosiliako near Agrafa, his statement that the fighter had 'sacrificed
his life for his country' gave expression to the growth in nationalistic feeling. For his part
Ali lost Veli Gega, a member of his Supreme Council. But for the moment Kapodistria and
the armatoli had to bide their time. Even if Ali was aggressively beyond control and the
Ottoman government a chaotic 'tyrannical and unjust domination' that had to be destroyed,
the Septinsular Republic was not at war with the Porte, but part of the French Empire.
Liberty, equality and fraternity were no longer the watchwords; Napoleon had crowned himself Emperor of the French in 1804, King of Italy in 1805 and Protector of the Confederation
of the Rhine in 1806, an equivalent post to that of Holy Roman Emperor previously held by
Francis II, the Emperor of Austria. For the future though, the siege of Santa Maura was a
boost to Kapodistria's standing during which he gained the confidence of the armatoli and
klephts, and the belief in the possibility of a free Greece.

Despite Ali's threats toward Parga, General Berthier was prepared to negotiate with him
for the sale of 300 horses for his cavalry. At the same time he persuaded Napoleon to let him
form the displaced armatoli into a regiment arguing that it was dangerous to leave them
unemployed. The volunteers left by the Russians were reformed into the *Régiment Albanais*
and they were joined by assorted Greek refugees who were put into their own *Battaillon
du Chasseurs à Pied Grecs* in 1808. The regiments were later amalgamated with the hope of
introducing some discipline into the Epirotes who had brought their families and flocks with
them and were prone to slipping back to the mainland for a spot of pillaging. In 1809 *Les
Chasseurs d'Orient*, a mainly Greek regiment under Colonel Nicole Papasoglu from Smyrna,
joined the Corfu garrison. Papasoglu and other members of *Les Chasseurs* were veterans
of the *Légion Grecque*, two battalions made up of local Greeks that had served Napoleon

in Egypt. They had been mainly active along the Dalmatian coast from 1806, particularly at the relief of Ragusa from the besieging Russians; a few were even present at the Battle of Trafalgar. Papasoglu had seen diplomatic service in Constantinople, and from Dalmatia he had been sent on a goodwill trip to Ali in Ioannina heading up a small group of artillery envoys and instructors. He used the opportunity to recruit some Greeks for the regiment along the way. A number of other Greeks transferred to *Les Chasseurs* from the Russian's own short-lived Greek Corps active in Wallachia between 1807 and 1808 with the help of the French consul in Bucharest.

The actions of Ali and the government had only succeeded in pushing the armatoli and klephts to making common cause. Coming together in the islands and with French encouragement a more coordinated and idealistic plan for the future began to take shape, a future without Ali Pasha. During 1807 the captains on Santa Maura, apocryphally including Kolokotronis, although he makes no mention of it in his memoirs, headed a call to link up with Nikotsaras, Palaeopolos, Blakavas and other klephts operating in Macedonia and the Pindus Mountains. The armatoli and klepht captains met at the Evangelistria Monastery on the Island of Skiathos where they swore an 'Oath of Freedom'. The islanders of Skiathos had taken part in the naval victory of Chesme during the Orlov Revolt and Nikotsaras decided to join forces with the Russian admiral, Dmitry Nikolayevich Senyavin, based at Tenedos whose fleet was preparing to attack Constantinople. In the meantime, under the first Greek flag (a white cross on light blue background) and assisted by the British frigate *Sea Horse* under Captain John Stuart the outlaws made raids on Ali's troops on the mainland Thessaly. During one such raid Nikotsaras was killed. Palaeopolos and Blakavas took their fight towards Ali in the mountain passes. The notion that a klepht confederacy was preparing to overthrow Ali was thought to be looked on favourably by some members of the Ottoman cabinet alarmed by the growth of his power. By the following year the actions of the klephts had became so serious that Mukhtar was dispatched with 4,000 troops to wipe them out. As the actions of the rebels degenerated into brigandage, inflicting damage on Greek and Muslim alike, support for their cause faded. Ali had set his web of informers to work and the band was caught at Kastri on the road to Trikkala in the Pindus after being betrayed by Deliyanni, a fellow klepht. Outnumbered eight to one there was only to be one outcome. Palaeopolos and Blakavas were taken and after two years in an Ioannina prison they managed to escape to Constantinople. Palaeopolos sought asylum from the French and went on to Moldavia. Blakavas was less fortunate. He procured a firman or decree of protection from the Porte and foolishly returned to Ioannina where Ali invited him to a conference at the end of which, true to form, Ali had him seized as he was leaving the room. Blakavas was put in prison where he was well treated during the time it took a messenger to go and return from Constantinople with a permission from the Porte for Ali to do what he pleased with his prisoner. Having got what he needed, Ali duly had him chopped to pieces; it was these remains that Byron and Hobhouse had witnessed hanging on display in Ioannina. Pouqueville claimed to have seen Blakavas suffering under the rays of the hot sun, tied to a stake in the court of the seraglio in Ioannina, his eyes flashing with defiance before suffering the calm death of a hero. In the aftermath Ali's army destroyed the fortified monastery of St Demetrius at Meteora where

Blakavas had sought refuge. His ally Katsantonis was only apprehended in 1809 when Ali learnt he was weakened by smallpox. Ali had him tortured to death and executed in public by having his bones crushed with a sledgehammer.

By now Ali was acting with increasing independence of the Ottoman government. His desire for control of his Adriatic shore, and therefore the islands lying just off the coast, had become so paramount that he was employing agents in London and Paris to further his interests and had even tried to influence the outcome of the Treaty of Tilsit with his own representative, an Italian priest captured with Pouqueville who had converted to Islam and was known as Mehmet Effendi. Contrary to official policy he had kept up relations with Britain and once the Ionian Islands were under the French, shifted his allegiance accordingly. Under pressure from Britain, Selim's faith in France waned and in November 1807 Ali had his first meetings with Captain Leake. The most important took place in secret (out of the prying eyes of Pouqueville) on the night of the 12th on the beach near Nicopolis. Britain hoped to exploit Ali's growing independence and Leake induced him to use his influence at Constantinople to help bring about a reconciliation between the Porte and Britain. In return Ali hoped to get Britain to invade the islands on his behalf. Bessières, now back in Corfu as imperial commissaire after a spell in Venice as consul, was putting his own pressure on Ali for the return of Butrint to France. Through an indirect source the French indicated that they might be willing to pay Ali for Butrint. Ali remained unmoved and his actions began to annoy Bessières. Aware of Ali's intentions to use the British against Parga, he warned him that his newly-formed friendship with Britain would sour his relations with France. At the capital the reforms to the ineffective army that the modernizing Selim was trying to introduce had proved too much for his enemies and the janissaries rose up in revolt. A short period of chaos followed, and in 1808 the Sultan was assassinated. Ali took the opportunity to move outside his jurisdiction by occupying Attica with a military force. Selim's successor Mustapha IV's reign of fourteen months was marked by rioting in Constantinople, and order was only restored when he was deposed and succeeded by Mahmud II, who carried on Selim's work. War along the Danubian front continued nevertheless and Ali responded by sending his sons Mukhtar and Veli.

In January 1809 Britain and Turkey made peace (Treaty of the Dardanelles) and next month Leake, promoted to major, was back from England with a present of artillery and ammunition for Ali to use against the French. From then on until March 1810 Leake was usually resident either at Preveza or Ioannina, from where he made frequent forays into the interior of Epirus and Thessaly. Leake had only been in Epirus a few months when Byron and Hobhouse arrived. Although relations were cooling between Turkey and France, Ali was still provisioning the French troops on Corfu. A testament to the complicated state of affairs was the deputation encountered by Hobhouse on 5 October on its way from Ali with letters to Bessières complaining of slow payment, just as the British Navy was occupying Cephalonia. The British Navy had defeated the French off Zante and was picking the islands off one by one, actions which had precipitated the revolt of the klephts earlier than anticipated. The *Battaillon du Chasseurs à Pied Grecs* who were defending positions on Zante, Cephalonia and Ithaca had been infiltrated by British, Russian and Turkish agents and despite their evident courage their loyalty was questionable. Captain Richard Church, a veteran of dealing with foreign recruits in Corsica and Malta, had been particularly active making his own contacts among the Greeks. They reportedly surrendered at the first shot and the islands fell to the British. As soon as Church took control of Zante he wasted no time in re-forming the Greek and Albanian fighters into the Duke of York's Greek Light Infantry under his command as major. The Greek infantry was quickly trained and put to work in the taking of Santa Maura the following year. Despite the fact Ali had hoped to take Santa Maura himself with British complicity, their success, intentionally or otherwise, had the effect of shoring up his position and changing the direction of future Greek insurrection. The desire for revolution was hardening and Kolokotrnis had ambitious plans. He had made an alliance with Ali Farmakis, an Albanian chief who had quarrelled with Veli, in the hope of forming a confederacy of Suliotes and other Albanian tribes under Hasan Tsapari to overthrow Veli and his father. Kolokotronis wanted to go direct to Napoleon, but when he informed General Donzelot, the governor of the Ionian Islands, of his plans, Donzelot approached Napoleon on his behalf. Donzelot put forward a proposal for 500 French artillerymen, 5,000 Greeks in French pay, a regiment from Corsica, funds for recruiting further Albanians and Greeks, and ships and other transport. To appease the Sultan, he was to be informed that the rebellion was not against the Turkish Empire but to rid it of the usurpers Ali and Veli, replacing them with a democratic government run by twelve Christians and twelve Muslims. Napoleon sanctioned the plan, but as the money was being made available and Epirote recruits raised the British arrived. Kolokotronis, tacking with the wind, joined Church's regiment with the rank of captain. Paxos and Corfu were tougher nuts for the British to crack. On Corfu, Papasoglu's regiment spent its time taking potshots from the batteries at passing British ships and on one occasion he bravely managed to break the British blockade.

British naval supremacy in the Mediterranean was taking its toll on French influence, bringing the Anglo-French conflict right to Ali's doorstep. As they made gains in the Ionian Islands, Ali's old and aged adversary Ibrahim Pasha of Berat, hoping for their protection, had put his faith in the French in return for exclusive rights to the commerce of Avlona and the right to station some artillerymen on his castle walls. As revolt raged in Thessaly, Ibrahim had gathered a league of Ali's enemies around him (Mustafa the former pasha of Delvino, Hasan Tsapari of Margariti, Pronio Aga of Paramythia, the Aga of Konispoli and the Beys of Himara and the Suliotes) and aided by French artillery he began attacking Ali's territory. Ali saw more gain in pinning his colours to the British cause, promising help in their attempt on Corfu and opening up his ports to British shipping. Learning of Ibrahim's plans he had not been prepared to allow French interests to infiltrate into his territory through a rival, opening up another front. With British aid behind him, Ali was able to isolate Ibrahim by bribing his supporters with gold and promises. Consequently Ali was besieging Ibrahim in Berat when Byron and Hobhouse arrived to pay him court at Tepelene. His army of 8,000 Greeks and Albanians was led by Omar Bey Vryoni a native of the nearby village of Vironi, who had seen action against the British in Egypt. An intractable year of skirmishing was brought to a conclusion with the aid of 600 Congreve rockets supplied Leake. When Berat fell, Ibrahim was obliged to retire to Avlona while Ali informed the Porte that he had been required to take Berat as all of upper Albania was in revolt due to the inability and infirmity of the aged pasha who was under the

Fig. 33: *Field Officer* Sir Richard Church in the uniform of the Duke of York's Greek Light Infantry by Denis Dighton.

influence of the French. Initially Ali held back from Avlona, deterred by news from Suleyman Divan Efendi[4] in Constantinople that the Sultan was displeased with Ali's attitude to Ibrahim, but once again in time-honoured manner the new Sultan Mahmud was forced to acknowledge

---

[4] The *divan efendi* presided over the council of the local governors.

a fait accompli as the best policy of maintaining internal order. Avlona's defences were poor and Ali soon had it in his possession; allowing him to tidy up his dominion over the whole coast from Durazzo in the north to Arta in the south, removing any notables that stood in his way. As a sideline he obtained the pitch mines (the basis of modern Albania's oil industry begun in the 1920s) between Berat and Avlona for a small fee from the Porte, allowing him to begin exporting through Avlona to Malta and the Italian coast. Mukhtar was duly installed as pasha of Berat, with Omar as governor, and Ibrahim was sent to languish in prison until, according to Pouqueville he was poisoned by one of Ali's doctors, who was then hung.

In 1810 Byron wrote a letter to Hobhouse from Patras saying that 'Ali was in a scrape'. Ibrahim, the pasha of Scurtari was descending on him with an army of 20,000 men having retaken Berat and threatening Tepelene. Veli, who was on his way to the Danube, was diverted back to Ioannina much to the annoyance of Sultan Mahmud and with 'all Albania in an uproar. The Mountains we crossed last year are the Scene of warfare, and there is nothing but carnage and the cutting of throats'. Byron had hoped to accept an invitation from Veli to review his army in Larissa but that had been sidelined. Byron and the energetic and exuberant Veli appear to have got on. Veli was good-natured and had a sense of humour, but he was constantly running out of supplies and money, as his begging letters to his father attest. Veli may well have inherited Ali's charm, but he also inherited his greed. The Abbot of the Olympiotissa Monastery summed up the general feeling in 1813:

> He [Veli] made a business of seizing villages through the use of menaces, honeyed words or coercion, and then taking them and making them his own by acts of treachery which he justified with specious excuses.

With Ali's actions becoming of increasing concern to the Sultan, a way to weaken him was the removal of Veli from the pashalik of the Morea where his greed was making him unpopular, and his relocation in the less important and closer pashalik of Larissa in Thessaly. Ali's nephew, Adem Bey, Shainitza's third and favourite son and governor of Libokavo whom Byron met on the way to see Ali the previous year, was dead, following another son Elmás who had also died young. There was also a report that Mukhtar had been captured by the Russians but this was to be dismissed as 'Greek Bazaar rumour'. Indeed most of Byron's information was suspect, perhaps a mixture of new and old news. In many ways Ali's star was still on the rise. Through Divan Efendi he knew Pouqueville was trying his best to undermine him at the Porte complaining that he had assisted the British in taking Santa Maura. The Porte did not accept the accusation but Divan Efendi was unsure. French intrigues at Constantinople may have influenced the Sultan's decision to relocate Veli, but Ali was still able to add the sanjacks of Ochrid and Elbasan to his territory and finally take formal control of Argyrocastro and Delvino in 1811. Turkish forces were being massed along the Danube where Russian preoccupations with France had weakened their efforts initiating a Turkish counteroffensive. It was expected that Veli would supply 20,000 men, Mukhtar, 10,000 and Ali would arrive with 30,000 of, according to Sir Robert Adair, the 'best troops in the Empire'. In the event Ali declined to go citing old age and ill health, but most likely he feared that he might be put in prison or worse, so he preferred to watch his back at home.

Tensions though between father and sons were real enough. Veli and Mukhtar were in Sofia, from where they made several requests for Haxhi Shehreti to visit them in confidence. Ali was reluctant, thinking they were going to conspire against him. Ali trusted Haxhi Shehreti enough to confide to him that some of his main concerns in life were his approaching old age and his 'children'. Although his hopes of gaining Santa Maura were dashed when General Sir John Oswald captured the island for the British and they kept it for themselves, he was happy to keep his friendship with Britain for the time being and Ioannina received a new British resident, George Foresti and numerous visits from high-ranking British officers. With the Ionian Islands on hold for the time being he had turned his attentions to outstanding business. The intrigues of the increasingly desperate French on Corfu had encouraged Mustafa Pasha of Delvino to keep in league with his former allies despite the peace between them and Ali. They had hoped to assemble their forces at Argyrocastro, nominally under Ibrahim Pasha but where Ali already had influence within the town through the marriage of his sister to Suleyman. A show of force, including artillery, proved all that was necessary for the gates to be opened to Ali. Mustafa and other leaders were given up by the townsfolk of Gardiki where they had sought refuge in the hope that Ali would spare them. Ali sealed his control of Epirus to the coast by promptly sending the Bey of Argyrocastro, the Bey of Konispoli and the pasha of Delvino and their followers to prison in Ioannina and putting his youngest son, Selim, hardly more than 10 years old, in charge at Argyrocastro. The two sons of Mustapha who were held as hostages by Ali were eliminated and eventually Mustapha and the other hostages vanished from amongst the living.

With the fall of its allies, Argyrocastro, Delvino and the pasha of Berat, Gardiki was left unprotected and exposed to Ali vengeance. Apparently urged on by his grief-stricken sister, Ali was reminded of his duty to her and his mother, and in 1812 he finally wrought his version of justice on the unfortunate town, massacring between 700 and 800 of its inhabitants in revenge for the outrage committed against them forty or so years previously. It is unlikely that he needed much encouragement and rather than being ashamed of the deed it seems he took great pleasure in its notoriety. He diverted Holland on his route from Tepelene to Ioannina with specific instructions to visit the scene of his crime. Having a force of possibly up to 15,000 men at his disposal, Ali was in a position to completely surround the town allowing no escape. Initially his Muslim troops were unwilling to make headway, perhaps fearing the consequence of their actions in attacking co-religionists. The attack was only successful when Thanasis Vagias from Lekil near Tepelene, and a party of fellow Greeks took the citadel. Once the town was taken Ali personally supervised the selection of those individuals to be sent for imprisonment in Ioannina or into slavery, including women and children, in parts of Albania, while those men he deemed in some way to be connected with the outrage of the past were bound together and herded within the courtyard of a large khan. The gates were then locked and the surrounding walls mounted with men who on Ali's signal opened fire. The slaughter continued until all were dead, some finished off by the sword. The thirty-six prominent members of the town sent as prisoners to Ioannina may have been seduced into

Fig. 34: 'The Vizier Ali Pacha, Giving the Fatal Signal, for the Slaughter of the Gardikiotes Shut up in the Khan of Valiare', from *Historical Portraiture of Leading Events in the Life of Ali Pacha, Vizier of Epirus, Surnamed the Lion, in a Series of Designs* by W Davenport, 1823.

thinking they had been spared but on arrival they were taken to a quiet spot and shot. At the site of the massacre a stone memorial was placed with a vindicating account and warning in verse in Greek of the fate that would befall anyone who sought to injure any members of Ali's family. Leake gives a rendition of the inscription in which the deceased explain Ali's actions:

> When Ali was a little boy, deprived of his father, with no brother, and only a mother, we ran with arms in our hands to cut him off. He escaped, skilful as he is, upon which we went to Gariani (Kariyanni[5]) and burnt his houses. It is now fifty years since. It is for that deed that he slew us at the Khan; that he has sent our chief men to the island of the lake of Ioannina, and there put them to death; that he has dispersed our families among all the kazis under his authority, has razed our unfortunate town to the ground, and ordered that it may remain a desert forever. For he is a very just man, and in like manner slew the Khormoites,[6] and ordered that not one should remain alive.

---

[5] Presumably the tiny village of Karjan/Karjani/Qarjani a few miles south of Tepelene, not far from Hormovo.

[6] The people of Hormovo.

Ali then concludes, 'When I consider this terrible slaughter, I am much grieved, and I desire that so great an evil shall never occur again: For which reason I give notice to all my neighbours that they must not molest my house but be obedient, in order that they may be happy.' If this massacre took place fifty years after the capture and molestation of his mother and sister, of which no mention is made, this would date that event at around 1760. The epithet 'little boy' would be more appropriate to someone born in 1750 rather than the earlier 1740 supporting the later date for Ali's birth. Shainitza's wrath was mollified when she received the hair from the victims' heads to stuff the cushions of her divan, but Ali was still not satisfied. Other villages in the vicinity that were in some way connected to Gardiki were also ravaged or destroyed and Gardiki itself left a shell with building materials from the best houses taken to be used in the building of his new seraglio at Argyrocastro.

Ali was now in his pomp and increasingly acting as an independent ruler. Over the next few years his court received a string of visitors, including a Persian khan and the deposed King Gustav IV Adolf (Gustavus Adolphus) of Sweden. Gustav's mishandled campaigns against Napoleon had resulted in defeat by Russia and a palace coup putting his Uncle Charles (XIII) on the throne. Ali's lavish receptions impressed his guests and Gustav presented him with a sword belonging to his predecessor Charles II. Ali's acquisitive nature was not satisfied. He was so impressed by a diamond in Gustav's possession that he bought it for 13,000 pounds sterling, no doubt easing the unhappy ex-monarch's financial situation. Ali went out of his way to please his European guests. At one party attended by Sir John Oswald in 1810 at Preveza an additional chef was imported from Santa Maura to join Ali's own head cook for the

Fig. 35: The quarantine station at Santa Maura from *The Ionian Islands: twelve plates* London, 1821 by Joseph Cartwright.

occasion and the shopping list showed a heavy Italian-Ionian influence. Organizational duties fell to the notorious Thanasis Vagias, who undertook everything from simple transactions to ambassadorial dinners. For his trouble Vagias was provided with five *okades* of wine every day for his personal use from a local wine-seller. All that was left to spoil Ali's satisfaction with his growing importance on the international stage was the irritating obstinacy of Parga.

In 1812, after years of invincibility, Napoleon was in retreat after his ill-fated expedition to Russia and Ali thought the time was ripe for another attempt on Parga. He sent his son Mukhtar, Omer Vironi and Agos Vasiaris and 6,000 men to lay siege. After some fruitless preliminary negotiation with General Berthier, his troops under his nephew Daut Bey took the outlying village of Agia, massacring and enslaving the population, their territory converted to *chifliks* for his favourites. Parga, to where the redoubtable Papasoglu had moved to take command of the castle after his dwindling regiment had been ordered to Ancona in 1813, was then besieged by land, and by sea with a fleet from Preveza. In one attack Daut Bey was killed by fire from Parga Castle. Ali ordered Daut Bey's body to be buried at the frontier in a mausoleum in view of the fortress at Parga as a reminder of what to expect. The French found themselves in an awkward position as they were not officially at war with Ali. So while the Pargians defended their town stoutly, the French resistance was lukewarm. At Anthousa, a hill between Agia and Parga that overlooked the town, Ali had a fortress built to use as a base of operations. When the British took Paxos, opposite to Parga, with the aid of the Greek Light Infantry, the Pargians decided to throw in their lot with Britain as the best policy for protection in the future and sidelining Ali who was now in a tricky diplomatic bind. They

Fig. 36: The town and harbour of Vathi, Ithaka from *The Ionian Islands: twelve plates* London, 1821 by Joseph Cartwright.

approached Captain Garland, and forces were diverted from the blockade of Corfu to take the town. After the French commandant refused to surrender it was agreed that if the inhabitants seized the town themselves, raising the British flag, the British forces would support them. On 22 March 1814, after a short struggle the Pargians took the town and raised the flag. The French garrison was exchanged for a small British one and the French were allowed passage to Corfu. Not only were the French in retreat from Parga, but they were also on the back foot and by May they had been defeated. The French ceded their possessions in the Ionian Islands and on the coast of Epirus to the British when in the Congress of Vienna of 1815 the British were given formal control of the protectorate of the Islands, the coastal towns were not mentioned, leaving the Pargians in limbo.

With any attempts to prise Parga from the British falling on the deaf ears of General Sir James Campbell, who was not to be taken in by any false claims, Ali turned to the Sultan. He accused Parga of being a nest of malefactors and along with the Suliotes, a danger to the Porte. When Campbell was replaced by Lieutenant General Sir Thomas Maitland as the governor of the Ionian Islands, the British Ambassador in Constantinople had been persuaded that a Turkish commissioner should be sent to Ioannina to treat with the various parties. Ali sent a deputy to Corfu on 16 March 1817 to inform Maitland that the Ottoman commissioner had arrived in Ioannina. Maitland was wary enough to have reinforced the thirty-man garrison at Parga tenfold while talks were under way lest Ali tried any pre-emptive moves. He was also aware that the Pargians would not take too kindly to any news that they might be ceded to Ali, so the garrison under Lieutenant Colonel Charles Philippe de Bosset was not there only to guard against any tricks by Ali but any violent reaction on the part of the inhabitants. While negotiations continued Ali set about undermining the population. The inhabitants were forced to repair the walls and prepare for attack in response to his feints and manoeuvres and he cut off supplies from his territories and grain from Cephalonia and Zante to create shortages. Finally on 17 May 1817 at Ioannina, the British, represented by John Cartwright, the British Consul in the Morea, and the Turks, represented by the Vizier Hamit Bey, signed a treaty ceding Parga to the Ottomans in return for Turkey resting its claims to the Ionian Islands. According to the treaty, it was left in the hands of Ali Pasha to guarantee the life, the security and the property of the citizens of Parga. Maitland promised any citizen who preferred to leave rather than remain under Ottoman rule would receive compensation for their losses. The Turkish government were unwilling to pay, but offered Parga to Ali if he were willing to pay. The first estimate by the Pargians was £500,000, the British and Turkish commissioners made separate assessments; the British, £276,075, the Turkish, £56,756. Nearly everyone in Parga chose to emigrate to Corfu, a humiliation for Ali and a burden to Maitland. The negotiations dragged on. In May, Maitland resolved the issue directly with Ali, an agreement was signed stipulating the terms including the compensation. The sum of £150,000 had to be paid by Ali before Parga was handed over.

On the Orthodox Good Friday, 1 April 1819, between 3,000 to 4,000 Pargians began their evacuation, carrying with them the disinterred bones or ashes of their ancestors, the images of their saints, flags and handfuls of soil as a reminder of their homeland; they took to the sea in boats provided by the islanders (the British vessels had not arrived on time) as refugees to start a afresh under British protection on Corfu, but always dreaming of their return. The sad moment of their arrival was witnessed by Kapodistria and his friend Dimitrios Arliotis, who described how the Pargians sat on the shore, gazing across the water to their former home with tears in their eyes, while Kapodistria gazed at them. In May Ali, who had been sniffing at the gates all the while, made his payment and marched into an empty town. On Corfu the commissioners distributed the compensation, after some niggling deductions by Maitland, and the exiles were housed and the poorest fed. The handing over of Parga was even at the time a highly controversial affair. The Pargians thought Maitland a dupe of Ali or in league with the Turks, nicknaming him 'Sultan Thomas'. Kapodistria blamed the tragedy of the 'sacrifice of Parga' on 'the bad faith and miscalculations of British agents' leaving the population 'obliged to deliver their old homes to Ali Pasha for a modest sum of money and carrying with them only the exhumed bones of their fathers'. The experienced Colonel de Bosset, a Swiss in the British Army who had fought at the Battle of Alexandria and was governor of Cephalonia between 1810–13,[7] was highly critical of Maitland's conduct. Maitland was accused of foolishly allowing Ali's men to make the evaluations for compensation and even of embezzling some of the money. It was commonly believed that he and the British had betrayed and sold Parga, not just to the Turks, but to Ali in particular as a cynical reward for his help against the French. The evacuation of Parga was a black mark for British foreign policy and national esteem but it became a symbol of Greek suffering and was turned to useful propaganda for the Greek cause.

Three letters from the Ali Archive give us an insight into his role in the affair and the nature of his demands while negotiating with the British Ambassador. In April 1818, Haxhi Shehreti and Elmaz Metze, his replacement in Constantinople, wrote to Ali informing him that the British Ambassador had been trying to find a solution favourable to Ali on the matter of the financial settlement and that he had met one of Ali's agents, Konstantis Agrafiotis, to say that the British government had agreed to contribute financially towards the compensation, which otherwise would have been Ali's responsibility. However, it transpires from a letter to Ali from Agrafiotis that the British did not accept the accusation that they were in any way responsible for the decision of all the Pargians to leave their homes. They could not have predicted such an outcome which was probably due to their fears linked with the massacre at Preveza, for as Holland put it, Ali had never forgiven the Pargians for their truculence and they in return 'regard him with a mixture of fear and detestation'. Also the cap that Ali had asked of sixty families maximum being allowed to leave could not be imposed retrospectively so the British had given permission for them all to leave their homeland. Parga would be Ali's last triumph. Having at last achieved his goal of complete mastery of the coast he reached the zenith of his power, but as he knew himself, he was sitting on a powder keg that a single match could blow up. Constantinople itself was a tinderbox, where a number of fires raged, said to be the work of discontented janissaries. Elmar Metze informed Ali that the Sultan had sought refuge from a fire in his unoccupied house there. Normally such a visit by the holy presence of the 'king' would require the house being closed down, but on being informed that

---

[7]   He was also the first collector of Mycenaean pottery.

the house belonged to Ali, the Sultan relented, allowing the building to remain in use; an act Metze reassuringly interpreted as all being well and Ali still in favour.

A quarter of a century of war between France and various European alliances was finally brought to an end in 1815 with Napoleon's defeat by Britain and Prussia at Waterloo and his exile to St Helena, ushering in the prospect of peace in Europe for the first time in generations. To preserve peace the major powers adopted a policy under the guidance of the Austrian foreign minister, Prince Klemens von Metternich, to uphold the balance of power by acknowledging each other's spheres of interest and opposing revolutionary or nationalistic movements. A weak link in the chain was the fragile Ottoman Empire, and its impending internal disintegration as the 'Sick man of Europe' became a headache for succeeding diplomats dealing with what was to be known as the 'Eastern Question'. For Britain a stable Turkey was important as a counter to Russian expansion in the East. The prospect of an entente and stability within the Balkans was not necessarily good news for Ali as it made him part of the problem rather than the solution. He could no longer rely on foreign allies to use as a veil for his ambitions, playing them off against each other and the new reality exposed him to closer scrutiny by the Porte. On the Ionian Islands the Greek regiments were disbanded and many klephts who had served under foreign flags had nowhere to go unless they joined the Neapolitan service or, paradoxically, the service of Ali Pasha. Having abandoned hope of getting the islands he turned his efforts to improve his towns and palaces, but signs of strain were beginning to show. In 1818 his beautiful new palace at Tepelene was struck by lightning and gutted by fire. His treasures valued at £2m were saved but his furniture was lost. Ali's relationship with his sons was one of lord and servant, or 'slave' in Veli's words in response to a request for financial assistance to repair the damage. All the revenue from their pashaliks was in Ali's view held in common, for him to dispose of. Ali's attitude to his family was that they were part of his networks. He would work to get them positions at court by force or through lobbying, sometimes financial, and they would give him undying loyalty in return. Ali continued the policy of securing his position through the tentacles of marriage alliances, as Hughes witnessed in 1814 when Veli's son Mahmet married the daughter of a bey of Larissa, but by 1819 the tide was turning and such tactics would no longer prove effective. His one-time friend, Ismail Pashabey, let it be known to the Porte that Veli had been depriving the government of its revenues from Thessaly. Veli was downgraded once more, and transferred to the tiny pashalik of Lepanto, which Mukhtar had to give up to his brother, curtailing Ali's power east of the Pindus.

In 1816 Ali had taken on a new wife, marrying Kyra Vassiliki, his favourite mistress, amidst much 'pomp and ceremony'. The beautiful, according to Hughes, Vassiliki Kontaxi was a Greek from the village of Pilsivitsa in Thesprotia near the Albanian border. She had come to Ali at the age of 12 to intercede for her father's life and after granting her father pardon, she was introduced into his harem. Vassiliki had been allowed to continue in her Orthodox faith and she undertook a number of charity initiatives and financed restoration work to monasteries on Mount Athos. Ali must have indulged her to some extent for she was reputed to have ameliorated some of his policies; and in 1818 she was bold enough to be inducted into the clandestine Filiki Eteria, the secret organization working for Greek freedom, directly recruited by Nikolaos Skoufas, one of the three founding members of the organization. It is said also that she had a brother, George Kitsos, who went on to fight in the Greek revolt. The society had begun to broaden its recruitment to include a certain number of women. Before his death in that year, Skoufas had suggested systematically contacting all women who by their proximity to institutions of power might be useful to the cause, specifically nominating Vassiliki. Skoufas was from the village of Kompoti near Arta and he had worked at various times as an apothecary, a commercial secretary and a hatter. As a merchant he had travelled to Russia, and while in Odessa he had become acquainted with Athanasios Tsakalov and Emmanuil Xanthos. Xanthos was a merchant from Patmos, but Tsakalov was a fellow Epirote from Ioannina who was in Russia to be with his father. Tsakalov had studied physics in Paris where he had been a co-founder of the Ellinoglosso Xenodocheio (the Greek-speaking Hotel), a secret organization whose purpose was to educate the Greeks for the struggle against the Ottomans. The three men came up with the idea of founding a new secret organization to prepare the ground for Greek independence.

To solve the problems of the Empire, Sultan Mahmud like his predecessor Selim, had returned to reform. With the Serbian uprising having been brought to a conclusion, creating a semi-independent state (1817), and other Balkan troublemakers brought into line, Mehmet Sait Halet Efendi, the Sultan's favourite minister, drew the attention of the Sultan to what he portrayed as Ali Pasha's continued disloyal acquisition of personal power. In 1814 his encroachments into the territory of the pasha of Salonika (Thessaloniki) where his agents had been active in a number of towns had caused complaints.[8] Ali's men had been collecting taxes from the region since 1808, causing problems with the local agas, and he had a network of informers to keep him aware of developments. Despite his excuses and the giving of gifts, his massacre at Gardiki had gone down badly with the Divan. With his stock falling at Constantinople, Ali looked to other means to safeguard his position, leaving nothing to chance. He decided that one way to nullify his enemies was to make secret moves to formalize what had in essence been true for a number of years, his existence as an independent state. Through Metze he tried to get his Greek diaspora friends posts as ambassador to Vienna and consuls to the Ionian Islands, Trieste and Leghorn (Livorno). The imperial dragoman, Michael Soutsos, said there might be a chance of Vienna, but by the end of 1818 he had been transferred to the post of *voivode* of Moldova. In 1818, in a bid for Russian support Ali let it be known that he was friendly towards the aims of the Filiki Eteria who were also looking towards the Russians for help. The Filiki Eteria, who were aware of Ali's manoeuvres were happy to encourage him to rebel, in the hope it would create the right circumstance for their own bid for independence. For his part Ali thought he could use the Greeks for his own ends and he approached those employed at his court, announcing that he would assist their organization. But the Greeks kept a distance in case he betrayed them.

Ali was used to double-dealing but his subsequent actions smack more of desperation than strategy as events at Constantinople took a more serious turn. The existence of plague at the capital, where it was never totally under control, gave Ali the excuse to create a cordon sanitaire, with lazarettos on the routes from Epirus to the capital, ostensibly to safeguard his people from its spread, but also as a means of control enabling him to intercept

---

[8] Karaferi, Negosti, Vodena—modern Veroia, Naousa and Edessa.

messages or anyone suspected of being sent from the Sultan to obtain his head. To counter the news from his spies that his enemies were turning the Sultan against him he increased his bribes, but his past was catching up with him. He had played fast and loose with his allies too many times. Ismail Pashabey, who had fallen out with Ali, switched his allegiance and fled to Constantinople where he gained a position of some influence with the authorities. In February 1820 Ismail put out a story that Ali had sent agents to murder him on the streets. Three Albanians were found who confessed under interrogation to being assassins and were executed. The whole thing was quite likely staged, but as a result Ali was declared an enemy of the Porte and Ismail was given the pashaliks of Ioannina and Delvino in Ali's stead. On hearing of this, while continuing his use of bribes, he tried to deflect attention by warning the ministers of the existence of the Filiki Eteria and hoping they would see it as in their interests to keep him in power. Soutsos, who had become a member of the Filiki Eteria, was now using his influence against Ali and used to hearing of Greek conspiracies the Porte ignored him, believing he was the greater danger. Ali responded by turning to the Ottomans' disaffected subjects, the Montenegrans and Serbs as well as the Greeks. He summoned the klephts to a conference in Preveza, promising arms and booty, and at a further meeting of Greeks and Albanians he offered money and a constitution, having approached Metternich to supply a model. The Greek revolutionaries listened but waited, happy to humour him for the moment. Never one to put all his bets on one play Ali also sought assistance from the British. He tried to persuade Maitland to help him promote an uprising against the Turks, something contrary to their policy. Maitland nevertheless referred the matter home. But when Ali met Maitland's representative Sir Frederick Hankey in April 1820 at Preveza, he had changed his tune declaring he wanted reconciliation with the Porte. This time he wanted protection from the British Fleet being aware that his flank was exposed to attack by the Turks from the Ionian Sea. The problem gave the confused Maitland a sleepless night. He was worried Ali might turn to Russia if Britain did not help, but Lord Bathurst, the colonial secretary, had given unequivocal instructions, there was no treaty barring Turkish warships from the Ionian Sea and Britain had no right to prevent naval operations by the Porte against the coast of Epirus.

Ali, of course, had not waited for Britain's reply but had already turned back to Russia offering more than he offered Britain: if Russia recognized his authority under the tsar he would raise his subjects in revolt against the Sultan and help Russia conquer European Turkey. The Russians gave little but a vague intention of support in the hope Ali might defy the Sultan. Having claimed to be a member of the Filiki Eteria he sought to curry favour with the Greeks and in the process impress the Russians by reduced taxes and cancelling debts and forced labour projects. There was even talk of him converting to Christianity. During May while Maitland awaited instructions he sent Colonel Charles Napier on a secret mission to Ioannina to assess Ali's military resources. On his own initiative Napier offered his services as military commander if Ali made a bid for Greek support by granting freedom to his Christian subjects, adopted a new military organization, and paid an advance £100,000. Napier reported:

> Ali has desired me to ask the Government's leave for raising troops in England, and my proposal was to assemble 8,000 troops at Parga before February next, if he

can maintain the contest for this summer. With these he might incorporate twenty-thousand Greeks; in a month I could make them all fit to take the field and attack the Turks in their winter quarters… England may make him an independent sovereign, not only of Albania, but all Greece, from Morea to Macedon. She can determine his frontier at her will, and by compelling him to accept a constitution favourable to the Greeks, she would form of those people a vigorous nation… The Greeks look to England for their emancipation. But if ever England engages in war with Russia to support the Turks, the Greeks will consider her as trying to rivet their chains and will join with the Russians.

The plan was too ambitious for either the British Government or Ali to take up. Ali was an opportunist but not a gambler and the stakes were too high. He was no longer a young man and the limits of his ambition and power were becoming clear. He had depended on Turkey for his power base, through defeating his enemies he had also kept in with the Sultan and without the support of one of the major powers he did not possess sufficient resources.

In July the Sublime Porte sent Ali an ultimatum. He was ordered to present himself within forty days to justify himself. Ali would have known it would be a risk to go, so he failed to turn up, but his insubordination played into the Sultan's hands by giving him a convenient excuse to use force against him. Ismail Pashabey was given the task of assembling a large army of regular troops under the pashas of Scutari and Larissa, the latter no longer a bulwark of Veli's protecting Ali's eastern flank. The combined force may have been chaotic but it was to prove effective. Finlay writes:

> The Othoman army was slowly collected, and it formed a motley assembly, without order, without artillery. Each pasha moved forward as he mustered his followers, with a separate commissar and a separate military chest. The daily rations and daily pay of the soldier differed in different divisions of the army. Ismael was really only the nominal commander-in-chief. He was not a soldier, and had he been an experienced officer, he could have done little to enforce order on the forces he commanded.

Ali was prepared. He had managed to swell the ranks of his army with volunteers persuaded to make common cause, but he was not going to take on the Sultan's army in open battle, preferring to fall back on defensible positions in the mountain passes. Omar Vrionis and 15,000 men were stationed at Metsovo to defend the approach from Larissa across the Pindus, while to the south-east Odysseus Androutsos held the mountain passes around Livadia, and to the north Mukhtar at Berat and his second son Hussain at Tepelene faced up against the pasha of Scutari, Mustafa Bushatli, son of Kara Mahmud Pasha. To the south Preveza, the key against attack from the sea, was held by Veli who had been driven out of Lepanto and Parga was under his son Mehmed. Ali himself remained at Ioannina with a garrison of around 8,000 men. For the first time in years and at the age of around 70, Ali was on the defensive and facing a large coordinated attack from all sides. The Ottoman Army advanced in a pincer from the south reaching the western coast. Here they joined the Turkish naval expedition from Constantinople consisting of three line-of-battle ships, five frigates and about twenty brigs, joined by squadrons from Algeria and Egypt. The Arab crews were more efficient; they had destroyed a Greek Fleet in the harbour of Galaxidhi on the north shore of the Gulf of Corinth. Control of the sea meant that Spyros Kolovos,[9] one of Ali's secretaries and intermediaries, was taken by the Turks while trying to obtain ammunition from Corfu, and tortured to death. If Ali's troops had remained loyal he may have tested the Porte's resolve as had happened on numerous previous occasions. As the strength of the opposition became clear even the loyalty of Ali's sons wavered. Faced with the choice of inheriting a share of their father's domain in permanent opposition to the Sultan or making peace each decided the best course was the latter, and with promises of pardons or another pashalik somewhere, they abandoned their positions. In the north Mukhtar surrendered Berat and Argyrocastro fell with Selim taken. The Turks used bribes to undermine Ali's troops and the Suliotes were invited from Corfu to take their homeland back. With their help the imperial force took Preveza from Veli, but they found Ali's fort of Kiafa a tougher proposition. Only Hussein Bey swore to die for his grandfather. As the Turks closed in Napier paid him a second visit at Ioannina, imploring him to spend money on his fortifications and on reorganizing his military force, but Ali was loathe to part with his money. Only when Ali's Odysseus Androutsos retreated from Thermopylae, and Omer Vrionis deserted to the Ottomans and his 15,000 men disappeared, and it was too late, did Ali make an offer of £2m to Napier to improve his defences. He was now slowly being surrounded at Ioannina as the 25,000-strong Turkish Army settled down for a protracted siege.

With winter, the discipline of the Ottoman Army, which was already suspect, deteriorated. Supplies were hard to come by and the country round Ioannina was mercilessly ravaged. In the words of an eyewitness the troops were 'raiding cities, townships and villages without the slightest restraint and stealing their last morsel of food from the mouths of poor Greeks'. Both sides employed Albanian mercenaries and Greeks, and their loyalty was prone to waver. With the devastation many of the Greeks turned back to Ali. His spies learnt that the presence of the Suliotes had caused a rift in the imperial force, with the local beys and agas threatening to desert. After the Suliots' failure to take Kiafa they were withdrawn from the main body of troops outside Ioannina and stationed in the most exposed positions and given little support when attacked. In consequence in December they opened negotiations with Ali, and left the Turkish camp for Suli, where Ali's commander at Kiafa handed over the fortress. In a strange reversal of fortune by January 1821 they were allied to Ali who had restored them to their homes and promised to provide money for their families in exile. Attempts by the Turks to try to win back their allegiance through the Greek metropolitan of Arta failed. With Ismail proving ineffective as commander of such a large force, the Sultan replaced him with the experienced Hurshid Pasha, who had taken over as governor of the Morea in November 1820. Hurshid had served as grand vizier and suppressed the revolts in Serbia. Energetic and capable he set about reorganizing the army. By now both sides were suffering from defections and the situation amongst the Turks was so bad that Hurshid felt compelled to stay in the camp.

---

[9] Often given as Spyridon Colovo.

Ali on the other hand was not content to just sit and wait but when he was tricked into making a sortie on 7 February he was severely defeated. Hurshid on the other hand was frustrated by his Albanian troops who wanted to prolong the campaign so they could continue drawing pay.

Alexandros Ypsilantis, the son of Constantine, a colonel in the Russian Army had taken over as leader of the Filiki Eteria. Apprised of the situation in Epirus he decided to use Ali as a diversion in a bid for Greek independence. He sent orders to Kolokotronis to encourage the klephts to join with the Suliotes, instructing them that any towns and fortresses taken from the Turks should be garrisoned by persons ready to declare for the Greek rebellion. In marching north to join the campaign Hurshid had weakened the Morea and when Mehmed Salik, the acting governor, announced that on top of the impositions already made to finance the war against Ali, a doubling of the *herach*, or poll tax, the situation was ripe for revolt. In February 1821 Ypsilantis moved an army made up of many Greeks in Russian service and Epirotes of Zagori into Wallachia, where Soutsos had become hospodar, in the hope of inciting a pan-Balkan revolution with Russian support. The Turks began to get jittery and in March they ordered the metropolitan bishops of the Peloponnese to go to Tripolitsa to confer on the subject of Ali's intrigues. The Turks still feared him more than a Greek uprising and wanted to nullify his bids for Greek support. They planned to hold the leading Greeks hostage, but the Greeks suspected the worst and made their excuses, stalling for time. By March, in response to Ypsilantis' move, the Peloponnese was in revolt but initially the Turks were still more worried about Ali than the situation in the Morea. The Sultan supported the policy of his grand vizier, Halet Effendi, who by ignoring the Greeks allowed them to consolidate. Halet's main concern was to discourage Muslims, and particularly Ali's Albanians, from cooperating with Christian klephts. On hearing of the Greek revolt, Ali sent Alexis Noutsos, who had commanded a force against Ismail in Zagori, on a mission to his compatriots to suggest a collaboration with the view to establishing an Albanian-Greek state under Ali's sovereignty. Ali's moves were coming too late to allay Greek suspicions and the momentum was already under way. Noutsos did not return. He joined the Greek leader Alexander Mavrokordatos at Missolonghi and the revolution.

Hurshid Pasha was now fighting a war on two fronts. While besieging Ali he had the Greeks biting at his heels to the south. In September at Peta near Arta, the Greek chiefs formed an alliance with the Suliotes and their Albanian allies to help Ali on condition that they got the freedom of the villages he had converted to *chifliks* under his direct control. Mavrokordatos who was still afraid that Ali might come to some arrangement with the Turks, persuaded Markos Botsaris, the Suliote leader, to desert the cause of Ali and to throw in his lot with the Greek chieftains besieging Arta. His brother Kostas Botsaris, a veteran of *Les Chasseurs* on the Ionian Islands and member of the Filiki Eteria, was already fighting for the cause. The Turks meanwhile tried to split the Greeks and Albanians. Ali's one-time ally and trusted general, Omar Vrionis, was sent to relieve Arta. He told the Albanians that Ali was at the end of his tether, and that the cunning Greeks were only fighting on their own account. When the Albanians found out that the Greeks lacked arms and ammunition and were destroying mosques, they deserted the Suliots and joined Omar. Meanwhile the Suliots slipped off home to Suli. By October the war of attrition had taken its toll and starved of supplies Ali burnt the town retreating to his last stronghold, the citadel of Itch-kalé on the promontory in the lake in Ioannina, where he shut himself up with the remnants of his harem and a small nervous garrison. He was described as living in a bombproof cellar, deserted by most of his sycophants, wrapped in a bundle of embroidered garments.

After a winter of stalemate the Turks broke into the citadel in January to find only 100 defenders left. Ali had retreated to his last and strongest tower, where his treasure and powder magazine were kept, threatening to blow himself up. Ali was prepared to play his last hand. He still had a vast treasure, although much reduced, and he was prepared to bargain with Hurshid who wanted to ensure that the treasure was not lost in any last-minute futile battle but retained for himself and the Sultan. Ali suggested a truce so he could belatedly put his case to the Sultan. Hurshid was prepared to agree if Ali signed an armistice, surrendered the fortress and retired to the little monastery of Agios Panteleimon on the island in the lake, while Hurshid applied to the Sultan for a pardon. Ali accepted, probably thinking he could convince the Sultan that he was still needed to fight the Greeks. Taking Vassiliki and his private guard Ali retired to the island to await the answer, supplied with delicacies and musicians by Hurshid. Once Hurshid had obtained access to the treasure, Ali was left with no bargaining position. Whether he was under orders that Ali should die or he was actually awaiting the Sultan's decree is uncertain. As with much in Ali's life, even the manner of his death is one of confusion and elaboration. On 5 February, Hurshid sent troops to Ali with instructions either to arrest him or to kill him; the accounts differ. Ali expected them to be delivering the pardon and in the simplest version, when the arresting officers entered the room and demanded his head for the Sultan, he opened fire on them. In the ensuing fight he killed two and wounded another before being shot through the heart. Another account portrays a more devious strategy on the part of the officer in charge. After some discussion with Ali in an upper room they left together and went out on the balcony. Ali made a low bow, and as he was off his guard the officer stabbed him in the heart, declaring 'Ali is dead'. Ali either died then and there or, in the manner of a horror movie, not having suffered the mortal blow he came back to life and crawled back into the room. The Turks, afraid to take him on, shot at him through the wooden floor, killing him. Another version has it that when the officer arrived with the document accompanied by troops, Ali realized it was not a pardon. Both sides opened fire, and after a confused struggle during which Ali was wounded, he took refuge in the upstairs room. The fatal blow was a shot fired up through the floorboards, wounding him in the groin. Finlay had not heard this version until he visited the monastery thirty years later and this is the one widely told today. Whatever the manner of his death, Ali's head was cut off, perhaps on a stone step outside, and shown to the remaining Albanian troops, who after a token show of resistance surrendered when they were promised their arrears in wages, whereupon they cheered loudly, 'The dog Ali is dead. Long live the Sultan.' Ali's head was then sent to the Sultan, the skin peeled off for transportation in the usual manner to be stuffed with straw and moistened for presentation. It was then exhibited on the gates of the Sultan's palace with the heads of his three sons and grandson, in the same way as the heads Ali himself had sent to the Sultan for his pleasure.

Ali's head may have gone to Constantinople but his body remained in Ioannina where he was buried with his first wife, Emine, in the citadel. Vassiliki was more fortunate. She was sent to the Ottoman capital, but alive as a prisoner. In 1830 she received a pardon and the newly independent Greek state, remembering her support for Greek liberty, gave her a medieval tower in Katochi, near Missolonghi, where she lived until her death in 1834. It was a Greek state that did not include Epirus. Ali's army and Ioannina had fallen into the hands of the Sultan and all of Epirus would not taste freedom until 1913.

Every year of Ali's life was spent in bloodshed and war. In mid-nineteenth century Europe his memory was synonymous with cruelty and despotism while it was acknowledged that some of his countrymen viewed him as a model governor. Summing up his life, the count-duke of Sorgo, a senator in the Dalmatian Republic of Ragusa who knew Ali personally, said that his system of government was fit for the country over which he ruled and no European would have brought Albania to the flourishing state it enjoyed during the last twenty years of his life. But in the words of Ismail Kemal Bey, the first head of state of Albania, there was a sense of wasted opportunity when he referred to the Greeks' insurrection:

> If Ali Pasha had been less a man of his time and better endowed with political forethought, he would himself have organized this coup in time, and Albania and Greece, with the whole of Thessaly and Macedonia, might have become an independent State and a kingdom of great importance.

Fig. 37: The tomb of Ali Pasha from *Constantinople and the Scenery of the Seven Churches of Asia Minor…* by Robert Walsh and Thomas Allom, London, 1836–38.

Chapter 5

Emissaries, Diplomats and Spies: Ali Pasha the Statesman

When Byron and Hobhouse arrived at Arta in 1809 they unknowingly stepped into a mire of intrigue and obfuscation. Beneath the glamour, confusion and squalor a sophisticated game of diplomatic chess was being played out, a forerunner of future power politics in the Middle East. Despite Ali's ferocious and cruel reputation, having him onside was seen as more important than ethical considerations or the welfare of the local population. Contrary to the image created by Western travel writers of Ali as a capricious Oriental, the slave to passions and emotions, the archival sources show a man capable of learning the techniques of statecraft. As Ali created his state within a state, he left his brigand roots behind, copying the bureaucracy of central government, running his own treasury and civil service, developing his own foreign policy and forming his own army. He was not alone in this. Pazvantoğlu, who was more forthright in his attempts to set up an independent state, went as far as minting his own coins and developing diplomatic relations with foreign states in the 1790s. As a friend of Rigas Feraios who was promoting pan-Balkan revolution, Pazvantoğlu was more politically motivated, and whether Ali bought into such ideas or not, he would have been influenced by the possibilities. Developments in international relations and political ideology were evolving as his own horizons were broadening, but aware enough as he was that he had to adapt, he only adopted those tools of government that would suit his purpose and maintain him in power. As the major holder of land and wealth in the Balkans his territory was a first line of defence for the Ottoman Empire against incursion from the west, especially during the Napoleonic Wars. In the knowledge that he held the key to the western front it became regarded as necessary for statesmen and heads of state to treat him on an equal basis. To this end four or five European powers would have consulates in Ioannina at a time and his charming hospitality to foreign visitors must be seen within this context. Dennis Skiotis has estimated that over fifty diplomats, military men, spies, gentlemen of leisure, scholars, doctors, adventurers, renegades, poets and painters took the hazardous trouble to pay him court, leaving a mass of memoirs and reports.

Ali's relationship with the Sublime Porte

Before Ali developed relationships with foreign powers his first priority was his relationship with the Sublime Porte. The vast size of the Ottoman Empire inevitably led to a devolution of power from the centre and communication over long distances and difficult terrain enabled provincial governors to act with increasing autonomy. To some extent it was a case of out of sight was out of mind; as long as the Sultan received his dues and a semblance of peace was maintained, everything was in order. However freely the provincial pashas

Fig. 38: Ali's Audience Chamber from *Twelve studies in double-tinted lithography of scenes in southern Albania* by George de la Poer Beresford, 1855.

acted it was still important to keep a presence at the capital in order to be kept up to date with developments and to ensure they remained in favour. The Sultan may have been the supreme authority ruling by divine will but he did not rule alone. At court and within the Divan different factions vied for influence, and a good word here or a gift there might mean the difference between promotion or death for some far-flung pasha. The methods Ali used to achieve his ends inevitably made enemies. It was vital for him to match his gains in power with influence at court that would ensure his actions were given the correct spin in the Sultan's ear and to nullify the 'lies' of his enemies. He also needed 'ears' at court aware of the mood so as to gauge his favour with the Sultan. In order to do this, along with the likes of Haxhi Shehreti, he maintained a coterie of friends in Constantinople willing to act on his behalf.

He had a well-developed network of allies, clients and informers that he could rely on. He cultivated relations with well-connected members of the Greek Phanariot community at Constantinople to keep an eye on both the Turkish and Greek situation. Stefanos Missiou had a warm relationship with Ali, calling himself an adoptive father to Ali's firstborn son, Mukhtar. An example of Missiou's news-gathering was his passing on of a rumour in 1801 that 'Captain Pasha', in other words Kutsuk Hussein Pasha, grand admiral of the Ottoman Fleet, had had some conflict with the English at Alexandria. This was the Siege of Alexandria during which the Turks helped the British against the French. Missiou promised to get back to confirm his information. At the same time he expressed genuine concern for Ali:

> I am doing you duty in telling you, my lord, as best as you can to pass your time peaceably because, apart from the fact that it will extinguish your purse, the fighting and these wars are not a good thing and in the name of God as much as you can you ought to avoid them and cut them out altogether.

This prescient letter coincided with others from his close friends, especially in Constantinople, showing general concern and fear that his involvement in troublesome activities and violence would backfire on him.

Dimitrios Razis, a doctor, had met Ali when he was on campaign in Vidin and formed a close friendship with him. Razis was interested in the European political scene and kept Ali informed on military and political developments. He had a son studying in Paris and through his links there he kept tabs on the Ottoman Embassy. During 1806 Razis kept Ali up to date with the progress of the war between France and Prussia and the presence of the British Fleet in the Dardanelles in a letter to be read 'secretly'. Sébastiani, the French ambassador at the Porte, was trying to persuade Sultan Selim to re-enter the war against Russia, and under request from Russia the British Mediterranean Fleet sent a squadron to prepare for an assault on Constantinople. Razis reported that the feeling at the Porte was that Turkey would end up at war whether it was desirable or not and despite Britain's show of force, Sébastiani prevailed. Turkey went to war with Russia, bringing it also into war with Britain, bringing the British Fleet and the Russian, under Admiral Senyavin, against them. Razis' interest in general politics kept Ali aware of broader issues such as the discontent in Russia, where the people wanted a Parliament 'like England has' and not 'him', the tsar, doing whatever he likes. But more pertinent to Ali's own situation, through intelligence from his contacts Razis informed him in advance of a deal that meant Preveza would not be included in the Treaty of Tilsit that handed the Ionian Islands back to the French. Razis, with his French connections, was biased towards France and he expressed sorrow when Napoleon was exiled to St Helena and towards the subsequent weakening of France, blaming the British interests.

On his own initiative, Razis devised a security system to protect his patron. In 1807 he explained to his contact Kostas Grammatikos that he was going to start numbering his letters so that if any got lost or intercepted it would be obvious and he would expect an acknowledgement of each received for his peace of mind. Though the letters were written in Greek it was no safeguard. Greek was the common language of communication even among Turkish officers, especially those in Greek-speaking areas of the Empire. With his professional hat on, as a sideline Razis sent pills and plasters to many of his correspondents and even a sick note on behalf of a woman who was to be sent to Ali 'for his pleasure' saying that she was suffering from an ailment. Razis worked closely with Georgios Marinoglou and they both corresponded with Mukhtar as well. Marinoglou, an elder from Zagori, kept Ali informed of events at Constantinople, passing on general information regarding the situation, including civil unrest and killings. As a person of rank Ali had connections within the ministries

Fig. 39: Tsar Alexander I of Russia and Napoleon I of France embrace after the Treaties of Tilsit (French Medallion).

of government. Suleyman Divan Efendi was one such source of information. As a member of the Turkish establishment he would offer a corroborative alternative to material from Razis alluding to diplomatic affairs. In 1807 he wrote to Ali concerning the meeting between Tsar Alexander and Napoleon prior to the Treaty of Tilsit and details of the negotiations between Turkey and Britain leading to the Treaty of the Dardanelles that concluded the war between them in 1809. Even though Ali tried to be up to date, the news from Tilsit, modern Sovetsk, in the Kaliningrad federal Russian enclave on the Baltic, took twenty days to reach Constantinople. And then it had to reach him in Ioannina, which meant his information could be at least a month old by the time it got to him. The Treaty of Tilsit was signed in July and Divan Efendi was writing in October. Ali's relationship with him was obviously cordial;

Divan sent Ali a slave girl and a woman for his pleasure from Larissa. He was prepared to help Ali in more ways. After unsuccessfully trying to cover up the death of Ali's nephew Adem Bey, in whose name Ali had purchased a lifetime lease, he was happy to bribe officials on Ali's behalf to find an alternative dupe who would hold it for Ali.

Internal security

Ali's friends in Constantinople with their contacts in Paris or Vienna also kept him in touch with developments closer to home and where there was discord within the Ottoman provinces. Ali kept good relations with low-ranking government officials and relied on many Greek notaries, merchants, community leaders and professionals to form a network of representatives, advisors and informants throughout the villages from Epirus to Macedonia. Brought together by a web of mutual interest and dependency, nevertheless it seems that these distinguished figures were genuinely devoted to serving Ali and had great loyalty to him. Marinoglou's sons, Kostantis and Christodoulos, continued to serve Ali after their father's death. Mukhtar was in contact with Marinoglou and Razis and from his letters to Ali, it is evident they worked closely together. A sense of warmth can be derived from their correspondence as when Marinoglou congratulated Ali on Mukhtar's instalment as pasha of Lepanto. Many of Ali's informers were his tax-farmers and tax collectors and therefore were gainers under his protection: Kostas Grammatikos and Georgios Marinoglou were tax collectors and administrators; Konstantinos Priskos was a lessee of the sheep tax for Larissa and Salona (Amfissa near Delphi), Alexis Noutsos, another notable from Zagori, a lessee of his area's sheep tax and a general tax administrator and Stergios Zotoglou was the sheep tax collector for Thessaly and Thebes. These were Ali's eyes and ears on the ground, but they were more than impartial observers.

International Diplomacy

During Ali's lifetime the increasingly volatile political situation in the eastern Mediterranean became the perfect breeding ground for aggressive diplomacy, intrigue and espionage. There was feverish activity on all sides as the various parties jostled for advantage: for the Sultan, he had to keep an eye on his insubordinate subjects, notables or otherwise, as well as on foreign manoeuvring and sedition; for Ali, he was aware that his insecurity increased as his gains in power were balanced against the threat this posed to the Empire; for the British, French and Russians, eager to exploit any opportunity to weaken the opposition, they had to be kept abreast of developments before their rivals; and for the disgruntled subjects of the Sultan, intrigue was the only way to foster their aims. This led to a situation not dissimilar to that in the Second World War, with Turkey awash with spies.

The information from his friends at Constantinople was important in his negotiations with foreign powers, but Ali did not rely on one source, he gathered news from various sources. He had the foreign newspapers translated for him and his own people created a kind of newsletter collated from European news outlets, called the 'Posta'. Hatzeris Beyzade, who is referred to in Ali's correspondence, was one of those employed to filter the news from the foreign press. When Edward Everett met him in Ioannina he was receiving the Lugano newspaper via Vienna, and the French state newspaper *Le Moniteur* on behalf of his protector. Everett calls Hatzeris, 'Prince Chanzerly of Joannina, the chief interpreter of the Pasha', saying he claimed to be the son of a 'Hospidar or Wallachian prince' and he had come to Ali's court to seek protection after his father's execution by the Sultan. He was indeed a prince of sorts and one and the same as the Phanariot 'Beyzady' mentioned by Hughes. Beyzade is Turkish for 'son of a bey' and Hatzeris can be identified as the son of Constantine Hangerli, one of two brothers who were princes of Wallachia and Moldavia respectively. Constantine was strangled and beheaded in 1799 for his lack of support against the rebel Pazvantoğlu. His brother, Alexander, fell foul of the authorities too but managed to flee to Moscow where he received sanctuary in 1805. The Hangerli family was related to and rivals of the important Ypsilantis family. With these connections to Russia and the Phanariot Greeks, Ali would see Hatzeris as a useful asset and would only be too happy to provide sanctuary. By the time of Everett's meeting Hatzeris was already a seasoned diplomat on Ali's behalf, having been entrusted with missions to Paris and Vienna, and to Napoleon when on his Moscow campaign (1812). At this time he would have been working with Manthos Oikonomou, an informer of Ali's and secretary.

As master of Epirus and controller of much of central Greece Ali became of supreme interest to the warring powers, sitting as he was between the prized Ionian Islands and the route to the Ottoman capital and Egypt. Up until this point open conflict in Epirus had been either internal or confined to that between Venice and Turkey, and most foreign intervention had been clandestine. The Venetians had exploited weaknesses in the local population and Russian agents had been at work inciting rebellion amongst the Greeks, most spectacularly leading up to the failed Orlov Revolt. The European powers had diplomatic relations with Venice, and therefore a consular presence in the Ionian Islands' dependencies was normal practice. That the French consul Lasalle in Preveza was making promises of military aid to Ali by 1792 was an omen of things to come. The French occupation of the islands in 1797 only brought in another player willing to encourage disunity amongst the various factions backed up with money and arms. But the French brought more, the idealism of revolution. To this end they sought to incite rebellion in the Mani Peninsula through their agents and spies. Dimo Staphanopoli and his nephew Nicolo, Corsicans of Greek descent, were particularly active. Dimo later acted as a military surgeon, but for now he was travelling to areas receptive to the idea of Greek liberation, including Himara in Epirus. Ali's attitude to the French vacillated between hostility and friendship fuelled by his contradictory desires to acquire a foothold on the islands and possession of the old Venetian ports while appearing to do his duty to the Ottoman government.

Even before the French had set foot on Epirote soil, in anticipation Ali was writing with fulsome admiration to Napoleon with offers of friendship. Napoleon was the commander in charge in Italy, and Albania came under his jurisdiction. The French forces in Italy were in need of Albanian grain and wood and if the troops on the Ionian Islands were to survive they too required supplies from the mainland. It was imperative for the French to initiate good relations from the start. Their garrison on Corfu was small and unpopular and Ali hoped to exploit their weakness by secretly pressing for control of their mainland possessions. He was soon making demands for free passage through the Corfu Strait and military aid from their commander, General Gentili, while piling on the flattery to the unfortunate Adjutant General Rose during their meetings. Ali's charm worked so well he even managed to acquire two gunboats and Gentili provided support for his massacre of the Himariotes, an action that was ostensibly carried out in the territory of his rival pasha, Mustafa of Delvino. At first, French strategy had been to play the warring pashas off against each other, in a similar manner adopted by the Porte, but when Napoleon wrote to Gentili he expressed the opinion that the unfettered strength of Ali could be to their advantage and should be encouraged. The idea of Albania as a French satellite state appealed to Napoleon and he was keen for Ali's support in case of war with Turkey, but in the end Ali decided his best interests were served elsewhere. Napoleon's attack on Egypt meant that France was no longer acting as a prop for the beleaguered Ottoman Empire and that role would pass to Britain. So when the Russo-Turkish alliance turned on France, Ali no longer needed to profess friendship, and would proceed to slaughter the inhabitants of Preveza. Initially however, even after the French defeat at the Battle of the Nile, Ali played a cagey game, continuing talks with Gentili's successor, General Chabot and Rose while through his informants he assessed the capability of Corfu to withstand a siege. However, once he had taken and tortured Rose and imprisoned Chabot, the cat was out of the bag and he made his demands for the Ionian dependencies to what he assumed was the losing side with the French in retreat in Egypt.

The British as yet were in no position to intervene in the Ionian Islands, but they were acutely aware of their strategic importance and hence of Ali Pasha's significance in relation to them. Spyridon and George Foresti, father and son, were Greeks from Zante in the service of the British Government. It was common practice for local consular services to be manned by natives of the region or of sympathetic countries. Before the outbreak of war between Britain and France, Spyridon Foresti had built up a large network of friends and business associates throughout the Ionian Islands, in southern Epirus and Dalmatia, and as far as Salonika and Constantinople, Asia Minor and Alexandria and with commercial agents and officials in Vienna, Bristol and London. Foresti had been appointed British vice consul on Zante in 1783 when it was under the Venetians, and promoted to consul in 1789 until the island was taken by France and he was incarcerated for a year on Corfu. He used this time productively as a spy, collecting information on shipping and the strength of the French Fleet for the Foreign Secretary, William Grenville. His efforts were so successful that Nelson attested that Foresti was one of only two consuls 'I have found who really and truly do their duty', and he recommended him to Lord Elgin at Constantinople, to the Foreign Secretary Lord Hawkesbury and Admiral Lord Keith. As an ex-sailor, Foresti's connections amongst the sea captains and commercial travellers helped him in the gathering of information and the sending of dispatches. Nelson had already indicated a wish to free the Ionian Islands but when they came under joint Russian and Turkish control Foresti was given a roving consular commission. He was in Venice and then with the Russian Fleet taking part in the Siege of Corfu before being reinstated as consul on Zante and becoming the British resident in Corfu in 1799. A long-term resident of Zante and friend of Foresti's was John Hawkins, a Cornish botanist and mining geologist who was making a study of local flora. Hawkins visited Ali Pasha in 1795 and 1798 where he was plied with gifts of antiquities. With his large network Foresti was perfectly placed to carry on his extra requirement of intelligence gathering for the military becoming the hub for the Adriatic and beyond. He kept Nelson informed of Russian intentions and naval capabilities and the general situation in Corfu and Albania with particular reference to Ali Pasha. He acted as a link between Nelson and Sir Sidney Smith in Egypt whose additional duty was to encourage Turkish opposition to Napoleon. Any such visit like that of Hawkins would have been useful to him. As early as 1798 Foresti was intercepting Ali's communications with the French and he was able to give inside information as to why the Turkish Fleet abandoned Palermo in 1799. There had been a revolt amongst the sailors and thousands of them were released from duty at Corfu from where they proceeded to join Ali. Even at this stage the British were interested in recruiting two regiments of Albanians to help them in Sicily and Foresti was given the task, but the time was not yet ripe.

Fig. 40: *Vice Admiral Horatio Lord Nelson* (1799) by Lemuel Francis Abbott.

With the establishment of diplomatic missions being part of the intelligence gathering process it was inevitable that Ali's court would come into the frame. Although Ali's domains were part of the Ottoman state, Ali was independent enough to warrant being dealt with as a separate entity. He could be used both as a conduit and as counterpoise to the Porte. In 1799, Thomas Bruce, 7th Earl of Elgin, was appointed as British ambassador to the Ottoman Empire in Constantinople where Sidney Smith's brother John was serving as chargé d'af-faires. Lord Elgin is remembered more for his interest in the collection of antiquities, most famously the Parthenon marbles held in the British Museum and commonly called after him, but he was in the post during a critical period of Anglo-Turkish relations. In his duties as ambassador he was able to travel in Greece accompanied by members of his staff. Philip Hunt, his chaplain, who aided him in his archaeological enterprises and was a keen collector of religious manuscripts, travelled extensively in the Aegean. This was a useful cover for the more serious business of intelligence collecting. In 1801 Hunt made a tour of the Morea with the purpose of discouraging local rulers from becoming involved with the French, from where he travelled to Ioannina. He spent three days there, and was received 'with high hon-our by Ali Pasha' having 'two long conversations on the politics of the time'. Touching on the repairs Ali made to the fortress at Preveza and the discovery of some statues that Ali described as only seeming 'to want breath', Hunt managed to get a promise from Ali to send Lord Elgin any future antiquities he discovered. Behind the bonhomie there were serious developments in the air. On his arrival in Corfu, Hunt heard rumours of impending peace between Britain and France, rumours borne out early next year with the Treaty of Amiens beginning a short interlude in hostilities.

Hunt was not the first choice from Elgin's staff for such a mission, but William Richard Hamilton and John Philip Morier, his private secretaries, were unavailable. The new political climate offered Ali an opportunity to make more formal approaches to Britain, so when in early 1803, he requested Lord Elgin to send an emissary offering cooperation against France, it was Hamilton who was duly dispatched. Hamilton had been in Egypt, where he had seized the Rossetta Stone from the French and returned to Athens with Leake in 1802. Here they met Elgin and picked up some of the marbles from the Parthenon for transportation aboard Elgin's ship *Mentor*. Caught in a storm rounding the Peloponnese at Cape Matapan, the tip of the Mani Peninsula, and overladen with antiquities, the ship sank after striking rocks off Cerigo (Kythera), an outpost of the Septinsular Republic. Lord Elgin had to spend the next two years retrieving the marbles from the seabed. In the meantime he was travelling in Boeotia and contemplating visiting Ali himself, but such thoughts had to be postponed as the British consul in Athens, Spyridon Logotheti of Levadia, working on Elgin's behalf, had made him-self unpopular with the local peasantry by seeking paid protection from Mukhtar. By May of 1803, relations with France had broken down once more. Impatient with Ali the French were arming the Suliotes, and Hamilton was in Ioannina just before war was officially resumed on 18 May. On the 6th, he had written to Lord Hawkesbury, giving a glowing impression of Ali.

He is prompt in his measures, full of energy, and professes a very quick and nice discernment of Individual Character; but his want of education, and life spent in arms, have rendered him in his Government cruel and despotic, because he found it to his advantage. He has however established the most perfect tranquillity, and security of Persons and Property throughout his dominions, whose Inhabitants, Greeks and Turks, are richer, happier, more contented than in any other part of European Turkey.

Ali had once again worked his charm, and no doubt giving the impression to the British he was someone they could do business with. Hamilton broached the possibility of the British Navy accessing stores through 'Panormo', Porto Palermo in Himara, and in a secret interview discussed Ali's intentions on the resumption of war with France. Ali indicated the possibility of the British using the ports for military purposes, garrisoning and building fortifications along the coast and opening up trade between Albania and Britain. Hamilton passed on the information to Hawkesbury, Nelson and Sir Arthur Paget at Vienna who was responsible for the alliance, the Third Coalition, against France that year. By 26 May he was travelling back through Thessaly to Athens. The following year he was in Vienna before returning to London. Elgin had already left his post and was unfortunately caught in France when war resumed and was detained there for three years.

Hamilton was followed by Morier who was born in Smyrna and came from a family of career diplomats; his father had been Consul General in Constantinople. Morier was appointed British Consul General to Albania, the Morea and adjacent territories of the Ottoman Empire to continue to discourage local alliances with France and gain intelligence as to the disposition of the inhabitants and their military capability to repel invasion. Early in 1804 Morier had an audience with 'His Excellency' during which Ali turned on the charm, offering assurances of his 'entire devotion' to the British government and underlying the threat from the Russian occupation of the Ionian Islands, which he also saw as a connivance by the Porte to reduce his power. Ali offered the use of his ports and even of 3,000 men to the British in return for arms, ammunition and artillery officers. Ali impressed Morier with his predictions of the collapse of the Ottoman Empire and the possibility of using him as a bulwark against other 'Christian' nations in return for protection and acknowledgement of his independent status. Needless to say Ali kept quiet about any dealings, previous or otherwise, with the French. Meanwhile from Corfu, Foresti was also acting on orders from Nelson to see if Ali would offer trade privileges. The need for timber and port facilities was becoming acute but it was important that the negotiations were kept from the Russian and Turkish governments and Nelson wrote to Ali in cipher. The intelligence was not immediately acted on but became useful in the later stages of the war. The value of Corfu as 'an observatory over the whole of European Turkey' had become apparent and it was a major motivation supporting the British invasion of the islands in 1809. The close relationship between Foresti and Nelson came to an end with his death at the Battle of Trafalgar the next year. John Morier was only in Ioannina a short time as his brother, the 20 years old David Richard Morier, arrived via Veli's base in Tripolitza in the Morea to take up his appointment as secretary to the political mission to Ali's court. John performed his duties as Consul General from Zante from where he could liaise with the Russians and update Nelson on the situation in Albania. While the

Ionian Islands were under Russian control Foresti was working with their plenipotentiary, Count Moncenigo, on the mainland with instructions from Hawkesbury to support the rebels in order to frustrate the endeavours of the French and from Nelson as to his intelligence requirements.

The British were not to have Ali all to themselves however. Julien Bessières had arrived at the same time to act as a conduit between Ali and the French. The loss of the Ionian Islands made it more imperative than ever for the French to have good relations with Ali. Two years later Bessières was replaced at Ioannina by François Pouqueville, sent by Napoleon to counter British influence. Pouqueville had been a physician to the Commission of the Sciences and Arts that accompanied Napoleon on his Egyptian campaign in 1798, when he had been forced to head home by bad health; only to be captured off Calabria by pirates from Tripoli on the Barbary coast along with a number of high-ranking officers including Bessières. Many of these pirates were actually Turkish or Greek, and Pouqueville was taken to the Peloponnese where the Bey of Navarino (Pylos) gave him the freedom to explore the region. From there he was sent to Constantinople, where he was again well-treated and allowed to travel, until

Fig. 41: *Portrait of François Pouqueville* (1830) in front of Ioannina by Henriette Lorimer.

his eventual release and return to France in 1801. His report of his experiences published in France in 1805 was of great interest to Napoleon. The fate of Bessières and four others was less fortunate; they were sold by the corsair captain as slaves in Butrint where Ali acquired them. By chance he had been given access to French military expertise without having to bargain for it and he promised them liberty after two years' service. Treating them well, he quickly set them to work organizing his artillery, defences and small fleet, but the captives were not content and made a bid for freedom. In 1800 Bessières and two others made for Corfu, now under the Russians where they were imprisoned in the Fortezza Nuova on Corfu. After only a year they managed to escape and return to France. Bessières' experience and inside knowledge of Ali's court was of great use to French diplomacy. Once Bessières had introduced Pouqueville to Ali, he took up the position of Consul General to Venice and from 1807 to 1810 he was imperial commissaire, in charge of all civilian affairs, on Corfu, and Pouqueville's superior. Pouqueville served as consul at Ali's court until the end of hostilities in 1815. While Ali was expressing disappointment to Morier that his requests through Nelson and others for arms, shot and cannon and officers to train his men in return for safe haven for ships and timber, and men against French attack had met with silence, Pouqueville had Ali's ear. His medical experience gave him special access to Ali for whom he acted impressively as a personal doctor, increasing his status within Ioannina and giving him official recognition by the Porte. Despite the loathing of Ali's deeds expressed in his memoirs, Pouqueville promoted Ali both to Napoleon as a useful ally in the region and favourably to the Porte. Through his efforts Pouqueville claimed Sébastiani, the French consul at Constantinople, had gained Veli and Mukhtar their pashaliks of the Morea and Lepanto to contain the Russians. French and Ottoman interests were coalescing round the desire to oust the Russians from the Ionian Islands from where they were propagating revolutionary ideas amongst the Orthodox populations in Dalmatia and the wealthy Greek merchants of Albania. Napoleon also wanted a bulwark against Austrian and Russia expansion into the Balkans, to which end he was happy to supply military aid to the Porte. To the British, Ali expressed distrust at the Russian influence at the Porte and disappointment with the French for not honouring their payments for his support, his conviction that the Ottoman Empire was near collapse, and how Britain could count on his future assistance while the Greeks would not rise up in support of the French because he indulged their vanity and easy-going natures. Military aid was indeed slow in materializing from the French, but at the same time as he was making Pouqueville welcome, even accompanying him on his travels and archaeological excursions, he was getting as much out of the French as he could by appearing to help them without committing himself. He was aware that Colonel Papasoglu was recruiting Albanians for his *Chasseurs d'Orient* his thinking was that with good relations with France they might provide extra manpower he could utilize.

After Elgin's departure from office, the painter Giovanni Battista Lusieri continued the excavations in Athens on his behalf. The outbreak of war between Britain and Turkey in February 1807 forced Lusieri out of Greece, but as he was leaving, Ali, one never to miss an opportunity, ordered that all the antiquities in his possession be sequestered. Ali then required samples of vases to be sent to him for his inspection. Lusieri suspected that Logotheti had become friendly toward the French and that he was really behind the request, but it transpired from a communication from Pouqueville to Louis-Sébastien Fauvel, the French consul in Athens and Elgin's rival who was collecting antiquities for France, that Pouqueville had put Ali up to it. As the sculptures were too heavy to transport over land they had satisfied themselves with vases intending to send them on to the Emperor. Ali was well aware of the growing philhellenic sympathies in Europe and the importance of preserving and reconnecting with the birthplace of European civilization and was content to pander to these sympathies for his own ends. He did send some of the vases as a gift to Napoleon, but they never reached him. Pouqueville informed Foresti in 1814 that Mehmet Effendi,[1] who was put in charge of their delivery, left them in Spalatro (Split) in Dalmatia when he was told that he had to go all the way to Vilnius in Lithuania to meet Napoleon. Apart from demonstrating Ali's long reach, he was in effect in control of Attica and Athens at this time, the acquisition and disposal of the vases illustrates his canny use of diplomatic sweeteners. It was during 1807 that Ali was seeking French aid in his endeavours to take Santa Maura and he was doing everything to improve relations only to be undone by the Treaty of Tilsit and the transfer of the islands to France despite his diplomatic efforts to affect the outcome. Mehmet Effendi had been on his way to the Baltic as Ali's emissary to the negotiations with the hope of impressing on France and Russia the need for Ali to possess the former Venetian territories in order to create a viable Albanian state. In the end Napoleon forced him to roll back his demands leaving only his obsession with Parga. In response he increased the duties on grain, wood and livestock exported to the islands. From then on French diplomacy would turn to creating an Albanian league of rival Beys against Ali to counter growing British influence in the Adriatic. Initial British policy had been to persuade Ali to comply with the Treaty while the Porte wanted him to create amicable relations with Britain. When Britain and Turkey briefly went to war, David Morier, who had been left in total charge of the mission to Ali, found the continuing discord between the governments undermined any progress and he was transferred to Sir Arthur Paget's mission in the Dardanelles, and then attached to Sir Robert Adair's embassy negotiating a peace treaty with the Turks. When Lusieri returned to Athens in 1809 he retrieved most of Elgin's statuary, but the vases were irretrievably lost. Even the acquisitive Veli Pasha, enjoying his apogee in the Morea, had managed to gain access to his house and stores, taking vases as gifts for the French. Once the Treaty of the Dardanelles was signed between Britain and Turkey, Ali became full of eagerness to please towards Elgin, sending him gifts through Foresti and offering him aid in retrieving his antiquities, but by now he was no longer in control at Athens.

In November 1807 Captain Leake appeared on the scene. As a young captain in the Royal Artillery he had been seconded to the British Military Mission to Turkey in 1799, travelling from Constantinople to Syria and Egypt before arriving in Athens to meet with Elgin. After the wreck of the *Mentor* and a short sojourn in London he was sent back East to assist the Ottoman government by assessing the state of their defences against possible French attack from the Adriatic, travelling extensively throughout Greece and Albania. This was a genuine concern and Foresti in Corfu was keeping Nelson informed of a possible French invasion. Leake's fact-finding missions did not go down well with the French, and when war broke out between the Porte

[1] Ali's secretary, see Chapter 6, p. 7.

and Britain they connived to have him arrested in Thessalonika as a spy. It was on his release, after nine months' confinement that he had his secret meeting with Ali concerning the peace negotiations between Britain and Turkey. Leake found Ali to be a man of ability but unstable, a fantasist convinced of his own importance and on bad terms with the Sultan. The feeling of the new Foreign Secretary, George Canning, was that Ali's claims to independence should not be encouraged while the Sultan stood up to Russia and France. Leake induced Ali to act as a go-between to bring about a reconciliation before returning to Britain. Although Pouqueville and Bessières were keen to use Ali they did not hesitate to take a hard line in order to safeguard French interest. Bessières was under no illusions. He routinely wrote to Ali in an annoyed and displeased tone, making no secret of his distrust of him, but he was also eager to present himself as Ali's ally. He wrote to Athanasios Psalidas explaining the lengths he had gone to by being required to write to Napoleon regarding Preveza, which Ali had held on to, explaining Ali's position in an effort to reduce the bad impression Ali had made. The situation over the dependencies was becoming more fraught. General Berthier announced that Parga was formally under French protection but the French still had to do business with Ali when needs must. In December 1807 Bessières was in discussion concerning the possible purchase of 300 horses for the use of the French cavalry and in the following March he was asking for help in order to take possession of 'the village of Vouthroto' (Butrint). He followed with a more threatening letter and still having achieved no result, Mula Mehmet next wrote to Ali offering indirect payment for Butrint on the behalf of the French. Until the French lost the Ionian Islands, Ali continued to provision the French troops at an increasing cost, but as the situation dragged on his relationship with Bessières deteriorated. He continued to refuse to honour the agreement over the French possessions in Epirus and Bessières was aware that Ali was favouring Britain in order to get what he wanted, possession in the islands. He warned Ali that if they continued in the same vein he would be forced to become indifferent to Ali's affairs, implying that he could not be held responsible for his future behaviour towards him. In fact the French were encouraging the formation of a league of dissenters and klephts against him based on the islands.

In October 1808, Leake was back in Epirus with supplies of artillery and ammunition as promised for use against the French. The following January, Sir Robert Adair wrote to Ali from HMS *Seahorse* in the Dardanelles, addressing him as 'Most High, Magnificent, and Powerful Prince', to thank him for his help in securing peace; but Adair was wary of entering into any further direct correspondence with him. Ali was quite likely to misconstrue the content of any letter in his favour. He claimed to have letters from Admiral Collingwood promising him Santa Maura and Parga and blamed Adair for blocking his plans. Instead Morier was to be dispatched to communicate in secret. In February Leake took up official residence at Ali's court, and from that time until March 1810 when he returned to England armed with his researches on topography and military capabilities, he was usually either at Preveza or Ioannina, from where he was able to continue travelling throughout Epirus and Thessaly. Leake's relationship with his counterpart Pouqueville was cordial enough for them to pursue some of their archaeological and geographical surveys together. With the French back in possession of the Ionian Islands, Spyridon Foresti had been exiled to Malta from 1807 to 1809 and it was there that he met with Byron and Hobhouse. Spyridon seems to have been largely responsible for Byron's

Fig. 42: *William Martin Leake* by Christian Albrecht Jensen.

visit to Albania and Ali. Unbeknownst to Byron, Spyridon was assisting Admiral Collingwood, commander-in-chief of the Mediterranean Fleet, in a plan to take the Ionian Islands back by hoping to exploit French unpopularity and the islanders' desire for British protection. Also Ali had his eyes on the islands, particularly Santa Maura, and Parga, and the British seem to have given him mixed assurances as to their intentions. In March 1809 Adair was implying that Ali should not give in to the French and with the supplies he had received from Leake and his cooperation, he was in a good position to get what he wanted 'with little trouble and expense'. On 12 June, Collingwood wrote to Wesley Pole at the Admiralty:

> What the sentiments of the islanders are towards Ali Pacha, - their detestation of the Turkish Government, - and the abhorrence of the Pacha personally -, I have before had occasion to state to their Lordships, His view of subduing the islands is well known, but he can only make himself master of them by aid of the English; - and this introduction to putting the Republicans (now merely a name) under the protection of the British, is not improbably the expedient they have adopted to detach us from

any Co-operation with the Pacha of Ioannina in his projects against them, - which will at least preserve them from a fate more dreaded, than their previous condition, but is diametrically opposed to the assurance Captain Leake is directed to give him.

Adair wanted to take Parga and the Ionian Islands and re-establish the Septinsular Republic but was quite happy to use Albanians and Ali in order to do so, and at the expense of giving up the dependencies of the Republic on the mainland to Ali if necessary. The pro-Russian Kapodistria blamed the unrest on the islands and the support for Britain on Ali. This significant support for the British was bolstered by the many disaffected Greeks from the mainland who later went on to join the British Greek regiment. Lusieri, still endeavouring to get his lordship's marbles back to him, arrived in Preveza that same June, presenting Ali with another opportunity to pander to the British and their lust for antiquities. Ali offered to smooth things over in Athens on Elgin's behalf. When the subject of the vases came up Ali said they had been spoils of war and the emperor had received them with thanks. Ali said that nobody had wanted the residue so, presumably in response to the shift in the diplomatic wind, he had given the vases, which were small and of poor quality, to Leake who was loathe to give them up. Unfortunately Ali's word did not carry enough weight at Athens and Lusieri had to approach Constantinople for his permits.

The handsome Byron was part of a plan cooked up by Foresti to sweeten Ali. After seducing Byron and Hobhouse with the delights and gossip of Malta, where Byron even had time to have a fling with John Spencer-Smith's wife Constance, he was able to persuade the footloose pair to head East by way of a diversion to Preveza and hence to Ali's court at Tepelene. Whether they knew or not a force of 1,800 men was only three days behind them heading for the Ionian Islands, it was something neither of them ever recorded. Byron's arrival in Ioannina was not greatly appreciated by Leake; he was in the midst of a tense situation as Ali was threatening to take him hostage in case Britain abandoned Ali to the French. Sir Robert Adair, ensconced as ambassador in Constantinople, had to send letters of reassurance on Leake's behalf to Ali. While the high profile tourists were at Ioannina, Hobhouse records in his diary a rumour that the Russians were about to attack Constantinople and that sixty men-of-war from the British Adriatic Fleet were already in the Dardanelles putting pressure on the Turks to make war with the French. The Greeks were supporting the Russians, and there were fears that a Greek uprising would put the British in Ali's territory in danger. However the British diplomats gained assurances, with the help of a few bribes, that Ali would honour his friendship. In the event the rumour proved false. Foresti was happy to give the impression that, although Byron was a lord, he was actually more elevated than that, perhaps even a son of George III. When Peter Howe Brown, 2nd Marquis of Sligo, visited Veli Pasha in the Morea and was mistaken for Byron, he was told that Veli had assumed Byron was a nephew of the King. Either way, Ali was duped into thinking he was highly honoured in receiving such an important guest. The Marquis, who knew Byron from Eton and spent some time with him in Greece, is better remembered for his later career as governor of Jamaica, where he acquired the unofficial title of 'liberator' for his reform programme.

George Foresti, who succeeded Leake as English resident in Ioannina (he was there in 1814 when Charles Cockerell visited), wrote to Colonel Lowe in January 1810 of the efficacy of Byron's visit to Ali and the subsequent offers of aid by Ali in the taking of Santa Maura and Corfu. Byron also wrote to Lowe, who he was keeping abreast of developments of Turkish advances at the expense of Russia, expressing his surprise at the outcome. Leake was in a difficult position. He had been told by Collingwood to encourage Ali in his desires on Santa Maura and Parga. When Leake supplied the rockets and artillery to take Berat, Ali opened his ports to British cruisers and merchant ships, and supplied provisions for the army in Spain and Portugal. In return Ali allowed the British to actively recruit mercenaries from the population but as these were generally taken from the Greek peasantry this did not go down well with the Ottoman authorities in the prescient knowledge these would-be soldiers might one day turn against them. Ali had ignored British requests to send troops to help the Austrians push the French from the Dalmatian coast. Such manoeuvres were having an effect on Leake who was feeling the pressure. He was trying to protect his sub-consul at Preveza who had played host to Byron and Hobhouse in Arta. Signor Commeniuti, in other words a Greek, Panos Kominiotis, was aided by his illiterate brother; 'a rogue' according to Hobhouse's dairy. From a letter to Ali by Stergios Zotoglou, one of Ali's informers and tax collectors, it appears that Ali wanted Commeniuti removed, and that Leake was unhappy with the behaviour of 'Mr Forestis', probably Spyridon. Pouqueville on the other hand was complaining directly to the Porte concerning Ali's assisting the British in taking Santa Maura. Although the Porte did not accept the accusation, Divan Efendi, Ali's contact in Constantinople, expressed his doubts about Ali's position in a letter to him in May 1810. The French ambassador had been working hard influencing top members of the Ottoman government to put pressure on the Sultan to declare Ali a rebel.

Although Adair wanted to keep Ali onside against the French he thought his claims for Parga unacceptable and the British position regarding the Ionian Islands and their dependencies was that they should be kept together. If they gave the impression otherwise they equally did not trust Ali's double-dealing. George Foresti was in contact with Stratford Canning, who had replaced Adair in Constantinople, informing him that Ali, their one true Balkan friend, was more anxious than ever for an alliance with Britain and that he had been responsible for the overthrow of the pro-French Alemdar Mustafa Pasha, the grand vizier, and that Britain should redirect its Baltic Fleet for his protection. These reports were backed up by Ali's agent Suleyman in Constantinople who was also in contact with Canning and passing all correspondence from the French Embassy via Canning before sending it on to Ali. Although Canning was aware of Ali's exaggerations he also knew that the French garrison on Corfu had grown to 10,000, swollen by the 2,000 Albanian fugitives from his rule, and they were putting pressure on him for supplies. Ali claimed he was only being a dutiful subject but he informed Canning secretly that the grand vizier was pushing him to supply the French. He also informed him that the British blockade of Corfu was ineffective and was easily being broken and in consequence he had to look to his own coastal defences. The British saw Ali's continued support of the French as a test of his loyalty towards them. As a result they tightened their grip and Foresti's agents monitored every harbour, intercepting boats and making arrests. Foresti wrote to the Foreign Office urging action to take Parga from the French but the British preferred to let the course of events unfold in the belief Parga would fall of its own accord. Ali, after sending his advisor and dragoman Spyros Kolovos to London to no avail, resorted to force. When the British pre-empted him by encouraging the Pargians to take the town themselves passing it to British protection, he resorted to diplomacy once more, appealing to Lord Castlereagh, the Foreign Secretary, and Earl Bathurst, the Colonial Secretary. They responded that the status of the islands and their dependencies was as determined in the Congress of Vienna which respected the previous Treaty of 1800 ceding Parga to the Porte. The complicated process whereby the Porte could not afford the compensation required for the inhabitants without Ali's financial assistance gave him a foot in the door, leading to the extended negotiations that eventually gave him possession of his long illusive prize.

Meanwhile at Ioannina, Hugues Pouqueville, who had joined his elder brother as a consul in 1811, was making complaints about Ali's duplicity that would eventually reach the ears of the Sultan. The fearful Ali's refusal to go to the Danube front suited British interests, so to counter French reports to the Sultan of Ali's duplicities, many of them instigated by themselves, Canning supported Ali's decision. The philhellenic Canning was never fully committed to Ali. If the Ottomans remained strong Britain was prepared to fight alongside Turkey, but during the Dardanelles negotiations, he secretly floated the idea of supplying arms to Ali and supporting any other insurrectionist groups within the Balkans and even some form of independent Greek state in return for services rendered if the Ottomans failed to hold Constantinople. It was thought that an independent state under a tyrant could be a transitional phase in the establishment of a free Greece, for, once he was no longer needed Ali could be easily toppled; preferable to the messy affair of supporting a full-blown revolution against Turkey. Canning continued to give the illusion of fostering Ali's ambitions without antagonizing him, for instance dissuading him from appointing a permanent delegate at London. As the French threat in the Adriatic faded Ali's usefulness to Britain diminished.

In the age of sail, the dissemination of information from the embassies was slow. Spyridon Foresti's messages could take up to two months to reach London depending on conditions and the state of the war. He utilized King's Messengers as they passed through Corfu on their way from Constantinople to London or if the dispatches were important a special express boat might be engaged. If available a naval ship provided quick and secure transmission, or if he knew the reliability of the captain, a merchant ship. Express or other boats were shared by nations and surprisingly little concern was given to the security of sealed packages. Messages to the fleet were quicker, being sent through their own system of communicating ships. Land routes were used from Ioannina to the east, and through Trieste and Vienna across Germany and on to London, but they were hazardous, crossing difficult terrain, prone to attacks by bandits and interceptions by the French through Italy. Foresti did not have access to ciphers despite his requests. That letters were intercepted is borne out by one that fell into the hands of Pouqueville that described how at Gardiki, after the soldiers had rounded up hundreds of women and delivered them to Ali's sister, Shainitza, she told Ali that she meant in future always to sleep on a mattress stuffed with their hair.

As Ali consolidated his position in Albania, French intrigues against him at the Porte increased. Napoleon's foreign minister and chief diplomat Talleyrand initiated a propaganda campaign through the chargé d'affairs at Constantinople, Latour Mabourg, stating his acts of aggression and violation of neutrality. Ali countered with accusations of secret French activities and intrigue with rebel groups. Ali's stock at the Porte had suffered since he declined to go to the Danube front in 1809. As a result the French upped their demands, threatening a break in diplomatic relations and war on Ali unless he returned captured boats and French fugitives at his court, expelled British corsairs from his waters and lifted the grain embargo on Corfu. Talleyrand's increasingly aggressive tone eventually brought results. The Porte dispatched an inspector, Celal Efendi, to look into his administration and foreign relations. The Porte trod carefully. In consequence of his report, as a sanction they removed Ali from his newly acquired sanjaks of Ochrid, Trikkala and Elbasan to placate the French, while at the same time impressing on Ali to retain good relationships with the British. But once the British had settled the Parga affair they became indifferent to his advances and his last-ditch approach in 1820 during which Colonel Napier was sent by Maitland to assess his military capabilities lead to nothing. Other matters were taking precedence.

Filiki Eteria

Ali Pasha's positioning of his regime in opposition to the Ottoman state suited the agenda of Western provocation and as his attitude hardened he provided, wittingly or otherwise, an ideal incubator for Greek nationalism. By making Ioannina stronger for his own advancement he had provided the Greek merchant class a platform from which to expand their horizons. They took full advantage of the opportune climate of relative stability creating a network for the advancement of trade; but the merchant diaspora could also be used to further the nationalist cause or 'the mystery', as it was called in Filiki Eteria parlance, or 'the school', as Patriarch Gregory V in Constantinople referred to it in correspondence. Under the pretext of such a 'scientific school' or 'Greek Museum', the patriarch and clerics, such as the Metropolitan of Old Patras, Germanos, could openly gather funds for the uprising and even mention it in correspondence with the Sultan.

As a result the most important clandestine activity in the region was carried out by the Greek underground movement, the Filiki Eteria. Widely spread throughout the towns and villages, and with support from klephts and intellectuals alike, the organization had infiltrated to the heart of Ali's administration. After years of subversive activity stoked by the Venetians, Russians and French, and a growing bourgeoisie and literate class, Epirus was fertile ground for revolution. The proximity of the Ionian Islands under their various rulers provided access to Western ideas and a haven to radicals and renegades. Through the growth in Greek trade internationally the Filiki Eteria was able to establish a wide reach, from Moscow and Vienna, to Constantinople and Greece itself. In Russia Greek nationalism was welcomed and encouraged, but in Austria and Turkey it was a dangerous affiliation. Rigas had been captured by the Austrians and handed over to the Turks to be executed. Therefore there was an imperative need for complete secrecy. The Filiki Eteria established the classic forms of recruitment and cells keeping the identities of the chain of command secret from the members. To do this

Fig. 43: *The Oath of Initiation into the Society* (1849) by Dionysos Tsokos, depicting Theodore Kolokotronis joining the Filiki Eteria. Tsokos came from Epirus and was taught by Nikolaos Kantounis from Cephalonia, a member of the Filiki Eteria.

correspondence was carried on in code. Important members were referred to by a number. The first spot, number '1' was kept vacant until a leader could be found, eventually filled by Alexander Ypsilantis, the son of Constantine who had made the attempt to liberate Greece via the Danube principalities with Russian help in 1806. Koloktronis was '118'; Perraivos '114'. Non-members had code names: Kapodistrias, who turned down the leadership was 'the man of good deeds', Ali was known as 'the father-in-law', the tsar, 'the philanthropist' and Sir Thomas Maitland, 'the old man'. Code words were used for sensitive information, betraying a certain sense of humour: the 'wine drinkers' were the Phanariotes, the 'unfortunate ones' were the bishops, the 'trees' were the muskets, the 'flock' was the fleet and the 'singer' was the cannon. Correspondence was carried on using a cryptographic alphabet, switching letters and numbers for the Greek alphabet. Some members of the Filiki Eteria were not Greek. When George Petrovich, known as Karađorđe, the leader of the Serbian uprisings, had to flee to Moldavia from Ottoman retribution he became a member. He was assassinated in 1817.

Christoforos Perraivos, whose name as the author of the *History of Souli and Parga* was written using the cryptographic alphabet, was a close friend of Rigas and was arrested with him in Trieste by the Austrians. Unlike Rigas he was released and went on to serve in the French and Russian foreign regiments on Corfu and helped with the defence of Santa Maura against Ali in 1807. With the British occupation of the islands he left for Odessa where he met the leaders of the Filiki Eteria and became an early member. In the preface to his *History*, Perraivos identified three Filiki Eteria and key members of Ali's circle who fed him information through 'allegorical signs'. Their names only became known in 1857 with the publication of the second edition of his book in Athens when there was no longer any danger or risk involved. The first edition had been published in 1815 in Venice by Nikolaos Glykys, a merchant from Ioannina, while Parga was still under threat from Ali. The key men in question were Athanasios Psalidas, whom Perraivos respectfully refers to as the teacher of Ioannina, Stephanos Doukas and Manthos Oikonomou. For Perraivos these men were members of what he termed the 'first Etairia', followers of Rigas, whereas he was a member of the second brotherhood from 1817, and they had kept their vow. Strangely, Oikonomou, who had initiated Kolovos, Ali's envoy to London, into the organization, was praised by Perraivos for his dedication to Ali. He was an important advisor in his administration, but his role as a patriot is questionable. After Perraivos' first edition was published he was Ali's negotiator for the sale Parga and was influential in the defection of Omer Vironi and others to the Sultan's troops during Ali's final war. When he tried to defect himself he ended up in the wrong hands and was executed by Mahmud Pasha. Oikonomou has been seen as a benefactor, looking after the interests of his home region of Zagori, and supporter of the Filiki Eteria but also accused of being one of Ali's unscrupulous enforcers. The intelligence Oikonomou, Psalidas and Doukas provided was used by Perraivos 'for the benefit of the Souliotes and Pargians' but with the outmost care not to leave any written or oral signs of their activities, as he was aware that Ali would immediately get rid of anyone who might compromise him 'from the root'. In Perraivos' view the three advisors had an ameliorating influence on Ali, but Archbishop Ignatios, who he knew was one of Ali's secret advisors, he held responsible for the events at Preveza before his defection to Santa Maura.

The aristocratic Ioannis Kapodistrias, who had defied Ali on Santa Maura in 1799, was a Liberal and a Democrat who then served in the ministry of the Septinsular Republic under the Russian occupation. Through Count George Mocenigo he joined the Russian diplomatic service taking a leading role in countering the attempt at Austrian domination of Europe under the policies of Metternich. Metternich, whose driving idea was stability within the *anciens régimes* of Europe, had no time for Kapodistria's progressive ideas and he kept a close eye on his movements. While he was in Russian service he had not forgotten about his native land and hoped to influence Tsar Alexander. In 1816 his secret police files record that Kapodistria was in Vienna where he was in contact with a number of Greeks, including the wealthy merchant Ioannis Stavrou, alleged to be 'the secret correspondent in Vienna of Ali Pasha of Ioannina'. Stavrou's son George was an old friend from his St Petersburg days. Closely involved with the Filiki Eteria, George made regular contact with leading conspirators when on commercial journeys abroad. The family were intimately connected with the Turkish chargé d'affaires in Vienna, a Phanariot, Alexander Mavrogenis, whom Kapodistria also visited. Mavrogenis was the son of a former Hospodar of Wallachia once employed by Rigas. It all amounted to a suspicious web to Metternich.

With the induction of Kira Vassiliki into the society in 1818 by Skoufas it is hardly surprising that in November, Ali informed the dragoman of the Russian consulate in Patras, Ioannis Paparrhigopoulos, that he knew of the existence of the Filiki Eteria and was conversant with their secret signs. In 1819 the Filiki Eteria had intensified its attempts for Russian support and Ali, through Paparrhigopoulos, began pressing for his own plans for a Russian-backed insurrection against the Sultan. At the same time he had opened up communication with his old enemy Kapodistria, and Paparrhigopoulos, who travelled regularly from Patras to Ioannina and from there on to Corfu, carried secret messages between them. It is suggested that Kapodistria had now come to the opinion that he could use Ali by encouraging him to rebel against the Sultan. Kapodistria was not beyond intrigue of his own. He passed on this information to Baron GA Stroganov at Constantinople, along with news that he had been forced to intervene to release the two sisters of Dimitrios Mostras, secretary to Bishop Ignatios, kidnapped by Ali. From Stroganov the message was sent to the Tsar, probably through the hands of Strogonov's secretary, Gabrial Katakaziz, who was also a member of the Filiki Eteria. By now Maitland, who was proving to be an unpopular governor on Corfu, was keeping tabs on Kapodistria. After a mishandled trip by Kapodistria to London to gain British support, Maitland was of the view he was a subversive and set his agents to intercept his messages. On one occasion Paparrhigopoulos was forced to play cat and mouse with a British ship sent to intercept him when he was crossing back to the mainland. He visited Ioannina again before returning to Patras to pass on an oral message from Kapodistria to Ali advising him to be loyal to the Sultan but act with humanity towards his subjects. This conciliatory tone was in effect encouragement to rebel because with the goodwill of his subjects he was increasing his chances of gaining independence. Kapodistrias was cautious, rightly wary of Ali's approaches to the Greeks, and reluctant to let the klepht captains become too closely drawn into Ali's web. After his round trip Paparrhigopoulos returned to Patras where he told his fellow conspirators, Consul Vlasopolos and Bishop Germanos, that Ali was primed and ready. The complexity of the relationships is summed up by the fact that Ali was back in correspondence with his old ally Bishop Ignatios who had left the Septinsular Republic in haste with the Russophile Count Mocenigo for St Petersburg. Appointed Bishop of Moldavia and Wallachia (Ungrovlachia) he was forced to leave Bucharest when the Danubian Principalities reverted back to the Ottoman Empire, to eventually find exile in Pisa from where he acted as a coordinator of the European philhellenic movement.

Kapodistrias' caution was proved correct as Ali vacillated between seeking British help in promoting an uprising against the Turks only then to say he wanted reconciliation with the Porte and its protection, while all the while making offers to Russia through Paparrhigopoulos. During the summer of 1820 Paparrhigopoulos was busy once more travelling from Patras to Constantinople, to visit the Filiki Eteria there, then to St Petersburg, where Kapodistrias had travelled. Ali's new tack was to own up to the Tsar to being a member the Filiki Eteria, having been initiated by Oikonomou. Paparrhigopoulos was dubious about this claim and on questioning denied the existence of the brotherhood. He knew that Greeks in Ali's service, the secretaries, Manthos and Alexis Noutsos, the physician Ioannis Kolettis and several klephts and armatoli had been enlisted but the organization had refrained from recruiting Albanians.

Fig. 44: Germanos, Archbishop of Old Patras by Adam Friedel.

It was Alexis Noutsos who was keeping Alexandros Ypsilantis informed of events in Epirus as he made preparations for the uprising before openly declaring himself for the Greek cause in Missolonghi in 1821.

In the end Ali ran out of friends. So accustomed to the practice of flattery and deceit, blackmail and extortion he was unable to develop the sophisticated tools to match his ambition. His diplomacy was so based on fickle alliances, double-dealing and hollow promises for the furtherance of his own ends that he was unable to keep the support of any of his major sponsors or the loyalty of the local beys and chieftains. The Porte was wise to many of his dealings with the foreign powers, playing one off against the other, and through its endeavours to keep a check on them inhibited his success in acting as an independent ruler. By never fully committing to breaking from the Ottoman sphere neither France nor Britain saw any long-term gain in continuing to support him. After pandering to the Sultan by informing on French clandestine activity in the Morea, his final bid to ally himself to the Filiki Eteria was a desperate last ploy. He had run out of options.

Chapter 6

Life under Ali Pasha

I have never followed any road previously travelled by Ali Pasha without seeing
some newly filled up grave, or some wretches hanging on trees. His footsteps are
stained with blood.

Richard Davenport

When Thomas Hughes stepped ashore at Preveza the town presented an oriental
prospect 'with its gorgeously painted seraglio, forts, and minarets'. At Konitsa,
north of Lake Ioannina, where there was an ancient fortress, a more peaceful
aspect greeted them. Here, where Ali had a serai, they found one of the 'best specimens of an
Albanian city that we saw':

> its houses stand for the most part separate, and the courts being planted with trees,
> a very pretty effect is thus given to its external aspect. It contains 5,000 inhabitants,
> about two-thirds of which are Mahometans. It is a bishopric. The bazaar is particu-
> larly neat, and the habitations in general extremely good, being built of stone, with
> handsome shelving roofs. We rode at once up to the grand serai of the vizir, and paid
> our respects to its Albanian governor… the intimate and confidential friend of Ali.

The governor was at dinner 'with a Turkish dervish and six other Albanian friends, clothed
in their sheep-skins, and eating a thick rice soup with wooden spoons'. Hughes and his companions were invited to join them; 'common politeness forced us to gulp down a few spoon-
fuls of this horrid pottage'. Every whim of the European guests was catered for. Desirous of
seeing the ancient ruin the aga supplied a body of men to escort them. To add to this picture
of contentment, by the side of the road to Ioannina there was 'a beautiful fountain beneath a
neat cupola, which contains seats for the accommodation of travellers' where one could take
'an excellent breakfast', and a new khan nearby and ferry station on the lake. For a moment
everything seems peace and tranquility in Ali's kingdom.

The Western narratives lurch from Oriental fantasy to harsh reality. Behind Preveza'a
picturesque facade were the 'miserable huts of the town… concealed by these edifices'. In the
imagination the people of Epirus may have been inhabiting a land plucked from the Arabian
Nights, but beneath the extremes and caricatures that the travellers found so fascinating a
state had to function. Ali's overblown persona, with its ambiguities and contradictions, played
into this dream but it also reflected the real-life uncertainties of his regime, poised as it was
between the old and the new; a land facing a world of possibilities waiting to be embraced, yet
caught in a medieval time warp of tribal loyalties. For a moment in time Epirus appeared as if

Fig. 45: *Ali Pasha hunting on the lake of Butrinto* after a print by Louis Dupré from *Voyage à Athènes et à Constantinople* (1825).

it might forge a new path, creating a new dynamic synthesis between two worlds where progressive ideas could even flourish. Given the condition of the floundering Ottoman Empire, Ali's autocracy was viewed by some as a lesser evil. Like any totalitarian regime it was selective in those whom it favoured, and for the fortunate there were opportunities within the semblance of security Ali provided, but at a price. He was running what amounted to a police state on a constant war footing, and as ever, it was the poor that felt the brunt of a rule that was based on expediency rather than justice.

In bare terms, Epirus, the heart of Ali's regime, was summed up by *The British and Foreign State Papers* for 1823–24 as having an estimated population of '375,000 souls' who had suffered 'in the midst of the chaos of the administration' of the 'most monstrous' tyrant, Ali Pasha.[1] In continental Greece the *Papers* reckoned the ratio of Christian to Muslim to be around five to one. In Epirus the numbers of Muslims generally increased progressively northwards and in Albania proper the mix would have been much more even. From the population of Epirus alone, not including his takings from Thessaly, Macedonia (with a larger population) and Acarnania, Ali extracted a tribute of two million piastres to hand over to the central government at Constantinople, and a further ten million which he kept for himself plus the exactions and revenues of his relatives. His personal income from Epirus was approximately equivalent to the total export value of all its seaports along the whole coast from Preveza as far north as Durazzo. At the time of writing after Ali's fall, the *Papers* described the Province as containing 'only ruins and solitude' and 'a feeble commerce with the Ionian Islands and the Ambracian or Artan Gulf'. Although it is evident Ali was regarded as a rapacious despot,

---

[1] Other estimates put the population in excess of 400,000.

the implication is that the quality of life had been reduced after his death. The stark contrast between Ali in his pomp and the condition of Epirus after his eclipse gives an indication of his impact on the region.

Ali's Court

From the grand displays and energetic building projects that Ali undertook it is clear that he was not satisfied with being yet another petty pasha in the accepted manner. Once Ali had established himself in Ioannina, he began to acquire the trappings of a potentate and develop a state apparatus in imitation of the Sultan. Having a capital allowed him to receive deputations from his subjects and delegations from foreign powers in the style of the Sublime Porte at Constantinople. At Ioannina, 1,500 staff attended visitors from far and wide. Hughes was there at the same time as a khan of Persia was paying his respects. The centre of Ali's administration was his court, which, like the progress of a medieval monarch, he moved around his domain from palace to palace. While the main seats of his power remained his palaces at Ioannina and Tepelene, he was said to travel throughout his fiefdom each year keeping a watchful eye on his allies and dependencies alike. For his subjects getting as close as possible to the 'throne' was a means to securing advantage, and gaining entry into the court circle itself was a highly prized method of social advancement. Notables from the villages of Zagori were as eager to show loyalty as the high placed citizens of Ioannina. Ioannoutsos Karamesinis, the most influential headman from Kapesovo, known as the 'Romiopasha', was a close ally and he entertained Ali in his mansion in the village on several occasions.

At the heart of the court was the harem, some of whose members moved with Ali from seraglio to seraglio, while others would remain *in situ* on a more permanent basis. At the Sultan's court the harem included female slaves and servants, eunuchs, wives and concubines and unmarried female relatives. The Sultan's mother played an important supervisory role within the imperial harem and when Ali took over the leadership of his clan from Hamko, she was said to have been pushed aside into the harem. Whether this was an amicable arrangement on not, she maintained her own small seraglio at Konitsa, her home village. Ali's first marriage had been for strategic reasons, but the route to his heart came from elsewhere. The mother of Selim Bey, Ali's youngest son, was a Circassian slave. Circassian women from the Caucasus were admired for their beauty and regarded as the pick of the concubines in the imperial harem and they were highly prized throughout the Empire. Selim's mother retained her favoured status with a position of authority over the harem at Tepelene. Kyra Vassiliki, who entered the harem at a young age, became in his later years his favourite mistress and eventually his wife. She gained such respect that she was recognized as a person of influence in her own right. Her position was secure enough for her to intercede on behalf of her fellow Christians and Greeks, finance restoration work at the monasteries in Mount Athos and even to become a member of the Filiki Eteria. That Vassiliki was content to play along with Ali, either through genuine devotion or expediency, was to her advantage, but as the story of Euphrosyne shows, others were not so willing. In some versions, she is depicted as heroically resisting Ali's advances and the shameful prospect of entering the harem. That such a prospect was damaging depended on individual circumstances. Slaves and captives ended up there, and also volunteers who saw it as an opportunity. Slavery was not banned in the Ottoman Empire until the early twentieth century. Non-Muslim young boys as well as women could be taken as slaves and used for sexual purposes, but more commonly they were used as attractive workers in bathhouses and coffee shops. That visitors to Ali's court were served by handsome youths was therefore not unusual in Ottoman society. It is well-attested however that Ali's harem included boys, called Ganymedes after the beautiful youth abducted by the god Zeus in classical myth. If there is any truth in Ali being, as Vaudoncourt euphe-mistically put it, 'almost exclusively given up to the Socratic pleasures', the name implies that many of the boys, or most of them, were abducted, and probably for more than their looks.

Slaves in Ottoman society could reach positions of high status and similarly a number of Ali's slaves and members of his harem went on to prosper. Odysseus Androutsos, who later would become a prominent figure in the Greek War of Independence, was taken and brought

Fig. 46: *Ali Pasha and Kira Vassiliki* (1848) by Paul Emile Jacobs.

up in Ali's seraglio from a baby, becoming, at the age of 12, Ali's favourite pipe-bearer. Born in Preveza, he was the son of a brigand leader who had spent years fighting Ali until, during the conflicts of 1789, his father was betrayed by the Venetian authorities. As Odysseus grew his exploits became notable enough to be celebrated by the balladeers; he was said to be able to divine water amongst the rocks and leap over the backs of seven horses. In a piece of typical bravado he pitted himself against Ali's swiftest stallion. As George Waddington recounts it in his *A Visit to Greece in 1823*:

> The race was to be performed on rising ground and the man to keep pace with the beast till the latter should fall down dead. In case of failure he was to forfeit his head to the indignation of his noble competitor. The Pasha accepted the challenge for his horse, as well as the condition proposed by the challenger, the execution of which he prepared to exact with great fidelity. The animals ran in his presence, - the biped was triumphant, and became from that moment the distinguished favourite of the master.

As a prize Odysseus was given a bride chosen from the harem. Whether this is fable or not, when he was 18, he had become trustworthy enough for Ali to appoint him the armatolic of Livadia, a position his father had once held. Rather than play the rebel though, in the next twelve years he carved out his own virtual fiefdom in Boeotia, which he ruled in imitation of his master with the same brutal efficiency. In 1821 when Ali was losing his grip on power, Odysseus cannily slipped off to the Ionian Islands. When the Greeks rose up in revolt he was then in a position to see an opportunity like Ali before him, gather 5,000 of his old comrades and set himself up in his old stamping ground as virtual dictator of the whole area known as Eastern Greece, from Parnassos to Athens.

Ali had a pragmatic attitude to captives. Captives were commodities and as such they could be expendable, used as bargaining tools or prove useful in some other capacity. Georgios Karaiskakis was born in a monastery near Arta, the son of an armatole and a nun, but soon he was running with the klephts of Antonis Katsantonis in the southern Pindus. He exhibited such daring and cunning that by the age of 15 he was leading his own band, much as Ali had done himself. Eventually, along with Katsantonis he was rounded up by Ali's men and sent to prison in Ioannina, but unlike Katsantonis who underwent a brutal death, he survived. His strong character must have shone through for he made such an impression that he then rose up through the ranks in Ali's service to become his bodyguard. This harmonious relationship was not to last. Karaiskakis fell out of favour and returned to the life of a klepht. When the Greek insurrection broke out he too joined the ranks of the revolutionaries. Unlike Odysseus he was content to fight for the cause, helping to lift the siege of Missolonghi and distinguishing himself in battle at Arachova and Distomo. He died trying to raise the Ottoman siege of Athens.

This 'meritocratic' aspect of Ali's rule was a mirror of life at Constantinople, where apologists for Ottoman rule point out that the Turks operated an open system of advancement. All the peoples of the Empire could reach the highest ranks if they progressed through the proscribed channels, the harem being one, conversion to Islam being another. Non-Muslims who were 'people of the Book', the Bible, in other words Christians or Jews, while being allowed to practise their religion were required to pay extra in taxation and were restricted in their activities and rights. Each religious group was organized as a separate entity (*millet*) within which it looked after its own affairs and disputes according to its own laws. In line with Ottoman practice Ali too tolerated Ioannina's significant Jewish community and paid due respect to the Greek Orthodox priesthood which wielded considerable authority amongst its followers. In Constantinople, the Greeks from the Phanar district had overcome their disadvantages to such an extent that they became indispensable to the Ottoman government. One of the attributes of the Turks often admired by Westerners was their perceived nobility and disdain for commerce. On the fall of the Byzantine Empire, the urban Greek, Jewish and Armenian populations found that the most profitable course open to them was either as a merchant or a dragoman (an interpreter, official guide and often all-round fixer between the Turks and their non-Ottoman contacts); the obsequious Levantine of this type became a caricature much despised in the West. The Phanar Greeks gained such wealth and influence through commerce that they were able to maintain their own educated professional class. The Turks found they required their expertise and Phanariotes began to occupy vital diplomatic positions within the Empire, infiltrating the government hierarchy almost to the top. After a time it was customary for Greeks to hold the posts of grand dragoman (official interpreter of the Divan, the Grand Council) or grand dragoman of the fleet. Eventually they even became princes or hospodars of the semi-autonomous provinces of Moldavia and Wallachia. The Turks' dependence on their Greek administrators would come back to haunt them. An extreme example was the Mavrokordatos family who achieved considerable success in a number of posts but their descendants would go on to be influential in the creation of an independent Greece. Alexander Mavrokordatos was the grand dragoman responsible for drafting the Treaty of Karlowitz (1699) between the Ottoman Empire and the Habsburgs. He was succeeded by his son Nicholas, who went on to be Hospodar of Moldavia and Wallachia, initiating a dynasty that lasted until another Alexander switched to the Greek cause. This Mavrokordatos became president of the first National Executive in 1823 and then prime minister of an independent Greece.

By Ali's time the use of Greeks in a clerical and professional capacity was common throughout the Empire, complementing their considerable influence at the capital. And as with the capital, so with Ali's Ioannina, where Greeks occupied several layers within his own administration. But at the Porte there was a significant difference; the official language of the court and government was carried out in Turkish. In the Balkans, Turkish was spoken by most Muslims except in Bosnia, Albania and southern Greece, where the local languages thrived amidst a mixed population of Slavs, Albanians, Greeks and Vlachs. In true Ottoman style, Ali maintained his own bureaucracy, but the language of his court was Greek. Ioannina was situated in a largely Greek-speaking region and under the Ottomans Albanian was not officially recognized; it did not become a fully written language with its own alphabet until the mid-nineteenth century. How proficient Ali was in written Greek is open to debate, but he was bilingual in both languages. Despite the low levels of literacy in the Ottoman Empire, written Greek was well established, so it was logical for Ali to call on his literate Greek subjects to staff his administration.

Ali retained four Greek secretaries to correspond with the various beys, agas, and gover-nors of his provinces. Hughes, who was not sympathetic to what he perceived as the Greeks' willingness to cooperate with Ali's despotism, describes two of the secretaries, named Mantho and Costa, as 'men of the most crafty and subtle disposition, the ready instruments of all the pasha's schemes of vengeance and of power.' The most trusted was Manthos Oikonomou from the Zagori village of Koukouli, who was Ali's private secretary and advisor. Oikonomou was given responsibility for the negotiations with the British for the purchase of Parga between 1817 and 1819. Like many of his compatriots he was able to fulfil these duties while at the same time, unknown to Hughes, being a member of the Filiki Eteria. The visitors to Ali tell of numerous secretaries, but it was a broad description. John Coletti (Ioannis Kolettis) from Siraco, high up in the Pindus Mountains south of Ioannina, was the secretary who met Byron and Hobhouse. Typical of many educated Greeks he spoke a number of languages: German, Latin, French, Italian, Greek, and Turkish. His birthplace may have been remote but accord-ing to Pouqueville and Leake it supplied capes for Napoleon's armies and also possessed a library where European newspapers could be found. Coletti or Kolettis, in fact a Hellenised Vlach, had studied medicine in Pisa in Italy, where he had come into contact with the Italian freedom fighters, the Carbonari. Kolettis was no ordinary secretary then, and on his return to Greece he served both Ali and Mukhtar as their personal physician, all the while pursuing his nationalist sympathies in the Filiki Eteria. Like Mavrokordatos, he would play his part in the Greek War of Independence, becoming a leading member of the initial independent administration and the first prime minister of the Greek State.

Leake tells us that Ali's less cultured rival at Berat, Ibrahim Pasha, employed a Greek trea-surer and physician, the learned George Sakellarios. Sakellarios who was born in Kozani was forced from his pleasant home in Ambelakia in Thessaly by Ali to fill this role. Educated in Hungary and Vienna, Sakellarios was also a poet. He is credited with introducing Shakespeare to Greece, but his association with Rigas and the Vienna circle of nationalists meant he had to be careful. Sakellarios too went on to be Ali's doctor. Evidently Ali's doctors had to be all-rounders, secretaries and interpreters as required. It appears Ali had four Greek doctors in total, three of whom were surrounding him when Holland paid his respects; along with Sakellarios the other two he names as Metaxa and Lucas Bia. The Bia family had cleverly attached themselves to Ali to such a degree that he sent Lucas to receive a medical education in Italy and Germany. When Holland was in Larissa he met Bia again where he had been called to give advice to another Greek doctor Ioannis Velara who was in the service of Veli, then pasha of Thessaly. Being a man of many trades would seem to have been either a require-ment or an advantage depending on your point of view. Psallida, the teacher in Ioannina who was met by Byron and a number of the British travellers, was required to double up his duties by providing his expertise in the local courts and councils. He was also employed as an advisor to Ali who sent him on several diplomatic missions. One of his reports on his activities in Corfu, where he had been dispatched to procure explosives, weaponry and other war-related materials, made a particular point of the high prices being charged by the British. His daughter was married to the doctor, Lucas Bia. Ability in languages was a prerequisite for a dragoman and important Western visitors were often supplied with a Greek interpreter and guide in this capacity, like Georgio Fousmioti who attended Byron and Hobhouse at Tepelene. Byron was an honoured guest so he was also attended by Ali's favourite dragoman and secretary, Spyros Kolovos. Kolovos had a strange reputation for acting on Ali's behalf as a sponsor of an alchemist who had the misfortune to be hung when his endeavours to change base metal into gold failed. Kolovos himself was captured and tortured by the Turks while visiting Corfu on a mission to procure munitions in 1820. Ali's other senior dragoman, described by Edward Everett as 'Prince Chanzerly of Joannina', was Hatzeris Beyzade, the son of Constantine Hangerli, the executed Prince of Wallachia.[2]

Not all the administrative posts were occupied by Greeks. Holland relates that 'I have seen a Christian, a Turkish and a Jewish secretary sitting on the ground before him… a principle which is carried through every branch of his government'. Although Leake tells us that Ali was his own 'Kehaya and Hasnadar', representative and prime minister, not even trusting his own sons and transacting everything himself that did not have to be done in writing, he surrounded himself with strong men willing to do his bidding. His most important servant was Suliman, who held such authority it was believed he might succeed Ali rather than Mukhtar or Veli. When Ali was not in residence at Tepelene he left the seraglio in the charge of Yusef Aga Arapi, a Moor, who Leake refers to as 'nominally His Highness's Hasnadar', whose duties extended to ridding Ali of any individuals that crossed him. Like the Sultan, Ali ran his own council or Divan where individual responsibilities did not have specified titles. His war council however was mainly made up of his most trusted Albanians, among them his sons Mukhtar and Veli, Abdullah Pashe Taushani of Elbasan, from an established Albanian family who guarded his northern frontier, Omar Vrioni and Veli Gega. In addition to his military duties, Ali entrusted Omar as his treasurer. An exception to the rule was his close councillor Thanasis Vagias or Athanasi Vaya, as Hughes calls him, 'his favourite and most successful general, who might indeed be styled commander in chief'. Intimate to Ali's deepest secrets, Vagias had free access to him night and day. A Greek from Tepelene, he had led the attack against Gardiki.

Ali employed a number of Europeans in various capacities, some voluntarily others not. Ali's 'prime minister' in Hughes' opinion was Mahomet Effendi, who he describes as:

> a silly old man who studies astrology and occult sciences till he thinks himself gifted with inspiration, and will pore for many hours together over an old globe, though he knows not whether the earth moves round the sun, or the contrary: it would be well if he were content to pronounce oracles upon science and politics; but he is withal a violent bigot, fierce and implacable against heretics or unbelievers, and ready to execute the most horrid commands of his despotic ruler.

Leake, who calls him Mehmet Effendi and Ali's secretary for foreign affairs, tells us that he was originally from Rome and called Marco Quirini (variously Guerini, Guéri or Gheri). That he was a persecutor of unbelievers shows that despite changing his religion he had not changed his zeal for orthodoxy; in Rome he had been a member of the inquisition. After a

---

[2] See Chapter 5.

period as a missionary in Aleppo he was in Malta at the time of the arrival of the French expedition to Egypt and with his knowledge of Arabic he was appointed by Napoleon as his secretary-interpreter. On his return journey to Europe, Quirini was travelling on the same Italian vessel, the *Madona di Montenegro*, as Pouqueville and Bessières and was captured by pirates to be sold as a slave and ending up in Ioannina where he decided that the best course of action, if he was ever to see freedom again, was to convert to Islam and enter Ali's service. Leake thought that for a 'man of acuteness, sense, and learning' it was a hard service 'among comrades with whom he can scarcely exchange an idea'. But Ali had 'according to his usual policy, already persuaded him to take a wife, and now that he has him in his power, scarcely gives him the means of existence'. Ali also employed, but rarely paid:

> a Milanese, who had previously been employed by the Pashás of Berát and Skodra, and who has undertaken to complete a foundry at Ioánnina: there are also a French engineer, a carpenter, who makes gun carriages, a Dalmatian watchmaker, and an Italian smith. These people, though really able men in their professions, will soon be forced to leave his service from the want of encouragement.

Many of Ali's foreign workers, such as landscape gardeners and architects, had either been captured or coerced into service. Other foreign experts, particularly military, he acquired through diplomatic means. In addition to these Ali's court included numerous minor officials and hangers-on. Mukhtar was able to run his own considerable court financed from his income as pasha of Berat.

Ali the Landowner

Ali's position of supremacy was consolidated through the acquisition of his own private estates to provide him with a constant revenue stream. Strong-arm tactics and force only achieved so much. Progressively Ali exploited the *chiflik* system to swallow up districts as his personal fiefdom and making him a major landholder;[3] a prime example of a local potentate who increased his private estates at the expense of the peasants. Some land, although not in Ali's name, could be controlled through marriage. Libokavo was a *chiflik* of Ali's sister not far from Argyrocastro through her marriage to Suleyman from a prestigious local family. Her son Adam went on to become governor. The more usual method was to establish a foothold in a village by acquiring some land, sometimes by merely claiming it as a right, then to put pressure on other villagers to sell to him by driving them into debt at high interest rates through extraordinary exactions, and sometimes by the expediency of quartering his Albanian soldiers in their houses. When the peasants could no longer pay, Ali took the village as his *chiflik* and the villagers became in effect his tithe-paying serfs. Ali did not always have it his own way, but the villagers held out at a severe cost. The inhabitants of Delvinaki were subjugated to a level of taxation which they could not pay, so the difference was made up

---

[3] See Chapter 1.

with an increased number of Albanian soldiers quartered on the town. Henry Holland was informed by a villager that this imposition was aimed at Ali 'obtaining proprietorship of the town'. The villagers were holding out possibly in the hope that Ali might increase the sum he was offering for the purchase. Holland comments that 'While on the one hand this bears the marks of unwarranted oppression, on the other it shews a somewhat more regulated despotism than might be expected from other acts of the man'.

In research carried out in 1835 by Professor Christoforos Philitas it was claimed Ali and his family held over 900 *chifliks*, mainly in Epirus, but throughout Thessaly and Macedonia as well. They held twenty-six villages in the Speracheios valley in central Thessaly alone. As Ali pushed south from his Epirus homeland, he acquired further fiefs in the Ottoman region of Livadia (central Greece). Here 107 villages have been identified as having belonged jointly to Ali and his sons. Ali held a further 13 himself and Veli Pasha owned 15 with 157 *zeugaria* of land, equivalent to around 157 peasant farms. Veli also held numerous villages in his own right around the Gulf of Corinth, yielding fifty-five *zeugaria*. Not all regions were suitable for this kind of appropriation. As Finlay noted, Acarnania in western Livadia was a region where 'property is generally private in a country of graziers and shepherds'. Even so Ali may have held some *chifliks* here that included forests as well as grazing land.

Although Ali's propensity for despotic behaviour was a cliché of the folk tales, the recollection of exactly how he acquired land became a matter of dispute even within living memory. After Greek independence the new Greek state laid claim to all Turkish owned land as state property. In the wrangles that followed, a legal battle with the residents of Desphina, a village of 200 inhabitants south of Delphi, ensued which illustrated Ali's technique of land appropriation. Desphina, in its upland location, had been favoured under Turkish rule as being allowed an element of self-administration and a low tax burden. The Greek State claimed that after Ali extended his rule into Livadia, in 1815 the villagers sold their private land to him. Ali used his classic methods, making economic demands through his agents on the villagers and demanding extra tithes. In Desphina's case he wanted triple the amount of grain harvest that had previously been reserved for the Sultan, thus marking it out for himself as a *chiflik*. The villagers claimed that Ali used violent means to seize Christian property contrary to Ottoman law, which recognized their special status. When his agents had failed to make any headway, he had brought four village elders to Ioannina by force, throwing two of them into prison. Here, before they died, they had replied to his threats saying they could only speak

---

Typical produce from Ali's Chifliks

Wheat	Beans	Flax	Oranges and
Barley	Olives and olive oil	Freshwater fish	lemons
Rye	Grapes	Hay	Figs
Oats	Hempseed	Mulberries	Pears
Corn	Saffron	Melons and	
Millet	Cotton	watermelons	

for themselves, not for the whole village. The villagers claimed that on this basis if any sale had been agreed it would have been invalid because the elders did not represent the other villagers. Ali had therefore arbitrarily seized the land and imposed the triple tithe. What was more, on Ali's death the Sultan himself returned their property and rights to them, recognizing as free any *chiflik* where Ali had seized land from either Turk or Christian. The villagers won their case.

Ali as a Ruler

Ali's harsh exactions on villagers had a debilitating effect on much of the countryside. Travellers noted the desperate state of many of the villages through which they passed. There was an air of decline and desertion in some places. This was partly attributed by Hughes on his journey through the country to a recent outbreak of the plague. When Byron and Hobhouse visited Zitza on their way to visit Ali in Tepelene, they were accompanied by Spyros Kolovos whose function on the trip Hobhouse describes in his diary as being partly 'His Highness Inspector of Villages'. Byron and Hobhouse were put up and entertained in the local monastery. For Byron, Zitza was the most beautiful place he had seen. Entranced by its magic he wrote in *Childe Harold*:

> Monastic Zitza! from thy shady brow,
> Thou small, but favour'd spot of holy ground!
> Where'er we gaze, around, above, below,
> What rainbow tints, what magic charms are found!

But Kolovos was not with them to enjoy the scenery. He used the opportunity to assess with the headman of the village the revenues due and then make a report to Ali. While they were in discussion one of the poor priests came to complain that they had rated the place too high. Zitza, populated solely by Greeks, only consisted of about 150 houses and 4 churches but paid 13,000 piastres in tax, which as Hobhouse states (expanding in his *Journey*) left them 'hardly sufficient remaining out of the produce of their labour to support themselves and children'. The village, located in Byron's idyll in a peaceful landscape where 'flocks play', was described by Hobhouse as being on rich soil and blessed with 'numerous flocks'. The village was famous for its local wine and produced corn, meat, fleeces and skins, but it was all sold, even the milk, to pay the tax. Hobhouse continues:

> They were starving in the midst of abundance; their labour was without reward, their rest without recreation; even the festivals of their Church were passed over uncelebrated, for they had neither the spirits nor the means for merriment.

Ali was forever blurring the line between government official and brigand as it suited him. All Albania was required to pay a tenth to the Sultan, of which Ali took a quarter. On top of this, the village being his *chiflik*, he took half its earnings plus labour and, in common with

Fig. 47: A view of 'monastic Zitsa' (photography Derek Smith).

several other villages nearby, protection money on demand. Even in his official capacity his requirements could be arbitrary. Troops or retainers could be quartered on villagers at any time and as an extra burden villagers were required to provide horses for travellers, which only the Westerners offered to pay for. To add to their material discomfort, the presence of Ali always loomed over them, for as Hughes recounts, he had a small serai, or palace, near the monastery, to which a granary was attached to contain their produce.

Ali's rapaciousness was in part a method of control, wearing down all opposition, but an undesired consequence was the devastating effect on the distribution of population. The verdict in James Bell's *A System of Geography* (1832) on the sanjak of Delvino was that the 'tyranny of Ali Pasha has left it in many places a desert'. As a result of his attempts to subdue and tax the Vlach and Sarakatasan pastoralists of the Pindus, hundreds or thousands of families fled to Thessaly and Macedonia where they found grazing on the eastern slopes of Mt Vernion, Mt Olympus, and as far as the Rhodope and Pirin Mountains in Thrace and Bulgaria. In central Macedonia his suppression of the rural population had a different result; they fled to the towns. Edessa, which Ali took in 1792, experienced an increase in population after his army had looted and plundered the neighbouring villages. When he made the village of Techovo (Karydia) into his *chiflik* the inhabitants deserted en masse to Edessa where they settled in the district of Techovtiki, named after their home. On the other hand Ali could force people to move if he wished. At the opposite end of his domain, at Saranda, the main port for the Delvino district, after he had taken control of the Himara coast, he built a small fort in 1801 and a new village to house farming communities from the neighbouring plain. These farmers were required to cultivate the depopulated area around the destroyed town of Nivitsa in Hamara whose survivors had been sent to his farms near Trikkala. Ali then took a third of the produce of the vacated land for himself.

Offering protection from government tax collectors to divert money into his own coffers or against the marauding activities of the klephts were two of his usual tactics for financing his regime. Some of his other schemes reveal his complex relationship with the Orthodox Church. In accordance with Ottoman practice the Church itself was supposedly exempt from tax. Even so a priest and a relation of Kolovos who was accompanying Byron and Hobhouse on their journey was going to petition the vizier to explain why he had defaulted on his protection payment. Ali took cuts from local clerics, such as a 'chanter's fee' offered to him on occasion of the ordination of a bishop. Holland tells us that Archbishop Polycarp of Larissa, an Albanian by birth, owed his position to Ali's favour. Having his man in position was a way of ensuring there would be no trouble, for the diocese was a lucrative one and a significant amount of its revenue was diverted into the coffers of Ali, his son Veli, as pasha of Thessaly, and to Constantinople. Despite these exactions, the clergy was dependent on Ali and prepared to be his ally. Correspondence in his archive reveals evidence of the priesthood pleading on his behalf to officials in Constantinople against the 'lies' of his enemies. Letters to Ali from his subjects are full of Oriental obsequious expressions of loyalty, while his replies are short, terse and factual. Ali may have wanted to underline his connection with his subjects by referring to them as 'My own...' but his terseness maintains his awareness of his authority.

Byron was not always in poetic raptures about everything he saw, and in a moment of down to earth sympathy he recounted to his mother how for women in the countryside life could be harsh:

> their women are sometimes handsome also, but they are treated like slaves, *beaten* & in short complete beasts of burthen, they plough, dig & sow, I found them carrying wood & actually repairing the highways. The men are all soldiers, & war & the chase their sole occupations, the women are the labourers, which after all is no great hardship in so delightful a climate.

Byron rather spoils his observation with his last throwaway comment, perhaps always feeling the need to end on an upbeat note for his mother. His sentiments are echoed by Hughes, who also could not resist attesting to the beautiful sunburnt features of the women. Near to Delvinaki, Hughes saw:

> women returning from the toils of agriculture with hoes, spades, and other implements of husbandry in their hands: one poor creature had two infants tied in a kind of bag over her shoulders. Almost all the cultivation of the ground in this

district is left to women, whilst the men are absent during greatest part of the year in Constantinople, Adrianople, Saloniki, and other large cities, where they carry on the trades of butchers and bakers.

To make ends meet the population had to be readily adaptable, often leading a double life. When this proved too much, the road of the klepht beckoned.

In an effort to be fair to Ali or to try and see something more than the caricature despot, some writers tried to put Ali's rule in a context while looking for the positives. As Cockerell explains:

> As for Ali Pasha's government, one has to remember what a chaotic state the country was in before he made himself master of it. The accounts one gets from the elders make it clear what misery there was. No stranger could travel in it, nor could the inhabitants themselves get about. Every valley was at war with its neighbour, and all were professional brigands. All this Ali has reduced to order. There is law — for everyone admits his impartiality as compared with that of rulers in other parts of Turkey — and there is commerce. He has made roads, fortified the borders, put down brigandage, and raised Albania into a power of some importance in Europe.

To weigh against the semblance of stability Ali had achieved, all descriptions of him include the words despot and tyrant. That Ali made improvements was accepted, but they were achieved with a heavy hand; he had brought order, if not law, by ruthless means. Ali's conquests were maintained only by a constant military presence. A string of fortresses kept vigil over Suli, in one of which at Kiafa was a fortified serai, and in the nearby village of Castriza thirty houses quartered thirty soldiers. Order was further maintained by a punishment regime that was often harsh and public. Byron had considered writing a tale based on the stoning of a pregnant 16 years old Turkish girl following an edict by Ali forbidding relations with a Christian, but he found it too terrible to relate. The mutilated remains of the priest Euthemos Blakavas that they had witnessed hanging in Ioannina, were posted there to send out a warning. In Ali's interpretation of justice he was obliged to subdue the robber bands that infested the country and this he undertook 'with the greatest severity; they were burnt, hanged, beheaded, and impaled'. Many of the harassed peasantry were sympathetic and in this he was aided and abetted by the local population. But Blakavas was not a thief. His band that threatened the Ioannina road to Thessaly across the Pindus was part of a general insurrectionist movement. In Ali's interpretation he would have had no alternative than to come down hard. When the band was defeated, his son Mukhtar 'cut to pieces a hundred of them on the spot', but the ringleaders were taken, for it would be necessary to make Blakavas an example. The outrage of Western writers at Ali's barbarism must be tempered with the knowledge that in Britain the last public display of murderers in a gibbet after hanging took place in 1832, until when theft was also a capital offence; burning at the stake was abolished in 1790, hanging carried out in public until 1868 and beheading and quartering for treason only abolished in 1870. Britain was not an exception, public executions by guillotine where carried on in France until 1939. The last men to be actually hung, drawn and quartered in Britain were five members of the Cato Street Conspiracy (1820) who attempted to murder the prime minister, Lord Liverpool, and members of his cabinet. Part of the problem was a matter of scale; Ali employed these harsh measures not merely to make the country safe for merchants and travellers, but to deter others who had revolt on their minds and to encourage others to turn them in.

The Ottoman system of justice was not based around capital punishment. Many criminal offences, even those as serious as murder and sexual impropriety, were dealt with by the imposition of fines according to the culprit's means. It was a system open to corruption, and by the eighteenth century open to abuse by local elites. By this time it was also on the decline and as the Empire moved into troubled times the recourse to other methods became more common. What shocked Western visitors as much as anything else was the scale of the barbarity and the tortuous methods used that guaranteed a slow lingering death. To put down revolt in Bosnia in 1809 and Serbia from 1804 the authorities impaled the rebels. Two hundred rebels were impaled in Belgrade in 1814, and in 1821 after the Greek uprising, revolutionaries and civilians alike were tortured and impaled; even the Patriarch Gregory V in Constantinople was taken on the orders of the Sultan directly from celebrating the Easter Liturgy and hung in full vestments for two days from the main gate of the patriarchate compound. Though Ali appeared to take a sadistic pleasure in ensuring his victims suffered in as humiliating and painful way as possible. Sometimes offenders were merely sent to prison, at Ioannina perhaps, but Ali also had more secure places of internment, such as the formidable mountaintop castle at Klissura (Këlcyrë). Here, Hughes observed some of Ali's 'state prisoners... wretched victims of his tyranny and suspicion'. A poor Greek from Lepanto was one who had been arbitrarily seized from his bed at night and then, after having served eighteen months in Ioannina, was banished to Klissura, 'where he had remained two years without even knowing the crime from which he suffered'. Another prisoner was a young black eunuch who had knifed one of Ali's pages and had become impossible to restrain. Imprisonment was another means of extracting money. Leake was informed that Ali kept a Jew in prison in Ioannina under threat of losing his head until he paid up forty purses. Ali's informers would let him know of any suspected improprieties, real or imaginary, going on in the villages so that he could impose cautionary fines, the proceeds of which went straight into his pockets. Despite the threat of such treatment, law and order continued to be difficult to maintain. When Hughes arrived at the dilapidated and hostile village of Ostanitsa (Aidonochori), he found that another traveller had discovered that four of Ali's soldiers had been murdered only a few days previously.

Nevertheless the consensus was that Ali's methods increased the safety of travellers, and with his improvements to the infrastructure, bettered the lot of some of its inhabitants, whilst also bringing in revenue for his coffers and prestige to his person. Bad roads and a lack of bridges had hamstrung the countryside for years. This was not just a restriction on movement; it aided the activities of the brigands and contributed to the general state of anarchy. Ibrahim Manzour claimed that the changes made meant that European travellers 'in the last ten years of the reign of Ali Pasha... could travel in complete security'. Things may have improved but 'complete security' sounds like wishful thinking on Manzour's part. An armed guard was deemed necessary to accompany Byron on his trip from Arta to Ioannina, because despite official efforts some bandits still operated. When Holland made his journey from Ioannina north to Tepelene he was provided with a passport and stern instructions that all his needs would be catered for. He writes that the instructions dictated that he was to be received as if Ali 'were present in person; that I should be supplied with horses wherever I required them; and that every house should be open to me. It concluded by the singular threat, "if you do not all this, the snake will eat you"'. In part these improvements were for Ali's own purposes, he had his own resting places, or small seraglios, along the routes of his journeys, easing his progress around the country. Better roads also meant his troops could move more swiftly to deal with trouble. Travel further afield remained arduous. To reach Thessalonika from Ioannina was an eight day journey in 1820.

As well as roads Ali built a canal to bring ships part way from Arta to Ioannina and his new roads and bridges were complemented by the draining of swamps. Near Delvinaki, Holland describes how a swamp or lake had recently been drained and turned to 'rich and profitable cultivation'. The road and causeway over the swampy marshes between Preveza and Arta were, according to Hughes, the best he had found in Greece, and as good as an English turn-pike; the handiwork of an Italian doctor, Ali's surveyor of highways, who found it easier to 'mend roads than constitutions'. Ali's meanness meant that the causeway was only partially paved, leaving Hughes in doubt as to which 'would first sink into oblivion, the pasha or his road'. Improvements had been made on the Arta to Ioannina road from around 1800, and despite the attempts at paving in some parts, Hobhouse found it tolerable for horses. Tolls of four paras were extracted at roadside *osteria*, or inns with an arch or adjoining barrack. This seemed to only apply to the Greek 'passengers' in his party when taking an overnight stop. By way of a backhanded apology for Ali's harsh reprisals, Hobhouse seems to accept that the means justified the end by saying that Ali 'by many wholesome regulations has acted the part of a good and great Prince, without perhaps a single other motive than that of his own aggrandizement'.

In essence Ali operated a system of divide and rule applicable in all his dealings. By showing favouritism across ethnic, religious and class divides he undermined tribal and community loyalties. Through his duplicity and the use of bribery he corrupted the elites, whether beys or agas, armatoli or klephts, religious or community leaders, or merchants.

Commerce

Bell's *System of Geography* tells us that:

> The commerce of Albania was greatly promoted by Ali Pasha. The exports are grain, timber, oil, tobacco, cotton, and wool; they are chiefly conducted through the gulf of Arta, but the merchants principally reside at Jaoannina. The grain is chiefly sent to the Ionian isles, Italy and Malta; the timber is excellent and grows almost on the shores; the cotton is received through Thessaly, and exported to the German and

Italian ports. The only manufactured article of export is the Albanian *capote*, a large woolen kind of great coat. The chief connections of the coast are with the Greek houses at Trieste, and Maltese house.

Cotton was a major export of Greece, four-fifths of it exported from Salonika in 1789 according to the *Encyclopaedia Britanica* (1824), the remainder from ports in Ali's control: Arta, Butrint and Avlona in Epirus and Volos in Thessaly.

One community that did well out of Ali were the merchants. There had long been a tradition of commerce within the region but it had been carried out in a hostile environment. The only towns that could flourish were either on the coast or hidden secure within the mountains and out of reach. Until Ali seized them, all the usable ports had been held by foreigners and precarious roads linked them to the prosperous villages of Zagori or across the Pindus to the town of Ambelakia in Thessaly, situated at an altitude of around 450m (1480ft) on the far off slopes of Mt Ossa. The merchants of these villages relied on safe passage for their extensive networks to flourish. The Ambelakians exported their unique red yarns by camel caravan across Epirus, where they were aided by their contacts, and on to important centres throughout Western Europe, even as far as England. As late as 1849 Edward Lear saw camels, 'ragged and hideous creatures… a great contrast to the trim and well-kept animals of our Arabs… known in our journey through the desert of Suez and Sinai' straggling along the road from the east coast toward Ioannina. Such enterprises needed security and this Ali could provide. Ali's seizure of the ports gained him the lucrative control of trade previously in the hands of the Venetians, and eased the flow of merchandise to and from the interior.

The crown of his achievements was making Ioannina into a thriving commercial and cultural centre. The city already had an illustrious history but it had been eclipsed by the coastal towns such as Parga, Arta and Preveza that had thrived through their connection to Venice. Arta and Preveza continued to flourish as mercantile centres under the French who used them as shipping points for timber for their navy at Toulon. When Ali brought them under his rule, they lost out to Ioannina when he made it his capital. According to Cockerell, the population of Preveza fell 'from 16,000, to 5,000 at the outside, mostly Turks'. Bell's *Geography* calls it 'now a place of small importance, but pretty well fortified'. Situated within an agricultural plain, Arta, 'an ill-built but active town with 10,000 inhabitants', could still rely on cattle, sheep and pigs for export to the Ionian Islands. But Hobhouse observed that while the Greek warehouses continued to trade in cotton, woollen and leather goods, tax revenues were down. Similarly, Trikkala, a city of the plain in Thessaly, though still one of the largest in Greece had, according to Leake, 'rapidly declined' since coming under Ali's government.

In contrast, Cockerell was impressed with Ioannina's rapid growth as a bustling market centre:

> The number and richness of the shops is surprising, and the bustle of business is such as I have not seen since leaving Constantinople. We understood that when the vizier first settled at Janina in '87 — that is, twenty-seven years ago — there

were but five or six shops in the place: now there are more than 2,000. The city has immensely increased, and we passed through several quarters of the town which are entirely new.

The population of the city was variously estimated at between 30,000 to 50,000 worshipping as to their religion in the 6 or 7 churches, 2 synagogues, 5 grand tekkes and 16 or so mosques. A series of fairs were held in towns in northern Greece in the summer; in Ioannina there were two large fairs a year and a smaller trade fair once a fortnight. For permanent trading Ioannina had a large covered market, an extensive bazaar, and a string of wooden booths through the intersecting streets where the bustle of business visitors found comparable to Constantinople. Wages, and prices, were among the highest in Greece. Ioannina's success was such that in 1833 a visitor declared it to be the Manchester and Paris of Roumeli. Cloth came in from Leipzig and even some rare highly esteemed English items could be found, the streets were abustle with artisans and metal-workers, and Greek merchants who travelled as far as Trieste, Genoa, Leghorn (Livorno), Venice and Vienna. Some of these merchants, such as the four Zosimas brothers who were based in Leghorn and Moscow or the Maroutsis family based in Venice, became extremely wealthy and were able to endow the places of their birth with schools and hospitals.

If the merchants prospered under Ali they still led a precarious existence. His relationship with the mercantile elite was a complex and volatile one. Some of the Greeks who held positions in local affairs and the administration did well out of Ali's financial and tax dealings, to such an extent that the Muslim merchants complained, saying they were forced to leave Epirus. A memorandum of 1814 states that 'He drove the agas out of their houses, their homelands, their villages… and he looks after the Christians, God forgive him'. But under Ali nothing was given for free, there was always a quid pro quo, or a payoff for himself. Nicolo Argyri, the Greek whose house in Ioannina was used by various foreign visitors, was one of the merchants who had business in Trieste. Ali regularly took what might be called commercial hostages. He allowed his subjects to travel abroad as long as they left their families behind. As Holland observed, Ali practised a system that never allowed 'a family to quit his territory, unless leaving behind some principal members of it, and their property also, to be responsible for their final return'. For this reason Ali was particularly displeased that the English ambassador allowed the entire population of Parga to emigrate following the agreement for the sale of their homeland, wanting to limit permission to only sixty families. In more modern times, a similar practice of tying families to a country by keeping some of its members within the boarders at any given time became common practice within the former Soviet bloc. According to Manzour, Ali imposed a further element of control over his citizens by obliging them to seek his permission to marry.

Nicolo's impressive residence was built by his father, the wealthy merchant and benefactor Anastasis Argyri Vrettos, who had endowed a hospital capable of treating 150 patients. After his father's death Ali shamelessly exploited Nicolo's house for the entertainment of his favoured guests. Cockerell, who made the memorable drawing of the courtyard, described it thus:

> The best room in this mansion was allotted to the English milordi: it was large and lofty, containing on the side next the court two rows of windows, between which ran a projecting cornice; the chimney piece was, according to the fashion of the country, a species of alcove, surmounted by an elegant leafy ornament, and handsomely ornamented with mouldings; whilst the divan was tastefully enough supplied with sofas and cushions of blue cloth.

If being constantly put upon by Ali was not enough, Nicolo's life was made even more complex as he was one of Mukhtar's retainers. In 1810 he was required to serve Mukhtar as his secretary at the siege of Rustschuk, modern Ruse, in Bulgaria during the Russian-Turkish war. Nicolo, who was not of a martial disposition, suffered further by receiving no recompense for either his personal losses or his services.

The notorious Kyra Frosini incident, which took place in 1801, was an example of the dangers of getting too close to or the demands that could be made by Ali. By the time Byron arrived in Ioannina eight years later, the story had already become obscured by rumour, but as the Ali Pasha Archives show, the 'beautiful Ephrosyne' was more than folklore. Byron and others all claim to have their conflicting information from first-hand sources; Leake of course already knew about it from one of the husbands of the victims. Kyra Frosyni (Euphrosyni Vasileiou) was the real wife of a successful Greek merchant, Demetrios Vasileiou. What the incident reveals is that rumour and suspicion were so rife that anything could be believed about Ali and his family and the raw material from such an event could be moulded to any purpose; to highlight the cruelty and arbitrary nature of Ali's justice and the corruption and lasciviousness of his court, while in some way preserving Euphrosyne as the victim. Ali could be either the strict preserver of public morals or the lascivious villain, but Mukhtar, renowned by all accounts for his publicly licentious behaviour, was always portrayed as a sexual predator. That the struggles to preserve one's honour against the advances of members of Ali's family were known to occur is apparent in a deleted passage in a letter Byron wrote to his mother, retrieved by his biographer Leslie A Marchand, where he decides against telling of the plight of a young Albanian girl caught in such a situation, preferring to cast Ali in a positive light. Euphrosyne was from an important family and moved in elevated circles, but this had its hazards as a letter from her uncle, Archbishop Gabriel VII Gagas of Ioannina, Nafpaktos and Arta, warning her of the risky nature of her private life shows. More is hinted at than spelled out, the archbishop had to be careful in case the letter fell into the wrong hands, but the implication is that she should retain the integrity of a married woman with small children otherwise the consequences could be dire. Whether she was the object of Ali's or Mukhtar's affection, the result accords with the rivalry between the two. The situation of Euphrosyne was typical of that between servant and master where the lesser is perpetually dependent on favours in order to procure and maintain advancement. Acceding to the wishes of an unpredictable ruler was a dangerous game. Whether Euphrosyne listened to her uncle, and was powerless to resist, or she was the willing dupe will never be known, but either way it led to her death. Once her possessions were confiscated, including the letter, and having made his point, Ali allowed the archbishop to look after her abandoned children.

Ioannina was the jewel in Ali's crown but other towns in the interior also revived their fortunes, particularly those of Ali's own region of southern Albania. Argyrocastro reached its apogee, growing to 15,000 inhabitants, with its prosperity reflected in the fine domestic architecture of the defensively built mansions that remain today. The people had not lost their taste for feuding, but as Pouqueville tells us, the relative peace brought commerce, and local goods including livestock, handicrafts, fabrics and dairy produce were exported within the Empire. The surrounding vale of Argyrocastro Holland described as thriving agriculturally with corn, maize, rice and tobacco sent to the coast for export. Tepelene, while in many ways as impressive as Ioannina, was never a rival, remaining essentially a military base. If Ali favoured some towns, other commercial centres still struggled. Ali was resentful of any kind of independence and particularly the further away from his heartland. The merchants of Ambelakia still plied their trade with some success until the town was hit by plague in 1813, but this was achieved despite constant harrying and disruptions by Ali's troops and his imposition of a heavy tax burden of 60,000 piastres. The merchants of Kozani in western Macedonia who had business in Germany abandoned their town when it fell into the hands of Ali, many seeking their fortunes in Constantinople.

Cultural Revival

Within Ali's household there was an ecumenical attitude to education, for, allowing perhaps for some stylistic exaggeration, Finlay tells us 'the children of Albanian Muselmans might be seen in one antechamber reading the Koran with a learnt Osmanli, while in another young Christians might be studying Hellenic grammar with a Greek priest'. Interesting in itself as a reflection of Ali's attitude to religion, this situation hints at a growing gulf between the aspirations of the Muslims and the Greeks. The Greeks looked to education to preserve their culture, but also as a means to reassert their national identity. By the late eighteenth century the Greeks of the Ottoman Empire were in the midst of a fever of renewed intellectual activity influenced by their diaspora communities, who in turn were in thrall to the French enlightenment. The scholars and writers of their own Greek enlightenment were often well-travelled and in communication with one another. The far-flung networks of Greek merchants enabled the flow of money and ideas to penetrate into the remotest of regions. The Ionian Islands were a natural reception point for Italian influence, but even in the interior mountain villages there were those eager to study abroad and bring their knowledge home. The connections with diaspora settlements within the Habsburg Empire and Russia were important in the fermenting of the revolutionary and nationalist sentiments of Rigas and the Filiki Eteria. Many of these mountain towns and villages had a strong Vlach presence. The Vlach pastoralists who roamed the mountains far and wide had made the passes their own. Moscopole, for instance, sitting on an important east-west trade route, exploited its prosperity and connections to become the leading Vlach and Greek intellectual centre until its decline after Ali's attack in 1788.[4] Particularly influential were the merchants and intellectuals to the south in the Zagori region, some of whom attained with important positions at Ali's court. Crucial to this revival was the finance redirected by merchant families into their home areas. Greeks from Delvino residing in Venice were part of a community known as the Brotherhood of Saint Nicholas who supported educational initiatives. The Zosimas brothers from Ioannina were important benefactors, setting up numerous schools and orphanages and sponsoring literary works. Their efforts were so noteworthy that the radical Greek journal *Hermes O Logios* (September 1819) printed in Vienna, reported that when the youngest brother was received in Moscow by Sophia, the mother of Tsar Alexander, she told him, 'the benefits which you confer everyday on your countrymen are known to my son and to me; continue them...' and turning to a company of his fellow Greeks, she added 'Gentlemen, this is a true ornament of your nation'.

With increased stability and trade, Ali's rule further opened up the region to outside influence. Ioannina already had a growing intellectual class with links to Venice and Italy, but it was enhanced as a cultural centre. Education for the Greeks of Epirus, funded by donations from successful local merchants, was generally in a better state than elsewhere in Greece. Schools often led a chequered existence under Ali. While not actively encouraging education, his ambivalence allowed it to prosper, perhaps valuing anything that could further his own ends. His capital possessed a number of schools and libraries. Two of the schools were usually referred to as academies or colleges while the others would be grammar or elementary schools. Some dated as far back as the seventeenth century, such as the Epiphaniou (1647) and Gioumeios (later Balaneios) schools (1676), and the prestigious Maroutseios School, founded in 1742. In 1797 the Maroutseios School was refounded and renamed the Kaplaneios School, when its benefactors, the Maroutsis family, ran into financial difficulties following the French occupation of Venice where they had business interests. Its new sponsors were the Kaplanis brothers. Students from the school went on to study abroad and on return make a significant contribution to Greek learning. Intellectual life had existed outside Ioannina too, particularly at Moscopole, where The New Academy or Greek Academy, had its own printing press, established there from around 1700, with a number of scholars from Ioannina as teachers. One teacher, Theodore Kavalliotis, was a native of the town who returned after studying mathematical and philosophical sciences at the Maroutseios School. Despite Ali's destruction of the city in 1788, a new school was established at the end of the century, funded by Simon Sinas, an Austrian aristocrat, diplomat and banker whose father came from the city, with the scholar and priest Daniil Moschopolitis, a student of Kavalliotis, who had published the first lexicon of the four native languages, Vlach, Greek, Bulgarian and Albanian, becoming headmaster in 1802. In Konitsa there was also a Greek school flourishing by the end of the 18th century run by a graduate of the Gioumeios School in Ioannina. During Ali's rule it closed briefly until it was reopened by Kosmas Thesprotos, a student of Psalidas.

Hobhouse and Byron met some of these teachers; a schoolmaster of Arta with sixty pupils was one who praised Ali saying he 'had civilized and improved all the country, which he had

---

[4] See Chapter 3.

conquered'. Most books available were translations of works sent from the diaspora print-ing presses, which passed through Arta and on their way to Ioannina. Byron was impressed with the cultural life of Ioannina, which he said was universally acknowledged amongst the Greeks as surpassing Athens in 'wealth, refinement, learning, and dialect of its inhabitants'. In addition to the Epiphaniou and Gioumeios schools he mentions that there was free edu-cation available in modern Greek, with reading and writing, taught to 300 boys in a school run by Valleno and funded by the Zosimas brothers. Athanasios Psalidas, who, when they met him, ran the Kaplaneios School with 100 pupils, giving instruction in French, Latin, Italian and Ancient Greek, already had a reputation as a major figure of the Greek enlight-enment. He had continued his education in Poltava in Russia (now the Ukraine) and Vienna, where he published his first work, *Real bliss*, in 1792, a philosophical treatise written in both Greek and Latin, and dedicated to Catherine the Great. Forced out of Vienna after being interrogated by the police for his liberal and French revolutionary sympathies he returned to Ioannina to become a progressive teacher. He introduced a controversial modern curricu-lum that included scientific experiments, a matter of consternation in conservative quarters. The abrasive Psalidas was fond of berating foreigners for their countries' part in the Fourth Crusade which devastated Constantinople, on the correct pronunciation of Classical Greek and their practice of removing antiquities, and failure to help Greece achieve her proper status in the world. In return the haughty foreigners were perhaps unfair on Psalidas, who provided the school with books and equipment, coming as they were from privileged back-grounds. Hobhouse was surprised that Pslidas possessed only a small library for a distin-guished scholar, and Cockerell was less impressed, admitting only that he was '… for this country, a learned man. Besides Greek, he speaks Latin and very bad Italian, but as far as manners go he is a mere barbarian'. Edward Everett somewhat agreed, casting doubt on the notion of his 'perfect' knowledge of so many languages.

When the Turks took the city in 1821 the schools were burnt or destroyed. It took some years before education returned. In 1828, the Zosimas brothers founded the Zosimaia; it was open to Greek, Albanian and Turkish students. Anastasios Sakellarios a student of Psalidas returned from a spell teaching in his home village of Vredeto in Zagori to become its principal in 1833. As well as schools, the Zosimas brothers financed editions of the works of the humanist scholar, Adamantios Korais. They had sponsored his studies in Paris where he witnessed the French Revolution. From there his works were disseminated throughout the Greek-speaking world. His belief in the importance of the Greek language in fostering national identity and that only through education would Greece achieve inde-pendence had an important influence on Greece's own revolution. He urged rich Greeks to 'multiply throughout Greece schools and libraries; at common expense to send prom-ising youths to Europe, that they may bring back her benefits to you; and entrust to them the education of our people'. Paradoxically, in 1802 when the Suliotes were fighting Ali he advised them as Albanian speakers: 'When you have a little peace, bring to your country a teacher to instruct your dear children in the Greek tongue. When the warriors of Souli learn from what ancestors they have sprung, nobody will be able to defeat them, either by guile or by force'.

War

'You will see that Ali Pasha, the successor to Pyrrhus will surpass him in every enterprise'. In these words Ali described himself to a dragoman employed by the French as an interpreter who relayed them to Sir William Eton. Ali was in preparation at the time for his attack of 1792 on Argyrocastro and had mustered 20,000 Albanians. With regard to this likening of himself with the King Pyrrhus, Leake remarked, 'Pyrrhus is the only great man of antiquity he [Ali] ever heard of except Alexander; of Alexander's father at least, whom Aly most resembles in character, I find he has no knowledge.' Ali was not content just to follow in his predecessor's footsteps; he wanted the connection between himself and Pyrrhus to go further, claiming in an inscription in Greek over the gate of his castle at Ioannina that he was descended from Pyrrhus. Claims and titles were one thing but living up to them was another. He reputedly earned himself the title of Aslan, the 'Lion' on the Danube front, but the assessment of Ali as a military leader, his prowess and the capabilities of his forces, and to whether he lived up to his boast, is not straightforward. Richard Davenport claimed to have seen with his own eyes a watch set in diamonds presented to him by Prince Potemkin as a testimony of the esteem held 'for his bravery and talents' during the campaign where he distinguished himself at the head of his Albanian troops in the service of the grand vizier, Yussef Pasha. The fact that Potemkin was on the other side during the hostilities of 1787 perhaps suggests that Ali's talents lay elsewhere; with his eye on Russia's intrigues in Greece, he was prepared to keep the lines of communication and his options open to further his own ambitions.

Warfare in the Balkans was a different affair to that carried out in the main theatres, on land or sea, during the French wars. There were no comparable set battles, certainly no Austerlitz, Waterloo or Trafalgar, even on a smaller scale. Ali owed his initial success to his brigand background, but he was astute enough to become aware of the more technical aspects of warfare. When on campaign for the Sultan he observed the discipline of the janissary units, but the janissaries were becoming a thing of the past. Like the Sultan, who was trying to modernize the Turkish Army, Ali was impressed by Western military advances. He became keen to adopt the latest models of army management and following the Sultan's lead he initially sought aid from the French. The nature of the terrain in Albania and western Greece suited small-scale engagements and limited the use of large weaponry, so, despite the fact that Ali brought a greater sense of purpose and organization, increased the use of artillery and improved defences, military action was still usually of a sporadic nature following the traditions of banditry and guerrilla warfare. The levies of local irregulars were accustomed to a style of warfare that involved much noise but little loss of life. Defending a position they would dig a shallow ditch surmounted by rough palisades (*tambouria*) for one or two men who, shouting threats and abuse, proceeded to fire into the air or without taking aim. Their opponents, often known to them, would reply in kind, rarely making a direct assault unless they had good reason to expect surrender. Ali only engaged with European trained troops in his confrontations with the Ionian Islands and their mainland coastal dependencies or on campaign along the Danube border. The European volunteers who rallied to the Greek cause during the War of Independence discovered to their cost the problems of trying to impose

Western ideas of military order on the Greek irregulars. The exceptions were the British who found themselves at advantage in that they had previous knowledge of the effectiveness of guerilla tactics from the Peninsular War.

During his alliance with the French Ali utilized their expertise in military training and fortification building, but as circumstances changed he was happy to turn to the British. An example of the different attitude to warfare comes from Signor Niccolo in Ioannina, if it is to be believed. The host of Byron and Hobhouse was at the siege of Berat for three months, where 'he used to smoke his pipe in the midst of the shooters, that though there were forty pieces of cannon in the castle, besides mortars and 6,000 besiegers, he once heard the list of killed and wounded, after a battle of forty-eight hours, three killed – two wounded'. The intervention of newly developed British technology was required to bring affairs to a speedier conclusion. The city fell eventually with the aid of 600 Congreve rockets. These had been brought over as a gift by Leake, who then trained the Albanian soldiers in their use. Such devices had appeared in 1807 at the siege of Alexandria in the campaign against Muhammad Ali Pasha, the Turks' nominal vassal in Egypt. The rockets were notoriously inaccurate but their explosion had a demoralizing effect, creating more terror than a cannonball.

In a letter to Stratford Canning, Foresti describes an engagement between Ibrahim Pasha and Ali in 1810. Encouraged by the French, the pasha of Avlona attempted to regain Berat while Ali was on his way to Larissa. Ali doubled back and in a pitched battle defeated Ibrahim, leaving 300 casualties. Such an event was 'not remembered to have taken place in Albania before where it is not uncommon for parties to contend for months without losing any men'.

During wartime, Ali reputedly could assemble an army of between 40,000 to 50,000 men in a matter of 2 to 3 days, and could double that number in 2 to 3 weeks. The estimates of his forces vary wildly; Holland: 30,000; Leake: 'not less than 16,000' armed with muskets; and Sir William Hamilton, former private secretary to Lord Elgin and ambassador extraordinary to the Sublime Porte in a letter of 1803 to Lord Hawkesbury the British Foreign Secretary, 'in the space of a few days he can raise 300,000 troops'. His regular supply of troops was drawn from his Albanian subjects, but others could be volunteered or persuaded to join his cause. Many of his Greek warriors later involved in the War of Independence received their training in Ali's army, but the most feared were his own men, for as Eton says, the 'good Turkish soldiers' used for his attack on Argyrocaster 'were the more formidable, as they were all Albanians'. Although Ali's janissaries and most of his Albanian levies were Muslim, he had a Catholic battalion, known as the Mirdites, recruited from the north of Albania. His

Fig. 48: Congreve Rocket troop in action.

Western allies were used to increase his manpower and supply modern weaponry. Once Ali had subjugated his provinces he undertook a comprehensive review of the defences of his territories, improving existing fortifications or building from scratch. Like his army, this had a dual purpose, to protect from foreign incursion, but also to keep under a hard-fisted control a population notorious for its bloody feuding and independence. Charles Cockerell gives us a picture of the situation at Ioannina in 1814.

> The fortresses on the promontory into the lake are of the vizier's building. He has always an establishment of 3,000 soldiers, 100 Tartars (the Sultan himself has but 200), a park of artillery presented him by the English, and German and other French artillerymen. We seem to have supplied him also with arms and ammunition in his wars with Souli and other parts of Epirus. Perhaps it is not much to our honour to have assisted a tyrant in dispossessing or exterminating the lawful owners of the soil, who only fought for their own liberty; but one must remember that, picturesque as they were and desperately as they fought, they were nothing but robbers and free-booters and the scourge of the country.

According to Edward Everett, the two forts at Ioannina possessed 29 pieces of 12 and 24 pounder cannon and five mortars supplied by the French under Vaudoncourt, and of the regular force of 8,000 in his provinces, Ali maintained 3,000 constantly in Ioannina.

Ali the Builder

The most immediate reminder of Ali Pasha in Epirus is the one he left in stone. Split between Greece and Albania, these remains are still relatively unexplored by visitors and historians. With the best known tending to be in Greece, this gives only a partial impression of his legacy. Foremost among these are the numerous fortifications attributed to Ali. Protecting his gains was a primary concern. To do this he either refurbished existing castles, many dating back to Venetian or Byzantine times, or built modern fortifications from scratch. Ali's building spree coincided with his success in courting the Western powers. This enabled him to gain access to the latest techniques of fort building through the aid of European architects and engineers.

The coastal towns and ports were of particular strategic importance and Ali expended much energy to bring them all under his control and keep them. Once he had secured the coast he set about improving existing defences and building new ones where necessary to create a defensive line from Preveza to Avlona. In many cases the improvements were minor. Avlona, when Leake was there in 1804, had an 'apology for a fort' with 'ruinous walls, with towers and a few cannon'. When Ibrahim Pasha was installed here after the fall of Berat, Ali must have been content to leave things be, perhaps preferring the town's defences not to be too secure. The centrepiece was still the Venetian sixteenth century round tower that acted as a citadel within the moated town walls, all of which was sadly demolished in 1906. South from Avlona, the truculent inhabitants of the Himara littoral were a different matter. They had been so harshly dealt with in 1798 that Ali appears to have deemed a minimum show of

Fig. 49: 'Ioannina the capital of Albania: Turkey in Europe' (1836) from *Constantinople and the Scenery of the Seven Churches of Asia Minor* by Rev. Thomas Walsh, illustrated by Thomas Allom.

force as sufficient. At Himara itself only small adjustments were made to the ancient castle. Further south in the bay at Porto Palermo a significant fort was built on the site of a much older castle. 'Ali's tower', as Pouqueville calls it, is a well-preserved fort attractively situated on an island within the bay and connected to the mainland by a narrow isthmus. Local legend has it that Ali built it in honour of his wife Vassiliki, whereas Hughes more realistically saw it as part of a plan to encircle the pashalik of Delvino, underlining that Ali's motives were to control the local population as much as to repel invaders. Over the entrance is a message from Ali: 'Who would dare touch these walls, the black snake will eat his eyes'. But it has been questioned how much of the work is actually his. Its triangular construction with cor-ner bastions is similar in style to the fifteenth or sixteenth century Venetian triangular fort at Butrint built prior to the evolution of the star design. The Venetian attribution is further enhanced by its general situation that suggests a seaward connection. In 1921 an American brigadier general, George P. Scriven, reported the castle at that time was called Venetian and the plaque above the entrance gate, which is now missing, was probably a carving of the lion of St Mark. The location under a hill from which it could be bombarded by cannon fire also suggests an early date.

As at Avlona, Leake and Pouqueville found Porto Palermo less formidable than at first sight. The garrison only consisted of ten men when Leake visited, armed with two four-pounders. Two years later Pouqueville counted 'a few guns, of no service either to command the entrance or to protect the shipping at anchor'. If it was built with the aid of French engineers it is surprising Pouqueville does not mention this. This less than impressive state of affairs in conjunction with his offer of the castle and port to the Royal Navy in 1803, suggests that Ali no longer feared insurrection from the local populace. The fort served as a Soviet submarine base under Albania's communist dictatorship and it has been suggested that the re-ascribing of its construction to Ali probably suited the regime's nationalistic agenda. Near the castle is a large church. Whether it was built by Ali along with other public works in an effort to win hearts and minds after his invasion, or for his wedding to Vassiliki, remote enough from the capital not to cause disquiet amongst the Muslim and Orthodox faithful as has been proposed in the tourist literature, is another Ali enigma. In contrast, although Ali ruined the mosque at nearby Borsh, he renovated the medieval castle of Sopoti. Similarly after he destroyed Nivitza, he erected a small square fortress just to the north at Agios Vasilis (Shen Vasil), which Pouqueville says was 'regarded by the Albanians, and for some time by Aly himself, as the key of the Ceraunian mountains'.

When Himara's loss of independence was followed by the fall of the strategically more important former Venetian ports, the more urgent work was begun to upgrade their defences. At the Skala of the Forty Saints (Saranda), Ali added a fortress (1804) with two round towers at the two opposite angles and a dwelling for the *bulu-bashi* or head of the military district in charge of a few soldiers. At Butrint, the retreating French Army had destroyed the triangular Venetian castle to prevent it falling into his hands, so he took over a fortified estate situated at the mouth of the Vivari channel belonging to a Corfiote family and began a series of improvements including the installation of gun emplacements. The reorientation of the main defences seaward shows that the fort was no longer protecting a link to Corfu but a border crossing and against attack from the sea. Despite its small size it became one of Ali's most important residences. It was upgraded again in response to the British capture of Corfu in 1814. Similarly at Igoumenitsa he built or rebuilt the harbour fort and set about major restructuring programmes at Preveza and Vonitsa.

At Preveza, despite the town having been held and fortified by the Turks and Venetians, the surviving fortifications are mainly the work of Ali. To guard their prize possession the Venetians built the Castle of Bouka overlooking the narrowest point of the inlet into the Ambracian Gulf, but they blew it up in 1701 before handing the town briefly back to the Ottomans. Constant attack and counter-attack had left the town's walls in need of an overhaul. So when Ali retook the town in 1807, he had grand designs. He hoped to make it his main coastal base and the necessary refortification was undertaken with the aid of French engineers, overseen by Colonel Vaudoncourt. Cockerell summed up Preveza thus:

> In Venetian days Previsa had no fortifications. Now the pasha has made it quite a strong place, with several forts and a deep ditch across the isthmus, though the cannons, to be sure — which are old English, ones of all sorts and sizes — are in the worst possible order, their carriages ill-designed, and now rotten as well. The population has fallen from 16,000, to 5,000 at the outside, mostly Turks.

Hughes agreed. He found the artillery was a hotchpotch of all types, many of which were unserviceable.

> the bastions of the surrounding wall are mounted with guns of all calibre, from old ship cannon, twenty-four and thirty-two pounders, to small swivels and light field-pieces, all intermingled together. Most of these guns are quite useless, and would either burst at the first discharge or at least shatter to pieces their rotten carriages.

Ali instigated a break with Ottoman traditions of fortress building and the remains of Preveza reveal his assimilation of Western ideas. Although he may have been eager to adopt new techniques he was not so hands-off to leave things to the experts as Vaudoncourt found out to his cost. Ali was incapable of allowing one man to get on with the job, often employing a number of architects on the same project and with conflicting aims. In consequence of his interference, greed and haste to cut corners the results were often inadequate, being built for show rather than for utility. The old town occupies the corner of the northern promontory facing inwards to the gulf. On the two landward sides of the town Ali built a 2km long earth rampart and moat using conscripted labour; by the time of Leake's visit in 1809, it was already beginning to crumble. At the north-east point where the wall projected into the gulf, it was augmented by the stone-built Pefkakia bastion with embrasures facing south to protect the port. At the opposite more exposed corner overlooking the seaward entrance to the gulf, the wall was reinforced with a fort known as the Castle of Saint George. Further to the south-west outside the town walls with gun batteries commanding the seaward approaches Ali built the pentagonal Pantokrator fort on the site of a church. Within the walls he refurbished most of the Castle of Saint Andrew, which the Turks had built as a replacement for the defunct Castle of Bouka, with a central tower protected by a rectangular wall and a defensive ditch. The two of its four corner towers that face the harbour are polygonal bastions that once had walls extending from them to enclose the port. On the site of the Castle of Bouka, he then had provided himself a seraglio with stones, Hobhouse informs us, plundered from the ancient ruins of Nicopolis nearby. On the opposite shore further into the gulf at Vonitsa, Hobhouse thought the existing fortress not very strong. Ali made improvements and when General Richard Church took the town in 1829 during the Greek War of Independence he reported it as the strongest of all the Turkish fortifications. On the route from Vonitsa to the offshore island of Leufkas, on which Ali had intentions, he built a further three forts.

Of the coastal towns, Parga was the exception, holding out until it was sold to Ali in 1819. As part of his strategy of encirclement Ali possibly refurbished the nearby sixteenth century Turkish Castle of Margiriti, which guards the routeway north, and when he took the closer village of Aghia in 1814, he built a new castle between the village and Parga. The architect of the Castle of Anthusa was said to be Don Santo di Monteleone, an Italian serving in Ali's army. Imposingly positioned on a hill visible from the town it is most likely it was placed there more as an act of intimidation as its guns would have been too small to put Parga within range. As at Preveza, the impression is superficial; the walls are too thin to withstand serious

Fig. 50: 'The Castle of Parga in Epirus' (1836) by Thomas Allom.

bombardment. Once he had possession of Parga, he built a citadel, serai and bathhouse on top of the old medieval and Venetian castle.

Inland the border of Ali's dominion was less defined. Ali maintained his defensive screen through alliances rather than by walls, but he did fortify or refortify places associated with his conquests and campaigns. Again the castles and walls of the established old towns were improved or new ones built, while in unruly areas new forts were imposed on the population, to form a latticework of key strongholds. To keep a vigilant eye on the Suliotes, high on a ridge on Mount Trypa, Ali built the Castle of Kiafa to control the passes into Suli. Built by a Greek, Kyr Petros, with bombproof magazines, casements and cisterns, and Leake thought, a large serai for the governor. Again most of the effort was expended on the imposing exterior, for Lear, who spent a night there, described the interior of the fort as having 'several dilapidated courtyards' through which one passed to reach 'the inner serai or governor's house – a small building with wide galleries round two sides of it'. At Paramythia, rather than building anew, the ancient Castle of Agios Donatos overlooking the depopulated town was used to house his Albanian troops. Ali built or upgraded the Turkish khans along the highways. Often these were more than just wayside inns for travellers. At the highest point (700m) of

Fig. 51: 'Seraglio of Suli' (1815) by Henry Holland.

the major routeway between Ioannina and Arta there was the important khan at Pente Pigadia (Five Wells). In 1818 Ali upgraded this to a two-storey fort with cannon guarding his newly paved road. This may have replaced an earlier nearby Turkish fort dating from around 1760.

To hold the land north of Tepelene he improved the medieval fortifications at Berat after ousting Ibrahim Pasha. Once he had subdued the country between Tepelene and Avlona he fortified the key points along the course of the River Vjosë, the main north-south artery. In the other direction upstream towards Permeti and Koritsa (Korçë), Ali built a castle and serai at Klisura (Leake's Klisúra), a strategic point where the Vjosë passes through a dramatic gorge. Ali's castle, the ruins of which are still to be seen, Leake describes as built on a prec-ipice 'at an elevation of about one-third of the summit of the mountain'. It consisted 'only of a square white-washed enclosure of a single wall, with a tower at each angle, but perfectly commanding the only road into the pass'. Built on the foundations of an ancient fortress to 'curb the spirit of this district', as Hughes put it, it overlooked a ragged and miserable pop-ulation in the village below. Even more ragged gypsies lived amongst the ruins of what must have once been a more prosperous settlement. In contrast not far away at Premeti (Përmet) Ali's youngest son Selim Bey, before he was removed to Argyrocastro, occupied a large serai above the town, which Hughes found

> fitted up with greater splendour than any we had seen except that of Tepeleni: it contained very fine baths and a beautiful kiosk, paved with marble, in the midst of which was a fountain: the serai is situated in a kind of paddock, to which extensive gardens are annexed; it is also surrounded by strong works.

Towards Argyrocastro and Delvino, at Gardiki (Kardhiq), the site of his infamous massacre, Ali reinforced the late medieval castle with his trademark polygonal towers. Despite Ali's desire to follow European fashion he still employed Ottoman architects. Ali's Ottoman master architect was Petro Korcari, Leake's Kir Petros. According to Leake the unfortunate Petro had not been paid after five years in Ali's service despite being responsible for the building of a number of castles and serai for Ali or his sons. Petros, who remained Ali's favourite architect from 1800 and 1812, was responsible for the magnificent Zekate fortified tower house or *kullë* in Argyrocastro built for Beqir Zeko, an administrator in Ali's government. The house is the finest example of one of 600 similar fortified houses built in the town around this time and the gun placements in the walls are a reminder of the still unsettled state of affairs, or to quote Pouqueville, 'distracted with sanguinary and endless contentions'.

The Zekate house was built at the same time as Ali refurbished Argyrocastro's impressive castle. The medieval castle of the Despots of Epirus on a high promontory overlooking the River Drino had been extensively improved by Sultan Beyazid II around 1490. From 1811, Ali modernized the fortifications, completing the full encirclement of the hill and adding emplacements housing numerous guns of British manufacture, employing around 2,000 workers; as usual in Holland's opinion, working too rapidly in order to appease the vizier's

Fig. 52: Zekate House in Argyrocastro built by Petro Korcari, 1811–12 (photo Malenki).

impatience. He added many new features, including a new seraglio within, accommodation for 5,000 troops, a curious clockwork mill for grinding corn designed by a Greek, and the Italianate clock tower on the eastern side. Leake had noticed a major weakness in that the site was deficient in water and Ali, to remedy this, built an aqueduct to bring water to the castle from a distance of over 10km from the surrounding mountains. A further drawback was that the castle was overlooked from above making it vulnerable to modern artillery, a point that Holland found it difficult to impress on him. In 1932 the castle was redesigned as a prison by the Italians at the request of King Zog.

Ali's legacy is not only military but most of his residences or palaces combined a defensive aspect. At Libokovo, Ali's seraglio and fort built between 1796 and 1798 as a dowry for his sister has four polygonal corner towers and a curtain wall surrounding a wide courtyard. Though nothing remains of the interior, Shainitza's grave can still be seen in the village. At Tepelene he created his grandest combination of fort, barracks and palace. He improved on the previous fortifications of the Byzantines and Turks determined to make his hometown a more impressive site. The castle built to enclose his palaces, and covering 4.5 hectares was finally completed in 1819. Hughes saw a town of 200 houses with an exclusively Albanian population and 'no architectural beauties… except the grand seraglio'. Ali had built this 'very spacious edifice standing upon a fine rock at the edge of the cliff' overlooking the Vjosë on a site originally belonging to his father, Veli Pasha. It was destroyed in a fire in 1818 and rebuilt; the money raised according to Hughes, by Ali begging for donations from his subjects at the gate 'seated upon a dirty mat, cross-legged and bare-headed, with a red Albanian cap in his hands'. The pedestrian bridge seen by Leake in 1804 that he built as a gift to the town to replace a ruined former one across the Vjosë, was apparently destroyed by flood by the time

Fig. 53: The fortress at Argyrocastro by Edward Lear showing the aqueduct.

of Hughes' visit and Ali was busy trying to construct a new one. This bridge links Tepelene to Beçisht, the village of his birth where the remains of his house are still visible.

At Ioannina, the main fortified area of the town, the *Phrourion*, is on a promontory jutting out into the lake with access gained by drawbridge across a moat. Ali replaced most of the old Byzantine walls adding round bastions and decorating its gates with ancient reliefs. Brewer suggests that in recognition of his title as the 'Lion of Ioannina' some of these reliefs show wild beasts. At the south-east corner of the *Phrourion* is the *Its Kale*, or 'inner fortress' built into the walls on three sides and in which Ali built a serai. Ioannina's topographical situation is said to resemble that of the peninsula of Constantinople but on a smaller scale. Ali may have emphasized this resemblance by building this residence here at the end of the promontory positioned in the same manner as the *Topkapi*, the palace of the Sultan. The Ottoman government was known as the Sublime Porte after the impressive gate leading to the headquarters of the grand vizier within the palace and it is possible Ali had this in mind when he commissioned the gate for his citadel. To provide building material for the walls Ali destroyed much of the Christian district of Litharitsia to the south of the *Phrourion*. As at Preveza, Vaudoncourt was Ali's chief architect and he was responsible for the Litharitsia, Ali's principal fortified residence containing the seraglio, completed in 1815. Outside the citadel there was the *Soufari Sarai*, 'horsemen's palace' or prosaically a cavalry barracks completed in 1820 which is still intact. In Hughes' summary Ioannina possessed 'two citadels, three palaces, besides a vast number of small serais'.

Within the citadel he extensively remodelled the fifteenth century Fethiye Mosque in 1795, making it the main mosque within the *Phrourion*. The graves of his first wife and of Ali himself are located in front of the mosque. His flexible attitude to religion is reflected in his endowment of mosques, tekkes, dervish shrines and even churches. In 1813, Ali built a monastery in honour of his revered Saint Kosmas Aitolos in Kolkondas, the place of his execution. Kosmas was held in particular high esteem in nearby Berat and in Himara and is seen as an important spiritual figure by both Albanians and Greeks. Along with his improvements to infrastructure Ali was eager to leave his mark on the civic landscape, usually to bolster his own prestige. He encouraged the building of khans and caravansarais, had travel lodges to stay in for his personal use and pleasant country retreats to hide away to, and dotted the landscape with numerous serai or houses on a more modest scale such as the new house at Arta that Hobhouse saw or his mother's fortified seraglio at Konitsa.

Archaeology

A perhaps surprising aspect of Ali's rule is his connection to archaeology. The height of his authority coincided with an upsurge in interest in the existing and tantalizingly uninvestigated ancient Greek remains. Intrepid Grand Tourists, whose interest in Classical Greece was a nostalgic reminiscence from their schooldays, were increasingly accompanied by numbers of serious scholars. When Byron left Epirus to exchange the wily embrace of Ali for the comforts of Athens, he met the Danish archaeologist Peter Oluf Brønsted newly arrived from Rome with his friend Georg Koës and they became friends and drinking companions.

Their group was enlarged by Cockerell, who had helped excavate the Temple of Aphaea on the island of Aegina. After conducting excavations on the islands of Kea, Aegina and Salamis, Brønsted joined Cockerell and the expedition of the Society of Travellers bound for the Morea where they gained permission from Veli Pasha to excavate the fifth century BC Temple of Apollo Epicurus at Bassae. Veli in the words of another antiquarian, William Gell, was 'the most amiable of tyrants, not thirsting, as he said himself, for blood, but only for money'. Always on the lookout for some antiquities that he could exploit, Veli had developed more than a passing interest in archaeology. He had excavated at Argos and Mycenae and had the works of the ancient travel writer Pausanias translated into modern Greek, but his motives were fuelled by material gain. Some of his plunder ended up as building materials; one column from the Treasury of Atreus ended up in a mosque in Argos, three others in the Marquis of Sligo's house in Ireland. The Marquis had continued work already begun by Lord Elgin. The carved green marble pillars would have flanked the entrance of the tomb.[5] The Society's most important find at Bassae was the temple frieze by Iktinos, one of the architects of the Parthenon. This was eventually sold to the British Museum, while the sculptures from Aegina went to Crown Prince Ludwig of Bavaria, the father of the future king of Greece, Otto.

In the autumn of 1812, Brønsted began to make his way homeward, first stopping off at Zante (Zakynthos) to see the tomb of his friend Koës who had died there of pneumonia. The next stop was Preveza where he intended to 're-examine the ruins of Nikopolis', the Roman city founded by the Emperor Augustus to overlook the site of his naval victory over Anthony and Cleopatra at Actium. On arrival Ali received him courteously, speaking good-humouredly in Greek and impressing him with his astuteness and interest. Learning of Brønsted's activities in the Morea, Ali became keen to know whether he had been one of those who had paid his son for the permit. When Brønsted answered in the affirmative, Ali showed even greater interest saying he also had some 'old stones' that could be excavated and that he would provide as many workers as required without cost on the understanding that he would have his 'share of the marbles, and any precious things we find.' By this stage Brønsted was eager to get home, but when Ali showed annoyance he reluctantly agreed to one visit to the ruins. A strange sight then ensued, Brønsted with Ali walking the length and breadth of the ruins, examining walls and discussing the history of the city, Ali being particularly interested in the Roman methods of construction. Despite Brønsted's protestations that the city had already been plundered Ali was still keen to dig, so again Brønsted relented pointing out a suitable spot. Brønsted then protested that they were ill-equipped; undeterred Ali set his men to work while sending for better tools. After finding a number of marble slabs and two Roman coins they returned to Preveza where Ali failed to persuade Brønsted to carry out further excavations in Albania. He finally let him go with the gift of one of the coins.

---

[5] Two of the columns were donated by his family to the British Museum in 1904; the missing parts are located in the National Museum of Athens and in several museums in Germany.

Fig. 54: Nikopolis by Edward Lear.

This excursion was not a one-off. Ali accompanied Henry Holland to the Nicopolis where he made a strange sight sitting among the ruins while the excavations were in progress. Hughes tells us:

> There is one spot, where the agents of the pasha had been making excavations, upon which some superb temple must once have stood: the numerous marble shafts and pieces of entablature that are discovered, are all carried off to be worked up in his forts and serai at Prevesa - thus perish even the ruins of Nicopolis; and the monuments of Augustus's glory serve to decorate the dwelling of an Albanian robber. Since our departure from Epirus I understand that his excavators have discovered a very fine bust of Trajan which now decorates one of the principal rooms in the Prevesan seraglio.

Ali may have pilfered the ancient stone to build his walls but he showed a curiosity about the ancient past. To Everett he inquired about the possible location of the important site of Dodona, unknown at this time, his interest probably as much stimulated by his vanity as his greed for treasures. It would have satisfied his pride to be the first to make such a significant discovery.

The Lost Legacy

> a vast but dilapidated khan as big as a Gothic castle, situated an a high range, and built… by Ali Pasha when his long, gracious, and unmolested reign had permitted him to turn this unrivalled country, which combines all the excellences of Southern Europe and Western Asia, to some of the purposes for which it is fitted.

On his way from Arta to Ioannina, the young Benjamin Disraeli was forced to stay for the night in one of the numerous hostels for travellers that Ali had built. In 1830, the future British prime minister was another young man seeking adventure on the tour of the Mediterranean and the Middle East, ostensibly for his health. Writing to his father from Preveza, he gives an indication of the condition Epirus had fallen into since the demise of Ali. Desiring to visit 'Southern Albania', part of Greece then still held by the Turks, on the pretext of delivering a letter from Sir Frederick Adam, the governor of the Ionian Isles, he obtained permission for an audience with Redschid, the new grand vizir at Ioannina.

Disraeli's letter makes no apologies for his awe of the oriental; the thrill of being surrounded by colourful sights, pashas, beys, agas, military chieftains, sheiks on camels, the vizir's troops, dervishes and the throng of the bazaar, with its mix of Turks, Albanians, Greeks and Jews, but unfortunately the country had become one he described as 'this savage land of anarchy'. From Arta, 'once a town… beautiful as its situation… in ruins, whole streets razed to the ground', the journey took them through country presenting a

> mournful aspect, which I had too long observed: villages in ruins, and perfectly uninhabited, caravanseras deserted, fortresses razed to the ground, olive woods burnt up. So complete had been the work of destruction, that you often find your horse's course on the foundation of a village without being aware of it, and what at first appears the dry bed of a torrent, turns out to be the backbone of the skeleton of a ravaged town.

Ioannina too was a pitiful sight:

> this city, once, if not the largest, one of the most prosperous and brilliant in the Turkish dominions, still looked imposing; but when we entered, I soon found that all preceding desolation had only been preparative to the vast scene of destruction now before me. We proceeded through a street, winding in its course, but of very great length, to our quarters. Ruined houses, mosques with their tower only standing, streets utterly razed – these are nothing. We met great patches of ruin a mile square, as if a swarm of locusts had had the power of desolating the works of man as well as those of God. The great heart of the city was a sea of ruin. Arches and pillars, isolated and shattered, still here and there jutting forth, breaking the uniformity of the desolation, and turning the horrible into the picturesque. The great bazaar, itself a little town, was burnt down only a few months since when an infuriate band of Albanian soldiers heard of the destruction of their chiefs by the grand vizier.

But something of the splendour of Ali's palace still remained, commandeered for use by the vizir.

> we repaired to the celebrated fortress-palace of Ali, which, though greatly battered in successive sieges, is still inhabitable, and yet affords a very fair idea of its old

magnificence. Having passed the gates of the fortress, we found ourselves in a number of small streets, like those in the liberties of the Tower, or any other old castle,
all full of life, stirring and excited; then we came to a grand place, in which on an
ascent stands the Palace. We hurried through courts and corridors, all full of guards,
and pages, and attendant chiefs, and in fact every species of Turkish population…
At length we came to a vast, irregular apartment, serving as the immediate antechamber to the Hall of Audience. This was the finest thing I have ever yet seen…
The Hall was vast, built by Ali Pacha purposely to receive the largest Gobelins
carpet that was ever made, which belonged to the chief chamber in Versailles, and
was sold to him in the Revolution. It is entirely covered with gilding and arabesques.

Despite the scenes of destruction witnessed by Disraeli, the complete erasure of Ali's memory was yet to come. Richard Burgess described passing the defences that Ali had put up
around Ioannina as he entered the city in 1834 as still being extant and he observed 'the
approach and suburbs of the meanest town in Italy may put to shame those of the capital of
Epirus'. The fortress 'battered on all sides' had fallen into ruin and the canal that connected
it into disuse. The population had been reduced by a third from that of twenty years previous.
The town's sixteen mosques and eight churches had been burnt by Ali. At Tepelene too, when
Lear visited in 1848 its former grandeur was a memory. The high fortress walls still stood
then as they do today, but little else remained but 'a short street of miserable bazaars' outside.
Lear had a Murray's *Guide* of 1840, so he knew what to expect: a ghost town, its population
reduced to 150 Albanian and 8 Greek families, a heap of ruins with its fortifications 'level
with the ground'. The same fate had befallen Tepelene as his seraglio at Preveza. Ali's palace,
eulogized by Byron, almost equal in size to that at Ioannina, its many rooms large in scale and
magnificently adorned, and the harem on its north side, was no more.

Chapter 7

Cultural Impact

When Ali Pasha heard this, his executioner he called in.
And while the klepht bowed, off went his head.

'Kolias', Klephtic song

F rom contemporary accounts we learn that tales and songs about Ali Pasha were already common currency during his lifetime. Music and storytelling were among the entertainments witnessed at Ali's court and a retinue of entertainers followed his family members as they moved from one residence to other. When Thomas Hughes was invited by Mukhtar to dine with him on the island of lake Ioannina, they were accompanied by a 'household fiddler, like the ancient bard, that invariable concomitant of the feast, stretching his lungs to the tortured catgut and celebrating in wild Albanian music the deeds of Ali and his valiant sons'.

In order to show his favour to distinguished European guests, it was usual practice for Ali to send musicians to their homes during the evening. Pouqueville tells of the entertainers in the retinues of Mukhtar and Veli; drawn from a wide area and including Jewish and Gypsy musicians and dancers, some from Constantinople, a Morlaque comedian troupe (from the Dalmatian coast), dancing bear trainers, *Buretinieri* (dice-box players) and acrobats. Pouqueville brackets the acrobats with prostitutes and he often compares musicians and acrobats to the courtesans and prostitutes of ancient banquets. Exotic as these entertainments must have been, the greatest impression on visitors was that left by the songs about their host. When Leake heard the war songs about Ali and the Suliotes sung in the guests' honour in the presence of the Albanian despot he could not help being moved and impressed. Ali liked to hear his deeds recounted, and the songs that told of his early exploits might be termed the 'official' record. As a counter there was the 'unofficial' version, also noted by visitors to Albania, that gave the alternative Ali story as witnessed by his subjects or his enemies. To have your praises sung was common practice and minstrels would compose eulogies in return for payment. Gavoyanios,[1] a famed old minstrel of Auspelatria in Thessaly living at the end of the eighteenth century, became wealthy composing songs for soldiers in the Turkish military, not a particularly popular undertaking, but he was prepared to extol their prowess for a large fee, the greater the praise the greater the sum. In contrast to the eulogies, the 'unofficial' songs praised the exploits of Ali's enemies and bewailed the excesses of his regime.

The most well known eulogy to Ali is the long epic song, the *Alipashiad*, which was composed for him in his lifetime. Written in Greek by the Muslim Albanian, Haxhi Shehreti, it gave

---

[1] Gavoyanios means Blind John; many folk musicians were blind.

a concertinaed and imaginative account of Ali's life to date, skipping lightly over his youthful exploits but not shirking from the brutal way in which Ali went about asserting his authority.

> He went in one end and out at the other,
> He tramples on bodies and still is not sated.
> Lord Ali had resolved not to leave a single soul,
> And his troops fell on them like maddened lions…
> All that were in the villages the snakes devoured;
> He smashed their legs and smashed their backs
> and smashed their buttocks.

Such details obviously were a matter of pride to Ali rather than shame. In song, Ali is often remembered for his cruelty to his opponents and to his subjects, but his opposition to the Sultan meant that he could be cast as both villain and hero. To the klephts, Ali was usually the villain.

In the song 'Kolias' (quoted at the beginning of the chapter) Ali is unequivocally seen as a double-crossing despot. In his study on klephtic song, Gabriel Rombotis saw the themes of capture and betrayal as a window into how Ali exploited the internal rivalries among the klepht captains. The captains were the dominant personalities after whom each band would be named. Rombotis lists the virtues and qualities for leadership a captain must have shown to gain his reputation:

> Determination, definiteness of purpose, supreme ability in the indispensable requirements of the profession, generosity when needed, gallantry, tenacity and inflexibility of character in the face of any event even death, fairness to his fel-low-Klephts, power of persuasion.

These strengths will have been those Ali himself possessed during his time leading a bandit life and once he became a pasha he was canny enough to know how to use his experience to turn the tables and exploit them as weaknesses. The virtues led to rivalry between the captains making it possible for pashas like Ali to 'attract them to their Palaces and treacherously to put them to death'; and Ali Pasha, quick to capitalize on any opportunity, would become a past master of the art. In the songs 'Kolias' and 'Katsoudas' (the same hero by another name) the protagonist is summarily beheaded with one clean blow by Ali's executioner, while in another version Kolias is given over to the pasha of Tripolitsa's men for a long process of torture and humiliation. 'Tripolitsa', Tripoli in the Peloponnese, where the song has moved the action, is where Veli held court. In the song the hero begs not to be taken through the mountain village of Vytina on the way to Tripoli so that his betrothed sweetheart does not see him in his perilous condition.

The French historian and philologist Claude Charles Fauriel collected these klephtic songs close to the latter years of Ali's life from expatriate Greeks living in Venice and Trieste and his translations were published in 1825 shortly after Ali's death. Fauriel was a radical and member of the *le comité philhellène de Paris* working for Greek independence. His pioneering work was taken up and expanded on by Arnold Passow who translated it into German in the 1850s. These two works brought the folk culture of Greece and Albania into the European mainstream for the first time and at an opportune moment. There was a growing interest within the Romantic and nationalist movements in folk song and culture. Using Furiel's work, the great German poet and writer Johann Wolfgang Goethe made his own adaptations of folk songs from Epirus following the adventures of another klepht, Liakos, who takes on Ali's principle deputy in charge of the passes and defeats him in single combat. From the German, the klephtic verses took on a new life in Bohemia. The Czechs, a subjugated people themselves under the Habsburg thumb since the seventeenth century, were creating their own national revival. Their Romantic nationalist poet Vaclav Bolemir Nebesky translated the klephtic verses, probably from Passow, into his native tongue and in so doing inspired Antonín Leopold Dvořák to set the results to music. 'Kolias', the story of Kolias, forms part of a suite of 'Three Modern Greek Songs' (1875). Two of the three poems relate to Ali Pasha, while the middle poem is of a pastoral nature akin to the mood of medieval romances. *The Lament of Parga*, the third in the trilogy, has been identified as a Suliote song in the heroic style concerning Ali's taking of the town. Dvořák's interest in this material chimes with his other work on nationalist themes, the *Slavonic Dances* (1878) and *Moravian Duets* settings of folk poetry (1875–81), that he composed during this period.

The mixture of resignation and national pride surrounding the events in Parga became a theme of numerous Greek folk songs. The moment when the Pargians dug up the graves of their ancestors rather than let their remains fall into the hands of the enemy (they had not submitted in life, so they should not submit in death), was felt to be memorably poignant. But the incident from Ali's life which is perhaps most famously commemorated in folk song, and also in this case dance, was the mass suicide of the Suliote women who preferred death rather than submitting to Ali's slavery, remembered as the 'Dance of Zalongo'. The dance is accompanied in song and there are versions in both Greek (*Horos tou Zalongou*) and Albanian (*Vallja e Zallongut*). In the Greek version, the women sing as they throw themselves over the cliff edge to their deaths:

> Farewell poor world,
> Farewell sweet life,
> and you, my wretched country,
> Farewell forever

The Suliotes' complex relationship with Ali is portrayed in *The Song of Ali Pasha* collected by Fauriel. It shows how soon after Ali's death events were already being manipulated to create a situation in which he could extol the bravery of the Suliotes. The song takes the form of a dialogue between Ali and his sons Mukhtar and Veli in the Church of the Pantokrator in Ioannina. The sons remind Ali of their collective wealth in order to reassure him. In response Ali says that he can neither rely on wealth nor on his regular troops but that his only hope against the wrath of the Sultan is the 'Greeks' who always fought against him with great heroism. He says that the Greeks emulate the French in their love of freedom, going on to single out the Suliotes, mentioning that not only the men but also the women 'preferred death to slavery' despite his promises of material goods, such as weaponry and coin.

With such songs disseminating across Greece and eventually abroad, and travellers' tales being rushed into print, Ali's notoriety was such that news of his death was rumoured prematurely on numerous occasions, with the result that foreign obituaries were penned before the event. But it was on his death that Ali achieved another level of fame, if not infamy. His life became not only the stuff of legend, but entertainment. Hardly had his head made its way to the Sultan before his own favourite puppeteer, Iakov, whose traditional bawdy Turkish *Karagöz* show Pouqueville had seen at Ali's court in 1799 and Hobhouse had witnessed in Ioannina, was quickly adapting his performance to one based on a life of Ali, which he then took round the countryside. A more sympathetic portrayal of Ali soon followed in an anonymous Greek poem, the *Lament of Ali Pasha*. The author appears deeply moved by the tyrant's death and attempts a closer characterization in fictional scenes between Ali, his son and the son of the Sultan. Ali is portrayed as majestic, caring and intimate in the days before his downfall. Three authentic persons, Manthos Oikonomou, Bairamis and Tzamis, known from the sources, are inaccurately put at Ali's side in his dying moments.

The first incident from Ali's life to have impact abroad was the fate of the 'beautiful Ephrosyne' recorded by Byron and the others. Already doing the rounds while Ali was alive, it became a fully developed tale within Greece and Albania and ready for adaptation into works by Western authors ensuring it an audience long after Ali's death. That the story was popular throughout Greece is recounted in Finlay's *History*. He includes a quotation from one of the many songs that mention the storyline of the ring, which he translates:

> I told you, Ephrosyne, dear,
> The ring, oh! do not take,
> Ali the news will quickly hear –
> He'll drown you in the lake.

The colourful detail that Mukhtar's wife had seen an emerald ring on the finger of Euphrosyne at the hamam (bathhouse), which was one and the same as the one that Mukhtar had earlier refused her, was found to be particularly emotive. Ali, who takes action after she goes to him to plead for vengeance, justifies his retribution as being necessary to uphold public morals. Although Euphrosyne in this version brings her fate on herself, *and* as the niece of an archbishop, was no obstacle to her becoming a martyr to the Orthodox Christians; the other sixteen or so victims (depending on the account) of Ali's rough justice, though perhaps less culpable, were not equally pitied. The real-life ambiguity of Euphrosyne, or Kyra Frosini amongst the Greeks, played into the hands of the storytellers who could embroider her tale for their own differing purposes, making her at one moment innocent victim, at another abused lover.

Euphrosyne became a popular folk hero to the Albanians too and was known as the maid Eufrozina. By the time her story was woven into a national epic poem about the Albanian struggle against the Turks, *The Highland Lute* (*Lahuta e Malcís*) written by

Gjergj Fishta in the early years of the twentieth century, it was her virginal qualities that were underlined.

> There are very many maidens
> But like that maid from Janina,
> Nowhere will you find her equal

Ali Pasha glimpses her as she 'dove-like stepped upon the terrace' and he immediately wants her for himself. Ali sends a Moor to fetch her but she refuses to 'renounce faith and honour' despite being warned that Ali will chop off her head. Ali sends the Moor again, warning him that he will end up in the lake if he does not bring Eufrozina. That night the Moor seizes her and embarks over the lake in a wooden raft with his cargo. Despite the Moor's threats she answers him:

> Yes, I'll go now to the pasha,
> But I need my bridal garments
> For I've made no preparations,

And so saying she,

> plunged into the water,
> Sank and vanished to the bottom.
> Word then spread across the country
> That Albania has such maidens
> Who, defending faith and honour,
> Sacrifice their young existence.

Despite the fact it is Ali, an Albanian, who wants Eufrozina, she is portrayed as being abused by a 'foreign' agent and so is transformed into a symbol of national struggle against the Turkish oppressor.

As was shown in the opening chapter, Ali's fame was closely linked to Byron's. Henry Gally Knight, who was a contemporary of Byron at Trinity College, Cambridge, also wrote verse in a similar vein, but in the shadow of his more illustrious competitor. Knight became an MP and a member of the London Greek Committee formed to support the Greek cause against the Turks. He travelled widely in the Middle East and to Epirus, and he and Byron were both publishing Orientalist verses at the same time, and with the same publisher, Murray. On learning that Byron's forthcoming poem, *The Giaour*, included an incident of a girl being drowned in a sack, Knight wrote to him in 1813 to make sure the way was clear for the publication of his poem, *Phrosine: A Grecian Tale* (1817), which he claimed he began around 1811. Knight was afraid they were using the same material and in his letter he explains that he heard the tale in Ioannina: 'the adventures of a certain Miss Phrosyne, whom Ali Pasha wish'd to get into his Harem, but her relations put her to death, to save her from infamy'. In this instance there is a similarity with the Albanian poem, where Eufrozina sacrifices herself, but in this instance she is willingly smothered by her female kin. It has been suggested by Michael Franklin that Knight was familiar with one of the Euphrosyne ballads through his allusion to the ballad's imagery in the letter. Knight follows the version of the tale that puts the maid at the hands of the rapacious Ali; the version that most chimed with philhellenic sentiment. In his poem, as Phrosyne dances with her fellow maidens she laments in song 'The lost delights of freedom's day' and the poem is unequivocal in its propagandist sentiments. It was in such symbolic identifications with Greece that Euphrosyne became the inspiration for the Greeks and their allies against Turkish domination.

On the news of his death accounts of Ali's life proliferated in the West, and something akin to Ali-mania broke out. Once again it was the story of Euphrosyne that captured the imagination first. Within seven months it had been transformed for the stage featuring the theme of the ring as the plot device as *Ali Pacha; or the Signet Ring* by the American John Howard Payne, who is mostly remembered as the writer of the song, 'Home Sweet Home'.[2] Premiered at the Covent Garden theatre in 1822 to 'enthusiastic expressions of delight' Payne was onto a winner, for as George Daniel wrote in the preface, 'the dramatist acts wisely who avails himself of extraordinary characters and events' and 'to have conceived a monster of greater ferocity than Ali Pasha, would have been to have to paint a devil'. Offering a spine-chilling evocation of oriental tyranny and grand spectacle the play became a tourist attraction. Britain was not yet officially involved in the Greek War of Independence and the portrayal of Ali, contrary to the facts, as the obstacle to freedom was a vehicle for arousing philhellenic sentiment. *Ali Pacha; or the Signet Ring* became one of a flurry of dramas and other works that appeared at the time supporting the cause, with Ali frequently cast as the villain. *The Maid of Athens* by John Baldwin Buckstone, which followed in 1829, was staged after the Battle of Navarino (1827) and Britain's official entry into the Greek War of Independence. It therefore gives a more nuanced characterization of Ali, who does not appear on stage, presenting him as a misunderstood tactician who could have saved Greece. *The Maid of Athens* is a reference to Byron, whose poem to Theresa Macri begins:

Maid of Athens, ere we part,
Give, oh! give me back my heart.

In the play, which also features Byron as a character, the maid is Madeleine, an English girl and daughter of a diplomat. Like the *Ali Pasha*, the play employs full dramatic licence. By the logic of melodrama the romance plot is concluded with Madeleine marrying Demetrius 'King of Greece', the previously unknown son of a Greek slave and Ali Pasha.

The reassuring portrayal of the death of Ali, the embodiment of the threat of tyranny and oriental despotism, gave the audience hope for the cause of Greek liberty. As the formation of a modern Greek State was becoming a reality, there was a vicarious thrill of danger for

---

[2]   According to a review in the American newspaper *Minerva* for 1822 (Vol. I No. 37) this was an adaptation of the play *Xenocles* by the French writer Mr Planchet. The protagonist in *Ali Pasha* is called Zenocles.

Fig. 55: Mr TP Cook as Zenocles, Ali Pasha's adversary in *Ali Pacha; or the Signet Ring.*

theatregoers who could fantasize about the prospect of travel to a land where the mystery of the Orient was still to be found. In music, Orientalist themes were already an established tradition. For the Austrians any such thrill was too real, for the Ottomans were their close neighbours, if diminishing as a threat. Mozart had been happy to absorb Eastern influences and storylines and for *Die Entführung aus dem Serail* (*The Abduction from the Seraglio*, 1782) he used fictional caricatures that include janissaries, Albanians, a despotic pasha, and the ever-intoxicating perceived licentiousness of the harem. But one year after Ali's death, Albert Lortzing from Berlin, turned to real life for inspiration with his first opera, the one-act *Ali Pasha von Janina*, first staged in 1828. Even though he was depicting almost contemporary events Lortzing remained wedded to Orientalist fantasy rather than any historical perspective, and using a plot resembling Mozart's, his opera tells of a Frenchman saving the girl he loves from the tyrant Ali's harem.

   Lurid biography and storytelling came fast on the heels of the swathe of travel memoirs and attempts at serious history published just prior to or after Ali's death. In E Mackenzie's *Choice Biography: Comprising an Entertaining and Instructive Account of Persons of Both Sexes and All Nations Eminent for Genius Learning Public Spirit Courage and Virtue*, published in Newcastle upon Tyne in 1829, Ali's dubious life sits alongside a hotchpotch of celebrities from

Canova and Rossini, to Marie Antoinette and Napoleon, and to virtuous nineteenth century British heroes such as Grace Darling. Ten years later Alexander Dumas (*père*) took on a similar exercise before embarking on his famous novels, but this time concentrating on the notorious. Dumas published his eight-volume collection of villains, *Celebrated Crimes* (1839–1840), based on historical records. Sitting alongside such notables as the Borgias, Mary Queen of Scots and the Man in the Iron Mask is 'Ali Pacha'. As was his usual practice Dumas used a number of collaborators and the lurid relating of the cruelties of Ali's court owes much to Félicien Malleville. Dumas was interested enough in the story of Ali to use the circumstances of his demise in his later novel, *The Count of Monte Cristo* (1844), where the death of Ali is used as a plot device and to introduce Orientalist colour into the narrative. Dumas' father had served in Italy and Egypt under Napoleon and stories of his escapades were another source of useful inspiration. Taking liberties with fact, Dumas has Ali betrayed by Fernand Mondego, a French officer who he had entrusted to plead for mercy from the Turks. Ali's young daughter, Haydée, witnesses her father's death and then she and her mother, the 'beautiful Vasiliki', are sold by Mondego to slave traders bound for Constantinople. On seeing Ali's head displayed in front of the imperial gates Vassiliki falls down dead. Haydée is sold on to Sultan Mahmud from whom she is purchased by Edmond Dantès, and then freed. Dantès, alias the Count

Fig. 56: *Haidée, a Greek Girl* (1827) by Sir Charles Eastlake (from Byron, *Don Juan*).

of Monte Cristo, uses Haydée in an elaborate plot to revenge himself on Fernand, who was responsible for framing him as a Bonapartist traitor, his imprisonment in the Château d'If and stealing his intended bride.

The name Haydée is self-consciously borrowed from Byron's heroine, Haidée in *Don Juan*, the daughter of a Greek pirate chief.[3] Dumas' heroine mixes a number of Orientalist fantasies. She is referred to as a princess, she is a Christian like her mother but the daughter of the nominally Muslim Ali, a cruel despot (whom she loves), and a product of the harem. A 'white slave' she has already experienced a number of masters, and, although they become lovers, placidly accedes to the count's demands. Educated in at least four languages, including Ancient Greek, her manners are oriental. She flounces amidst cushions on a divan, dressed in the Turkic Greek style, drinking Turkish coffee and eating oriental sweetmeats, and smoking a chibouk, the long-stemmed Turkish tobacco pipe sometimes used for smoking hashish. The mixture of the harem and slavery had an added frisson; Greek slaves had become a *cause célèbre* when reprisals by the Turks after the Greek uprising of 1822 led to an increased number of Christian slave-girls in the markets of Constantinople and Smyrna. In England, the Quakers used their commercial connections in the Levant to systematically buy them and then set them free. Depictions of the (often beautiful and scantily clad) Greek slave became a dramatic propaganda tool used by artists to promote the cause of Greek liberty.

Kyra Vassiliki did not die at the sight of Ali's head in Constantinople, but one memory of her may live on in present-day Istanbul. It is said that a large diamond once worn by her resides in the Topkapi Palace. The Spoonmaker's Diamond is the largest pear-shaped example at 86 carats (17.2g), but how it came to be in its present resting place is unclear. Although possibly commissioned by either Ali or Mahmud II, some of the tales relating to its appearance rely on fables worthy of the *Arabian Nights*, including one to do with a fisherman. If it was in Ali's possession first, it may have passed to Mahmud either as part of Ali's complicated dealings with the Porte or after his execution, when his possessions and treasure were confiscated. In another version of events it was the ransom paid for Captain Camus de Richemont after Ali's victory over the French at Preveza. Camus had been sent to Istanbul for questioning but was released through the auspices of Napoleon's mother, Letizia Romolino, in 1801; they were rumoured to have been lovers. Letizia sent a diamond reputed to have belonged to Marie Antoinette to Preveza as a present for Sultan Selim III. From there it went to Ali in Ioannina. As Camus was freed Ali must have felt bound to honour such an illustrious undertaking by sending it on to the Topkapi Palace. The mysterious allure of Vassiliki lived on as an adornment to a number of depictions of Ali by Western Orientalist artists.

The continuing Orientalist appeal of Ali Pasha was summed up by R Nisbet Bain towards the end of the century in his introduction to the novel, *The Last Days of the Janissaries: The Lion of Janina, a Turkish Novel* (1854) by the Hungarian writer Morus Jokai. Bain, Jokai's English translator, commented on the success of the writer in portraying Ali's dual nature:

---

[3] Byron took the name from a Greek folk song, a translation of which he appended to the first edition of *Childe Harold*.

Fig. 57: *The Greek Slave* by the American sculptor Hiram Powers (1843).

Fig. 58: *The Greek Slave* on display in New York. It caused a sensation in London where Elizabeth Barrett Browning was so moved by the work she penned an impassioned sonnet desiring Art to break up 'the serf-dom of this world' and show that the East was not grieving alone and the 'strong' would be overthrown.

The hero of the strange and terrible drama, or, rather, series of dramas, unfolded with such spirit, skill, and vividness … is Ali Pasha of Janina, certainly one of the most brilliant, picturesque, and, it must be added, capable ruffians that even Turkish history can produce. Manifold and monstrous as were Ali's crimes, his astonishing ability and splendid courage lend a sort of savage sublimity even to his blood-stained career, and, indeed, the dogged valor with which the octogenarian warrior defended

Fig. 59: *Ali Pasha and Vassiliki* by Raymond Monvoisin (1832).

himself at the last in his stronghold against the whole might of the Ottoman Empire is almost without a parallel in history.

The life of Ali Pasha may have provided numerous colourful episodes to delight European audiences and readers and a comforting feeling of superiority in comparison to oriental barbarism but his real-life exploits were tied into unfolding events in Eastern Europe and Greece in particular, providing useful propaganda material for philhellenes and other European nationalists. His reign and collapse was part of a drama in which European nations, for so long at war, might be forced to act together for an ideal. The confusion as to whom was the enemy for the Greek and Albanian freedom fighters, Ali or the Porte, was overlooked as the effects of his tyranny provided ample examples of brutal injustice to be exploited. The taking of Parga by Ali was an incident that struck a chord with the Romantic idealist and the suppressed political activist alike. When Missolonghi fell to the Turks in April 1826, the plight of the fleeing inhabitants including women and children recalled the fate of Parga in 1819. The story was widely known in France by the 1820s through accounts in the press, Pouqueville's writings and Madame Dufrénoy's history of Greece.[4] In a land where the cry for freedom still rang out, numerous poems were inspired by the event.[5] The radical poet Viennet prefaced his poem on Parga published in 1820 with a defence of liberty:

> But it is in the name of liberty that we support [the Pargians'] cause, because liberty has been profaned under our eyes, the governments must disapprove whatever is solicited in its name, as if liberty meant permissiveness everywhere, as if monarchy was synonymous with despotism... And the degradation of our principles is such that it is impossible to indict the despotism of the Grand Turk and his pashas without being accused of jacobinism.

Baron d'Ordre's poem of the same year stressed the exiles' devotion to freedom:

> *Ce people préféra la mort à l'esclavage*
> *Détruit, mais non vaincu, trahi du tout côté,*
> *Il s'écriait encore: liberté, liberté!*

> This people have chosen death over slavery
> Destroyed yet not defeated, betrayed from everywhere,
> They still cried out: liberty, liberty!

The Greek war had not broken out yet but by 1827 when the play, *Parga: ou, Le brulot, mélodrame en trois actes, a spectacle*, by Pierre-Frédéric-Adolphe Carmouche and Adolphe Poujol was performed the resonance of events at Missolonghi with those of Parga were raw. Pouqueville had described the Pargians praying for help from the Virgin, their protector. In the play they were shown as victims of their faith and their love of liberty.

Outrage and politics were not confined to the page. The moment of embarkation of the Pargians for Corfu was a striking mental image ideal to be put on canvas. The Romantic artist Jean-Louis André Théodore Géricault left pencil sketches of the Pargians streaming down from the town on its rocky promontory toward the shore as preparation for a monumental project, the *Reddition de Parga*, which he never completed. Some are depicted

---

[4] Adélaïde-Gillette Dufrénoy, *Beautés de l'histoire de la Grèce moderne* (1826).

[5] JPG Viennet, Parga, *Poème au bénéfice du Parganiotes* (Paris, 1820); TJ du Wicquet, Baron d'Ordre, *Les Exilés de Parga. Poème* (Paris, 1820); J Berchet, *Les Fugitifs de Parga. Poème traduit librement de l'italien* (Paris, 1823).

already aboard the boats, others are being carried on shoulders and some bend to kiss their sacred land farewell as a man points to the sky. The conflation of the events at Missolonghi with Parga is evident in a similar unfinished painting attributed to Géricault. Wrongly titled, *Scene from the Exodus of Missolonghi*, the same scene is repeated in more detail with disregard to Missolonghi being situated on flat land. The townspeople form the same procession to the sea with a youth being carried by an old bishop and their holy images mistakenly represented by the Catholic statue of the Virgin. As the people make for the waiting boats a group of British officers look on. In an allusion to the Pargians' refusal to leave any of their possessions to the Turks, a man shoots his horse. These same elements appear in a highly finished version by Alphonse-Apollidore Callet from 1827. In *L'Embarquement des Parganiotes* the procession has reached the harbour, but it is the priest who is carried by two men who points to the sky.

In Italy the cause of freedom had a different appeal. After the defeat of Napoleon the old order had been restored and Italy was divided under the rule of Austria and the House of Savoy. The plight of Parga and its close proximity provided a popular analogy for poets and artists yearning for their own freedom from foreign domination. Ugo Foscolo, born in Zante, was living in exile in London when he wrote his description of the fall of Parga, *Narrazione della fortune e della cessione di Parga*, published in 1821 during nationalist uprisings in Naples and Piedmont. It was immediately suppressed for being subversive. The preface for the 1850 edition outlined its militant revolutionary character. Foscolo's purpose was to expose the new doctrine of the Right of Nations for what it was; a false claim of legitimacy that allowed modern diplomats to carry out deadly acts of tyranny. Sharing the mixed Italian heritage of the Ionian Islands, Foscolo knew Dionysios Solomos and Andreas Kalvos, the Ionian poets of Greek nationhood. Solomos' verses became the words to the Greek national anthem. The poet Giovanni Berchet also turned to the theme of Parga. *I Profughi di Parga* (1821) appeared in *Il Conciliatore*, a periodical with contributions from members of the Federati, revolutionaries dedicated to ridding Italy of the Austrians. Berchet had to flee from the Austrian authorities in 1823 and join the Italian exiles in London. Translated into French by Fauriel, the poem appeared in London the following year. In the final part of the poem Berchet made an impassioned attack on British foreign policy. He saw Parga's fate as a symbol of the small nation at the mercy of a larger and more powerful one and yet again Britain's actions had unjustly snuffed out another Liberal cause. The last words of the Pargians became a rallying call to all of Europe: 'Time will bring our revenge, and God will endorse it, He who strengthens the spirit of Europe'. These verses became the battle cry of the Italian revolution and were sung across Italy.

The artist Francisco Hayez lived in Austrian-held Milan. He was an associate of fellow Italian patriots and radical intellectuals including Rossini and Verdi and the poets Leopardi and Manzoni. Working under Austrian censorship, Hayez made oblique reference to current affairs in a number of his paintings and he knew that Parga would be analogous to a situation every Italian would immediately recognize. He made three versions of the Parga incident. The earliest from 1831, *The Refugees of Parga*, focuses on the usual scene of the Pargians preparing to leave but with the added detail of the Turks making their way into the town perched on its rock. His 1832 version has echoes of Géricault and Callet but with emphasis on the Pargians pleading to God, an anonymous people of martyrs and heroes caught between the shore and the stretching sea with the infidels approaching in the distance. In *Boat with Greek Fugitives* the Pargians have set out into the unknown. Here the fragile storm-tossed boat is the universal symbol of Romantic iconography used to symbolize the fate of the entire Greek nation caught in the storm of revolution and fighting against overwhelming odds. Hayez's contemporaries saw his work as important in the forging of national identity and promoting the patriotic ideal. Giuseppe Mazzini, a leader of the Risorgimento movement for Italian unification, singled out *The Refugees of Parga*, praising its theme as an analogy to the state of Italy.

Parga was matched in the European consciousness by the drama and idealization of Suli and the Suliotes. Ali's massacre of the Suliotes in 1804 was immortalized in verse, drama and various paintings. Worthy of a mere footnote in Canto II of Byron's *Childe Harold*, by 1825 it had become a five-act tragedy, *The Martyrs of Souli or the modern Epirus*, written by Louis Jean Népomucène Lemercier. In 1828, Victor Hugo was content with an account in verse, *The Pasha and the Dervish* (*Un jour Ali passait*), in which as Ali is out riding he is harangued for his deeds by a dervish who foretells that his fate is catching up with him, he is a 'dog accurst':

Fig. 60: *The Refugees of Parga* (*I profughi di Parga*) by Francesco Hayez (1831).

for Janina makes
A grave for thee where every turret quakes,
And thou shalt drop below
To where the spirits, to a tree enchained,
Will clutch thee, there to be 'mid them retained
For all to-come in woe!

Ali, perhaps true to his real character, remains unmoved:

Ali deemed anchorite or saint a pawn –
The crater of his blunderbuss did yawn,
Sword, dagger hung at ease:
But he had let the holy man revile,
Though clouds o'erswept his brow; then, with a smile,
He tossed him his pelisse.

Unlike Hugo, David Morier had first-hand experience of Ali and as one-time British emissary to his court he was in a better position to write about the Suliotes. Morier supplemented his personal recollections with tales supplied by a Greek physician with whom he was compelled to spend a period of quarantine at Corfu, to create *Photo, the Suliote, a Tale of Modern Greece* (1857). Modestly described as an 'imperfect sketch' or 'fragment' he attempted to give a picture of contemporary Greek and Albanian life in the manner of his more literary brother James, the author of the popular *Adventures of Hajji Baba* based on his experiences in Persia.

As with the Pargians, the Suliotes provided dramatic inspiration for painters. The momentum for Greek liberty triumphantly fused the themes of romanticism and liberalism at the Paris Salon exhibition of 1827–8, with twenty-one works on modern Greek subjects being exhibited. Ary Scheffer showed two paintings on the theme of Greek women taking refuge from the Turks, once more linking events from Ali's past with the current Greek war; *Jeune filles greques implorant la protection de la Vierge pendent un combat* based on incidents from Missolonghi and *Les Femmes Souliotes*. In both paintings the women plead to heaven. The latter recalls the incident at Zalongo where the Suliot women and children are huddled on the edge of the precipice prior to throwing themselves over.

The narrative of the Suliot women's sacrifice was equally well known in France and elevated to an evocation of the Romantic ideal of patriotic heroism and resilience. Again Pouqueville's accounts provided inspiration. He had described the women singing and dancing as one after the other took the fatal step in his *Histoire de la régénération de la Grèce* (1824) an image taken up by the Romantic poet Alfred de Vigny in 'Helena' (1826) where the women go to their deaths singing in voices 'steady and devoid of sobs'. The politician and writer Abel-François Villemain, whose portrait Scheffer painted, referred to them in his historical novel *Lascaris* (1825) as 'these heroic and fierce mothers who, in order to escape from the barbarians, formed a funerary dance on the crest of a rock and leapt, one after another, over the precipice, holding their children in their arms.' His fellow politician, writer and Orientalist, Alphonse de

Fig. 61: *The Suliote Women* by Ary Shaffer (1827).

Lamartin, drew on Fauriel's folk song collection adding with indignation, 'Here is one of the prodigies of heroism and misfortune of which our age is a daily observer... And Europe just looks on!' Pouqueville's steadfast courage is replaced by fear and panic in Scheffer's version where the women evoke pity by being depicted at the extreme of despair, broken and without pride or dignity. This deviation from the story was noted by the critics. In his review carried by the *Revue encyclopédique*, PA Coupin expressed confusion as to the picture's purpose and Charles Farcy, in a statement echoed by many modern gallery-goers, said in the *Journal des artistes*, 'really, one needs the catalogue in order to find out exactly what is [the subject] of the picture'. If the critics missed the point, it was a shame as Schaffer, a radical and philhellene, had intentionally modified the theme in an effort to fit better the mood and imagery of Liberal philhellenism, appealing to the public's sympathies by showing pleading victims instead of heroic defenders, as the Greek cause hung in the balance before the intervention by the European powers. Ali's life may have offered a spectrum of themes to be manipulated, Orientalist despot of legend to cartoon villain and lesson from history to entertainment, but it was as a vehicle for the cause of Greek liberty and the oppressed of Europe that it had its most profound impact.

Chapter 8

The Aftermath

The nations knew nothing before the French Revolution. The people thought that kings were gods upon earth, and that the people were bound to say that whatever the kings did was well done.

Theodore Kolokotronis

T he death of Ali Pasha at Ioannina left a void and, with Turkish armies beset on all sides, how it was to be filled was in the balance. Ali's ambivalent policies had served him well. Nobody ever knew whether they were his enemy or his friend, and in truth his only interests were selfish ones. His ability to play political games ran its course as the dynamics of power changed. In the end it proved to be internal pressures within the Ottoman Empire that left him exposed when foreign powers no longer needed him. He had used both the Suliotes and the Turks equally for his own purposes; and both played their part in his downfall. The man Byron called the Muslim Bonaparte had overreached himself like his French idol, but unlike him, and to the dismay of his loyal followers, his life was not to be spared. Although the Turkish reaction was to clamp down hard on Epirus to bring it to heal, other forces were at play. The existence of Ali's breakaway fiefdom had created ripples that would lead to a momentous change within the Empire and affect the world order.

When Lord Byron died at Missolonghi in 1824 he became an international hero and symbol of the Greek fight for freedom. His fame and sacrifice was such that he almost took on a mystical persona. As John Galt put it in his *The Life of Lord Byron* (1830), 'the Greek people became impatient for Lord Byron to come among them. They looked forward to his arrival as to the coming of a Messiah'. For the Philhellenes and the propagandists for a free Greek state, Byron was a vital element in their efforts to promote their cause and as such he came to be seen as the obvious catalyst of Greek liberty. Galt was aware of the importance of the relationship between Byron and Ali Pasha and how in their own ways they had played a part in creating the new reality; but unlike Galt, for Hughes it was Ali Pasha who was the catalyst for the insurrection that followed. The Sultan's gains in putting down Ali's own bid for autonomy were short-lived. His audacity in creating an alternative state from within hastened the split of Greece from the Empire. Ali's reprisals against insurrectionists were motivated by his own greed rather any form of loyalty, while his indifference to, or even tolerance of, intellectuals when it suited him allowed revolutionary ideas to spread. By belatedly espousing the Greek cause, whether meant or not, he furthered the momentum for change from within and his constant undermining of the Sultan was an inspiration for Balkan freedom.

Ali's activities had blinded the Sultan to the real danger of insurrection, to such an extent that he preferred to believe that dealing with his irritating upstart was the priority. Resources were kept occupied watching him rather than concentrating on the undercurrent of national awakening. In 1874 the historian Karl Mendelssohn-Bartholdy made the case for the start of the Greek War of Independence as early as the flight of the Suliotes from Ali; creating a focus for a national fighting force outside Ottoman control. The unrest throughout the Ottomans' European provinces meant that the dream of Rigas for a pan-Balkan state was always a possibility. Through the Filiki Eteria the Greeks of the Danube provinces had allies amongst the Slavs and Rumanians and it was felt that another coordinated attack on the Empire from north and south could end Turkish rule in the region. When once again the flag of revolution was raised in the Morea in March of 1821, it was to coincide with the march of Prince Alexander Ypsilantis and his Sacred Band of Greek volunteers from all over Europe into Wallachia and on to Bucharest. The hope was for Russian intervention to inspire a general revolt in Greece. The lack of expected local support and the assembly of a large Turkish army crushed Ypsilantis before he could force the Russians to back the insurrection as a fait accompli. For Ypsilantis the war was over; he spent the next seven years imprisoned in Terezín before being allowed to retire in exile within the Austrian boarders through the intervention of Tsar Nicholas I. The banner of Ypsilantis' Sacred Band bore the device of the Phoenix rising from his ashes and despite this setback the fuse had been lit from Crete to Macedonia. The ever-truculent Maniotes in the Peloponnese were the first to rise up and by 21 March, the official declaration of the uprising when Bishop Germanos of Patras blessed the banner, the whole of the Peloponnese was up in arms. The Turkish preoccupation with Ali in Ioannina provided an ideal opportunity to strike for freedom. Ali's showdown with the Sultan took Hurshid Pasha and his troops from the Morea and initially the Greeks were successful against the diminished Turkish forces. This momentum was key to keeping the revolt alive in its first year, until Ali's death meant that the Turks could put their full weight behind dealing with the rebels. Theodoros Kolokotronis, hardened klepht and trained soldier under the British (he always proudly wore the helmet of the Greek Light Infantry), took Tripolitsa. It was while he was in the city that he learnt of Ali's death. Many of his companions then feared that the 80,000-strong army that went against Ali would now turn on them. Kolokotronis would become the main figurehead of the Revolution and his son, Gennaios ('brave', a name he earned in battle), became prime minister of Greece.

The fighters of the revolt were drawn from disparate sources, ex-armatoles and klephts, idealists and the dispossessed, peasants and foreign volunteers, and Vlachs, Albanians and Greeks. Ypsilantis and the Filiki Eteria had been hard at work and they had contacts in central Greece. Leaders such as Demetrios Panourgias (Salona), Athanasios Diakos (Leivadia), Demos Skaltsas (Phokis villages) and Vassilis Bousgos (Thebes) had served under Ali at some point in their earlier career. Bousgos had been under Diakos and Ali's favourite Odysseus Androutsos. With the support of Ali, Panourgias had acquired influence as an armatole. He was a member of the Filiki Etaireia and led the first revolt in central Greece. With the aid of Yannis Gouras, Diakos and Makriyannis he captured the Castle of Salona, on Easter Sunday, 10 April 1821; the same day that Patriarch Gregory V was hung in reprisal during the 'Constantinople Massacre'. It was Ali's constant warfaring that unintentionally created the perfect environment for the future Greek freedom fighters to learn the art of war. The constant need to expand his military might soaked up his pool of manpower forcing him to spread his recruitment net beyond his close retainers, taking in promising individuals into his forces who then became skilled and experienced fighters ready to offer their services to the Greek cause.

In early 1821, when Ali's enemies were closing in, Odysseus Androutsos had slipped away to the Ionian Islands so that when the Revolution broke out he reappeared with 5,000 of his old comrades to establish himself in his old haunts as virtual dictator of the whole area known as Eastern Greece, from Parnassos to Athens. From his stronghold in the mountains he was able to keep the Turkish advance at bay. But Ali's court had proved to be a dubious schooling. Brought up in the intrigue and faction fighting of the clans his career epitomized the independence of the klephtic leaders who found uniting under a common banner to be unsuited to their way of life; one they were reluctant to give up. By 1823 civil war had broken

Fig. 62: *Kolokotronis and his personal escort* (1828) by Pierre Peytier.

Fig. 63: *Nikos Mitropoulos hoists the flag at Salona* by Louis Dupré (1821).

out between Kolokotronis and the other leaders. With Ali gone the Turks could turn their full force on the Greeks. Ali's ex-Commander Omar Vironi was sent by Hurshid Pasha to crush the revolt north of the Gulf of Corinth joined by an army from Egypt under Ibrahim Pasha, son of the breakaway Muhammad Ali Pasha, to subdue the Morea. The revolt faltered with the insurrectionist forces riven by jealousy and infighting. Odysseus followed the example he learnt at Ioannina by seeing an opportunity to set himself up Ali-style within his own chiefdom. For Edward John Trelawny, who had followed Byron to fight for the Greek cause, he was an almost superhuman hero, 'a glorious being, a noble fellow, a gallant soldier, and a man of most wonderful mind' in the mould of George Washington or Simon Bolivar 'appearing in different parts of Greece at nearly the same instant' where he was able with 5,000 men to slay 20,000 of the enemy allowing them 'no leisure to fortify cities or throw up entrenchments'. Trelawny became a trusted friend of Odysseus, commanding his troops in his absence, but his hero-worship was not shared by Thomas Gordon. Gordon, in his *History of the Greek Revolution* (1832), called Odysseus violent, cruel, subtle, ambitious and paranoid, the perfect mix of Albanian brutality and Greek mendacity and devoid of religion, patriotism or idealism holding to the klephtic ways under the new legitimacy of revolt. Like his mentor Odysseus' self-aggrandizement went too far and he was imprisoned in 1825 by the Greek revolutionary government. He was murdered while awaiting trial under orders of one of his former lieutenants, Yannis Gouras, cousin of Panourgias of Salona. Trelawny had married Odysseus' half-sister with whom he had a daughter, but divorced her upon his return to England. In Epirus, Ali's army was at the disposal of the Sultan to use against the Greeks and Ioannis Makriyannis who had served under Ali was engaged in a guerrilla war of survival. Makriyannis knew Odysseus from the Ali days and he called his execution one of the darkest moments of the War of Independence. Makriyannis's *Memoirs* of the War became one of the classics of modern Greek literature. The Noble Prize-winning poet George Seferis rated the work as the most important piece of prose in the language.

The Ionian Islands had proved to be a valuable recruiting ground for the rebel cause and Richard Church, in charge of the Greek Regiment, had argued at the Congress of Vienna in 1815 for an independent Greek state. Church had kept in touch with his friend Kolokotronis and was eager to join the fray from the first. Byron too was hoping for the support of Church and his former colleague Colonel Charles Napier in beleaguered Missolonghi. As the war progressed, with the Greeks increasingly on the defensive, foreign fighters, including former enemies, the French, Russian and British, joined the cause. Although official international reaction was antipathetic to the Greek revolt, George Canning, now the commissioner in the Ionian Islands, was able to give logistic support while committees of Philhellenes in London and Paris raised funds and recruited volunteers. In 1823 Lord Byron was idly kicking his heels in Genoa when he heeded the call, putting action behind his fine sentiments; a decision that would cement his name in Greek hearts. With the backing of the London committee he set sail for Greece via Cephalonia to meet his old friend from Italy and revolutionary leader, Alexander Mavrokordatos, in Missolonghi. Mavrokordatos had been pushed back from his attempt on Arta by Reshid Mehmed Pasha, who had been at the siege of Ioannina. Mavrokordatos and Byron planned

Fig. 64: Detail of a painting (1822) by Theophilos showing Yannis Gouras fighting under the command of Odysseus Androutsos.

to attack Turkish-held Lepanto but before they could do so Byron fell ill. His death was a shock and internationally mourned and ironically a great boost to the Greek cause. Reshid was joined by Omar Vironi and Missolonghi was subjected to a long series of sieges. The siege of the town took on heroic proportions and its fall in 1827 and the massacre of the population, like that of the previous massacre on the island of Chios (1822), became a symbol of oppression. With the Greeks in disarray, Church was invited to take control of the army.

To the north Reshid had subdued Thessaly, taking over the sanjak of Trikkala and he turned towards Attica and Athens. In Epirus the Turks had gradually retaken control. The Suliotes were defeated in 1822 and forced to flee once again from their homeland, taking refuge in the Ionian Islands. Byron had not lost his admiration and affection for the nobility of the Suliotes and it was from them that he recruited a number to form his private guard prior to his arrival in Missolonghi. The Suliote leaders Markos Botsaris and Kitsos Tzavellas became distinguished generals in the war. Botsaris led a valiant attack on Karpenisi in the Pindus with only 350 Suliots where they ambushed the 3,000-strong vanguard of the pasha of Scutari's army. When Botsaris was buried in Missolonghi, the leadership of the Suliotes passed to Byron, and his courage was immortalized by a number of artists and writers. Byron lamented the death of 'the modern Leonidas' in his letters and his funeral was described emotionally by Pouqueville and Dionysios Solomos, who likened the event to the funeral of Hector in Homer's *Iliad*. One of the mourners was Georgios Karaiskakis, later commander-in-chief of the Greek Army. Bedridden at the time with TB, he is said to have wished that he might die the same glorious death as Botsaris. His wish came true at the battle in Faliro in Attica on St George's Day, April 1827. After the death of Karaiskakis, Lord Thomas Cochrane, a naval veteran of campaigns for independence in Chile and Peru, and Church took over the leadership. Botsaris and Karaiskakis are held to be amongst the most revered figures in modern Greek History. The special relationship between Byron and the Suliotes is attested in the lament for Byron's death by Solomos. Many other Suliotes lost their lives in the fight for freedom, especially defending the city of Missolonghi with Byron. Their role in the siege and the famous defiant sortie from the town in 1826 went down as a testimony to their bravery. The city of Missolonghi itself was proclaimed a Sacred City by Greece and the sortie is commemorated there on Palm Sunday every year. The date of Lord Byron's death, 19 April 1824, was designated as 'Day of Philhellenism and International Solidarity' by the Greek President in 2008. Botsaris' name too lived on abroad. James Fenimore Cooper quoted from the poem *Marco Bozzaris* (1825) by Fitz-Greene Halleck, the 'American Byron', in the *Last of the Mohicans*, which he was writing at the time.

They fought like brave men, long and well;
They piled that ground with Moslem slain;
They conquer'd; -- but Bozzaris fell,
Bleeding at every vein.
His few surviving comrades saw
His smile when rang their loud hurrah,
And the red field was won;
Then saw in death his eyelids close,
Calmly as to a night's repose,--
Like flowers at set of sun.

Fig. 65: *Greece on the Ruins of Missolonghi* (1826) by Eugène Delacroix.

Abraham Lincoln read the entire poem to the Union troops in 1862 before the Battle of Fredericksburg during the American Civil War.

In June 1827, the Acropolis in Athens, the last great stronghold in central Greece, fell to the Turks. The massacres, defeats and courage of the beleaguered Greeks coupled with the propaganda of the philhellenes and the growth of public support finally forced the great powers to act. With pressure from the Russians to help their Orthodox brethren and George Canning replacing Castlereagh, with whom he had fought a duel, as Foreign Secretary, Metternich's policy of non-intervention was unravelling. To pre-empt Russian unilateral action, Canning brought Britain, France and Russia together to sign the Treaty of London to force an armistice between the belligerents and start peace negotiations, something the Porte was unwilling to concede from a winning position. Canning's forceful actions had pushed him to the forefront, succeeding the Duke of Wellington as prime minister, but he died before he could see the results of his endeavours. To ensure compliance with the treaty the Mediterranean British Fleet was dispatched under Sir Edward Codrington, a veteran of Trafalgar. While the Greek provisional government at Nafplion was understandably ready to accept, the Porte rejected the terms of the treaty. Contrary to warnings from the Allies a large Turkish fleet gathered at

Fig. 66: *Botsaris surprises the Turkish camp and falls fatally wounded* (1860–62) by Eugène Delacroix.

Navarino and as the peace negotiations continued Ibrahim Pasha protested that he was being asked to uphold the ceasefire while the Greeks were carrying on operations; operations aided by Cochrane, who was organizing a revolt behind Turkish lines in Epirus and Church, who was besieging Patras. Turkish attempts to relieve Patras were foiled by Codrington's naval blockade and when he learnt of the devastating effects of Ibrahim's scorched earth policy that was reducing the population of Messenia to starvation his patience ran out. Reinforced by squadrons of the Russian and French Navy, Codrington acted on his own initiative, and without official sanction he engaged and destroyed the Ottoman Fleet. Although his victory did not bring about an immediate capitulation by the Turkish government, it was a turning point in the war, bringing European forces into play on the ground. With the Albanian and Egyptian mercenaries putting up little resistance to the battle-hardened French veterans of Napoleon's army in the Morea, and the Russians once again driving across the Danube towards Constantinople, the Porte was forced to recognize an independent Greek state in the Protocol of London in 1830 and the Kingdom of Greece was established in 1832.

During the war a number of provisional governments had been set up by the Greeks, all riven by faction fighting between idealists, pragmatists and opportunists. Finally in 1827, Kapodistrias, the most recognized Greek politician in Europe was invited to head the National Assembly. When he arrived in Nafplion it was the first time he set foot on the soil of the Greek mainland. The sick, forgotten and impoverished Ypsilantis had only recently been released from prison when he died in Vienna just days after Kapodistrias took up his post in January 1828. Kapodistrias struggled to impose the idea of national unity and revolutionary politics on the former klephts and independently minded Maniots and sailors of Hydra and Poros who had taken on the Turks. When Kapodistrias imprisoned Petrobey Mavromichalis he outraged the family and he was assassinated by Petrobey's brother and son on the steps of the Church of St Spyridon in Nafplion. In an effort to maintain order the great powers, contrary to the spirit of the revolution, imposed a neutral monarchy on Greece, King Otto of Bavaria taking up the crown.

A number of Ali Pasha's former advisors and allies fought for the cause and served in the Greek administration. Ioannis Kolettis, one of his numerous doctors, became the representative for Epirus in the First National Assembly. Kolettis was a determined politician and in his capacity as Minister of War and the Interior used Alexis Noutsos and Christos Palaskas, a Suliot captain, to block his rival Odysseus. Odysseus had them murdered in their sleep. Makriyannis believed Kolettis had done this in the knowledge that Odysseus would react in this way, ridding himself of two other rivals. Kolettis' former connections within Ali's court, including Ioannis Gouras, meant he knew and could influence many of the captains gathering them around him. His control of the British loan to the Greeks in 1824 gave him power to organize his own Rumeliot party representing central Greece against the 'Russian' faction supported by Mavrokordatos, Botsaris and Kitsos Tzavellas and the Peloponnesian grouping around Kolokotronis. After the death of Kapodistrias, Kolettis became one of the most powerful Greek politicians and author of the *Megali Idea* or 'Great Idea', the final unification of all the Greek lands including Constantinople and the coast of Asia Minor, a major fixation of Greek foreign policy until the reversal of 1922 when the present borders with Turkey

Fig. 67: *The Murder of Kapodistrias* (*c.*1870s) by Charalambos Pachis.

were established. He served between terms by Mavrokordatos as prime minister, and was succeeded on his death by Kitsos Tzavellas in 1847. The success of the War of Independence was only for the south. In 1854, during the Crimean War, Tzavellas led a revolt in Epirus supported by officers of Suliot descent. This time there was no British and French support; they actively supported their Turkish ally against Russia to maintain the status quo.

On his return to England in 1810, Leake, now promoted to major, was granted an annual allowance in consideration of his services in Turkey since 1799. His colleague Spyridion Foresti also received a pension from the British government for his vital intelligence service on the recommendation of the four naval commanders including admirals Nelson and Collingwood. In his retirement Leake set to work on his detailed and sober accounts of Greece and Albania, but he was not impartial. He saw Turkish rule as inept and the Muslim population as lazy. As a philhellene he was hopeful that the Greeks would someday throw off the degrading effects of years under Ottoman despotism. In a political pamphlet *Greece at the End of Twenty-three years of Protection* (1851) he criticized successive British governments for their lack of support towards a Greek state and for showing 'a preference for incurable barbarism to progress and civilization' which resulted in the continued 'abasement of Greece'. The border between the new Greece and Turkey still ran as recognized in 1830 from Arta to Volos and included Euboea and the Saronic and Cycladic Islands. Crete and the other islands

Fig. 68: Ali Pasha's statue in Tepelene, photo Derek Smith.

remained under Turkish control. The Ionian Islands were under British protection until they were handed over to Greece as a goodwill gesture in 1864. In 1881 Greece gained Thessaly. Crete broke from Turkish rule in 1898 only to become part of Greece in 1913 when Albania achieved its own independence, but Epirus, Macedonia and Thrace would have to wait until the border settlements after the First World War. The Dodecanese Islands only became part of Greece in 1947 after a period of Italian occupation from the First World War.

The immediate result of the Greek uprising for the rest of the Ottoman Empire was a reaction by the Porte to reimpose its grip on defecting regions. Through a combination of harsh reprisals, increased central control and long-needed administrative and fiscal reform the Sultan Mahmud fought to maintain the integrity of the Empire. His *Tanzimat* reforms introduced a council of ministers, European style clothing and laws, land reform and the final abolition of the janissaries setting Turkey on a course of modernization. In independent Greece there was a desire to wipe out the memory of Turkish rule and a programme of de-Ottomanization was introduced. Under King Otto, the second son of the fanatical admirer of ancient Greece, King Ludwig I of Bavaria, the new capital of Athens was transformed as much as possible into a neoclassical stage set. When Edward Lear travelled to the border at Lamia in 1848 he noticed that in Greek lands all traces of Turkish occupation had already been removed. In 1922 the final break with Turkey came with the exchange of populations removing Greeks from Asia Minor, and transforming Constantinople into Istanbul, and Turks from Greek territory. Despite the achievement of Greek and Albanian nationhood and the pride that accompanies it in Epirus, north and south of the border the memory of Ali Pasha could not be erased. Although he was ruthless without prejudice, for Muslim Albanians he could be seen as a patriot, for Christians on both sides he made Epirus important again and for all a source of fascination; Ali's exploits for good or ill leave a deep impression on the local populace.

Glossary

armatole, *armatoli* (p), Christian Greek militia within the Ottoman Empire
armatoliki, area administered by the armatoli
Filiki Eteria, Friendly Society, the secret organization for Greek independence
hospodar, lord, specifically in Moldavia and Wallachia
klepht, bandit, freedom fighter
palikar, warrior
voivode. voyvoda, governor

Turkish terms

aga, *agha*, honourific title given to a civilian or military officer
ayan, notable person
bey, governor
chiflik, *ciftlik*, system of land ownership
dervendji-pasha (*derbendler basbugu*), guardian or governor of the passes
Divan, council of the Ottoman state
divan efendi, presided over the council of the local governors
eyalets or *viyalets*, first level province; the Eyalet of Rumeli (Rumelia) encompassed most of
    the Balkans with its capital variously at Edirne, Sofia and Monastir
hamam, bathhouse
harach, poll tax
harem, separate part of a Muslim house for women; for the Sultan and ruling class this would
    include servants and concubines
janissaries, elite corps made up of Christian captives converted to Islam
khan, inn with a courtyard
millet, an autonomous religious community responsible for its own laws i.e. the Christian millet
pasha, a governor of high rank, an honourary title
pashalik, area governed by a pasha
sanjak, subdivision of an *eyalet*
seraglio, walled palace
serai, mansion, lodge
Sublime Porte, 'High Gate', the residence of the government in Constantinople/Istanbul, generally
    the government was referred to as the *Porte Sultan*, hereditary sovereign of the Ottoman Empire
timar, fiefdom, subdivision of a *sanjak*
vizier, high official or minister: grand vizier, chief officer of state with military responsibility

Bibliography and Sources

Fig. 69: Frontispiece to Lord Byron's *Childe Harold's Pilgrimage*.

Primary Sources

Adair, Sir Robert, *The Negotiations for the Peace of the Dardanelles in 1808–9: with Dispatches and Official Documents*, Vol. 2 (Longman, London, 1845).

Anon, Edward Everett, 'Visit to Janina and Ali Pasha', *The North American Review and Miscellaneous Journal*, Vol. 10, No. 27 (April, 1820), pp. 429–462.

Anon, *Threnos (Lament) of Ali of Tepelene, Pasha of Ioannina*, ed. Émile Legrand, Ekate, first published 1886 (Athens, 2009).

Andersen, Hans Christian, *A Poet's Bazaar (En Digters Bazar): A Journey to Greece, Turkey & up the Danube* (1841), translated by Grace Thomson (Michael Kesend Publishing, New York, 1988).

Arvatinos, Panagiotes, ed. *Sylloge demodon asmaton tes Epeirou* (Perres, Athens, 1888).

Beauchamp, Alphonse de, *The life of Ali Pacha, of Jannina: late vizier of Epirus, surnamed Aslan, or the Lion*, 2nd edition (L Relfe, London, 1823).

Bell, James, *A System of Geography, Popular and Scientific: Or A Physical, Political and Statistical Account of the World in All its Divisions*, Vol. II (Fullarton, Glasgow, 1832).

Bossett, Lieutenant Colonel Charles Phillipe de, *Parga and the Ionian Islands, comprehending a refutation of the mis-statements of the Quarterly review and of Lieut-Gen. Sir Thomas Maitland, on the subject, with a report of the trial between that officer and the author* (Warren, London, 1821).

Brønstedt, Peter Oluf, *Interview with Ali Pacha of Joanina, in the Autumn of 1812; with Some Particulars of Epirus, and the Albanians of the Present Day*, Jacob Isager ed. (The Danish Institute at Athens, Athens, 1999).

Byron, Lord George Gordon, *The Works of Lord Byron*, 4 vols. (John Murray, London, 1830).

Byron, Lord George Gordon, *The Works of Lord Byron: Letters and Journals*, Vol. 1, Rowland E. Prothero, ed. (John Murray, London, 1898).

Byron, Lord George Gordon, *Byron's Correspondence and Journals 02: from the Mediterranean, July 1809–July 1811*, Peter Cochran ed. (2012).

Byron, Lord George Gordon, *'Famous in my time': Byron's Letters and Journals*, 2 vols. Leslie Marchand ed. (Harvard University Press, Cambridge, Mass., 1973).

Church, EM, *Sir Richard Church in Italy and Greece* based on family papers (W Blackwood, Edinburgh, 1895).

Church, Sir Richard, 'A report on the Ionian islands for the Congress of Vienna, in which he advocated the retention of the islands under the British flag and the permanent occupation by Great Britain of Parga and of other formerly Venetian coast towns on the mainland, then in the possession of Ali Pasha of Ioannina', *The MS Correspondence and Papers of Sir Richard Church* in 29 vols. now in the British Museum (Add. MSS. 36543-36571).

Church, Sir Richard, 'Memoir of General Church', *The United Service Magazine*, Part 3 (London, 1831), p. 210.

Cockerell RA, Charles Robert, *Travels in Southern Europe and the Levant, 1810–17*, SP Cockerell ed. (Longmans, Green, London, 1903).

Dawson, CM and AE Raubitschek, 'A Greek Folksong Copied for Lord Byron', *Hesperia* X, IV, 1, pp. 33–57.

Disraeli, Ralph (ed), *Home Letters written by the late Earl of Beaconsfield in 1830 and 1831* (John Murray, London, 1885, reprint: Kraus Reprint, New York, 1970).

Dufrénoy, Adélaïde-Gillette, *Beautés de l'histoire de la Grèce moderne, ou Récit des faits mémorables des Hellènes depuis 1770 jusqu'à ce jour* (A Eymery, Paris, 1825).

Eton, Sir William, *A Survey of the Turkish Empire* in 4 vols, 2nd ed. T Cadell, junior and W Davies (London, 1799).

Fauriel, Claude ed., *Chants populaires de la Grèce moderne* in 2 vols (Didot, Paris, 1824–25).

Frewen, Lord Walter, *Sir Thomas Maitland: the Mastery of the Mediterranean* (T Fisher Unwin, London, 1897).

Hatzi Sechretis, *The Alipashiad* or *The Alipashias* ed. K Sathas, Istorikai diatrivai III (Tekna A Koromila, Athens, 1870).

Hobhouse, John Cam, *Travels in Albania and other provinces of Turkey in 1809 and 1810* in 2 vols (John Murray, London, 1813 & 1858).

Hobhouse, John Cam, *A Journey Through Albania, and Other Provinces of Turkey in Europe and Asia, to Constantinople during the years 1809 and 1810* (M Carey, Philadelphia, 1817).

Hobhouse, John Cam, *Hobhouse's Diary*, Peter Cochran ed. (2010).

Holland, Sir Henry, *Travels in the Ionian Isles, Albania, Thessaly, Macedonia, &c: During the years 1812 and 1813* (Longman, London, 1815).

Hughes, Thomas Smart *Travels in Sicily, Greece, and Albania*, 2 vols. (Mawman, London, 1820).

Ibrahim Manzour Effendi, *Mémoires sur la Grèce et l'Albanie pendant le government d'Ali-Pacha* (Paul Ledoux, Paris, 1827).

John Murray (Firm), *A Handbook for Travellers in the Ionian Islands, Greece, Turkey, Asia Minor and Constantinople* (London, 1840).

Kinglake, Alexander William, *Eothen* (John Oliver, London, 1844).

Knight, Henry Gally, *Eastern Sketches in Verse* (John Murray, London 1830).

Kolokotrones, Theodoros, *Kolokotrones, the Klepht and the Warrior: sixty years of peril and daring. An autobiography*, trans. Elizabeth Mayhew Edmonds, (Unwin, London, 1892).

Leake, William Martin, *Travels in Northern Greece*, 4 vols. (Rodwell, London, 1835).

Lear, Edward, *Journals of a Landscape Painter in Albania and Illyria* (John Murray, London, 1851).

Panagiotopoulos, Vasiles ed. *Archive of Ali Pasha*, 4 vols. with Demetres Demetropoulos and Panagiotes Michaelares; *Archeio Ale Pasa: sylloges I. Chotze, Gennadeiou Vivliothekes tes Amerikanikes Scholes Athenon*, Series: Kentro Neoellenikon Ereunon E.I.E. 95, Institouto Neoellenikon Ereunon Ethnikou Hidrymatos Ereunon, (Athens, 2007–2009).

Passow, Arnold, *Romeika Tragoudia* (BG Teubner, Leipzig, 1860).

Perraivos, Christophoros, *Istoria syntomos tou Souliou kai Pargas*, 3rd edition, (Typois Ph. Karampine kai K. Vapha, Athens, 1857).

Perraivos, Christophoros, *History of Suli and Parga, containing their chronology and their wars, particularly those with Ali Pasha, Prince of Greece*, translated into English from the Italian of Carlo Gherardini, who used the 2nd Greek edition (Venice: Printing House of Nikolaos Glykis, 1815), Edinburgh, Archibald Constable and Co.; and London, Hurst, Robinson, and Co., (1823).

Politis, Nikolaos G, ed. *Eklogai apo ta tragoudia tou ellenikou laou* (Estia, Athens, 1914).

Pouqueville, François Charles Hugues Laurent, *Voyage en Morée, à Constantinople, en Albanie, et dans plusieurs autres parties de l'Empire Ottoman*, 3 vol. (Gabon, Paris, 1805).

Pouqueville, François Charles Hugues Laurent, *Travels in Epirus, Albania, Macedonia, and Thessaly* (R Phillips, London, 1820).

Pouqueville, François Charles Hugues Laurent, *Prisonnier ches les Turcs & Le Tigre de Janina*, first published 1820 (Librairie Industrielle, Paris, 1893).

Pouqueville, François Charles Hugues Laurent, *Voyage dans la Grèce*, vol. 1 (Didot, Paris, 1820).

Pouqueville, François Charles Hugues Laurent, *Voyage en Grèce*, 5 vol. (Didot, Paris, 1820–1822), 20 édit., 6 vol. (1826–1827).

Pouqueville, François Charles Hugues Laurent, *Histoire de la régénération de la Grèce*, 4 vol. (Didot, Paris, 1824).

Pouqueville, François Charles Hugues Laurent, *La Grèce, dans l'Univers pittoresque* (Didot, Paris, 1835).

Pouqueville, François Charles Hugues Laurent, *Trois Mémoires sur l'Illyrie* (Académie des inscriptions & belles-lettres, Paris, 1839).

Pouqueville, François Charles Hugues Laurent, 'Voyages dans la Grèce', *The Foreign Quarterly Review*, Article VIII, 3, Vol. III. No. V (London, 1829).

Swan, Rev. Charles (with Markos Philippos Zallones, b.1782), *Journal of a voyage up the Mediterranean, principally among the Archipelago, and in Asia Minor: including many interesting particulars relative to the Greek Revolution, especially a journey through Maina to the Camp of Ibrahim Pacha, together with observations on the antiquities, opinions, and usages of Greece, as they now exist.* To which is added, an essay on the Fanariotes / translated from the French of Mark Philip Zallony, a Greek (Rivington, London, 1826).

Vaudoncourt, Guillaume de, *Memoirs on the Ionian Islands considered in a commercial, political and military point of view: including the life and character of Ali Pacha, the present ruler of Greece* (Baldwin, Cradock, and Joy, London, 1816).

Williams, Hugh William, *Travels in Italy, Greece and the Ionian Islands: in a series of letters, descriptive of manners, scenery and the fine arts*, Vol. 2 (George Ramsay, London & Archibald Constable, Edinburgh, 1820).

Secondary Sources

Arafat, KW, 'A Legacy of Islam in Greece: Ali Pasha and Ioannina', *Bulletin (British Society for Middle Eastern Studies)* Vol. 14, No. 2 (1987), pp.172–182.

Athanassoglou-Kallmyer, Nina, *French Images from the Greek War of Independence 1821–1830: Art and Politics under the Restoration* (Yale University Press, New Haven and London, 1989).

Baggally, JW, 'Russia, Great Britain and Ali Pasha', *The Slavonic Review*, Vol. 14, No. 42 (January, 1936), pp. 441–3.

Battacharji, Shobhana, 'I like the Albanians much': Byron and three twentieth-century British travellers to Albania', *The Byron Journal*, 38.1 (Liverpool University Press, 2010), pp. 39–48.

Baggally, JW, *Ali Pasha and Great Britain* (Basil Blackwell, Oxford, 1938).

Brewer, David, *The Greek War of Independence: the Struggle for Freedom from Ottoman Oppression* (Overlook, New York and Duckworth, London, 2011).

Brooks, Allan, *Castles of Northwest Greece: From the early Byzantine Period to the eve of the First World War* (Aetos Press, Huddersfield, 2013).

Carvajal, Jose C & Ana Palanco, 'The castle of Ali Pasha at Butrint', *Butrint 4: The Archaeology and Histories of an Ionian Town*, edited by Inge Lyse Hansen, Richard Hodges, Sarah Leppard (Oxbow Books, Oxford, 2013).

Carvajal, Jose C, Ana Palanco & Nevila Molla, 'The castle of Ali Pasha at Butrint: from gateway to defence line', *Antiquity*, www.antiquity.ac.uk/projgall/carvajal323/

Chessell, C I, 'Britain's Ionian Consul: Spiridion Foresti and Intelligence Collection (1793–1805)', *Journal of Mediterranean Studies*, Vol. 16, No. 1/2 (2006), pp. 45–63.

Clogg, Richard, *The Movements for Greek Independence 1770–1821: A collection of documents* (Macmillan, London, 1973).

Cochran, Peter, *Byron and Hobby-O: Lord Byron's Relationship with John Cam Hobhouse* (Cambridge Scholars Publishing, Newcastle-upon-Tyne, 2010).

Cochran, Peter, *Byron and Ali Pasha*, www.newsteadabbeybyronsociety.org/works/downloads/byron_pasha.pdf

Dakin, Douglas, *The Greek Struggle for Independence, 1821–1833* (BT Batsford Ltd, London, 1973).

Davenport, Richard Alfred, *The Life of Ali Pasha of Tepeleni, Vizier of Epirus, surnamed Aslan or the Lion* (Tegg and Son, London, 1837).

Demir, Ilker, 'Ali Pasha and the West: a history of his relations with France and Great Britain 1798–1820', *Masters Thesis* (Bilkent University, Ankara, 2007).

Dictionary of National Biography OUP, www.oxforddnb.com/

Dumas, Alexandre, 'Ali Pascha', *Celebrated Crimes*, (first published, Paris, 1839–40) (PF Collier, New York, 1910).

Eisner, Robert, *Travelers to an Antique Land: the History and Literature of Travel to Greece* (University of Michigan, Michigan, 1993).

Finlay, George, *History of the Greek Revolution* (Oxford, 1877; Zeno, London, 1971).

Fishta, Gjergj, *The Highland Lute* (*Lahuta e Malcís*), trans. Robert Elsie & Janice Mathie-Heck (IB Tauris, London, 2005).

Fleming, K E, *The Muslim Bonaparte: Diplomacy and Orientalism in Ali Pasha's Greece* (Princeton University Press, Princeton, 1999).

Franklin, Michael J, 'Jousting for the Honour of Greece and a "certain miss phrosyne"': Baron Byron and Gally Knight Clash over Costume, Correctness, and a Princess, *The Modern language Review*, Vol. 103, No. 2 (April 2008), pp. 330–349.

Howarth, David, *The Greek Adventure: Lord Byron and other Eccentrics in the War of Independence* (Collins, London, 1976).

Hugo, Victor, 'Les Orientales', *Oeuvres Complètes de Victor Hugo* (Hetzel, Paris, 1829).

Hunt, Philip and Smith, AH, 'Lord Elgin and his collection', *The Journal of Hellenic Studies*, Vol. 38 (1916), pp. 163–372.

Ingram, Edward, *Anglo-Ottoman Encounters in the Age of Revolution: The Collected Essays of Allan Cunningham*, Vol. 1 (Routledge, Abingdon, Oxon, 2013).

Jelavich, Barbara, *History of the Balkans*, Vol.1 (Cambridge University Press, Cambridge and New York, 1983).

Johnson, William E, *The Crescent Among the Eagles: The Ottoman Empire in the Napoleonic Wars* (The Nafziger Collection, West Chester, OH, 1994).

Kaser, Karl, 'The Balkan joint family household: seeking its origins', *Continuity and Change*, 9.1 (Cambridge University Press, 1994), pp. 45–68, http://journals.cambridge.org/abstract_S0268416000004161

Koliopoulos, John S, *Brigands with a Cause, Brigandage and Irredentism in Modern Greece 1821–1912* (Clarendon Press, Oxford, 1987).

Mackenzie, E, *Choice Biography: Comprising an Entertaining and Instructive Account of Persons of Both Sexes and All Nations Eminent for Genius Learning Public Spirit Courage and Virtue* (Mackenzie & Dent, Newcastle upon Tyne, 1829).

McGrew, William W, *Land and Revolution in Modern Greece, 1800–1881: The Transition of Land Tenure and Exploitation of Land from Ottoman Rule to Independence* (Kent State University Press, Kent, OH, 1985).

Minta, Stephen, *Chateaubriand and Byron: Atala* and *Childe Harold's Pilgrimage I and II* (Proceedings of the International Association of Byron Societies, Valladolid, 2011).

Muse, Amy, 'Encountering Ali Pasha on the London stage: no friend to freedom?', *Romanticism*, 17.3 (Edinburgh University Press, 2011), pp. 340–350.

Peters, Rudolph, *Crime and Punishment in Islamic Law: Theory and Practice from the Sixteenth to the Twenty-First Century* (Cambridge University Press, Cambridge, 2006).

Plate, William, 'Ali Weli-Zade Tepeleni', *The Biographical Dictionary of the Society for the Diffusion of Useful Knowledge*, Vol. 2, No. 1 (1842).

Plomer, William, *Ali the Lion* (London, 1936, reissued as *The Diamond of Jannina* Jonathan Cape, London, 1970).

Rombotis, Gabriel, 'The Klephts in Modern Greek Poetry: an inquiry into a Graeco-Turkish cultural conflict', *Open Court* 46 (1932), pp. 759–773.

Scriven, Brig. Gen. George P, 'Some Highways of Albania and a forgotten Riviera', *Geographical Review* Vol. 11 No. 2 (American Geographical Society, 1921), pp. 198–206.

Shaw, Stanford, *History of the Ottoman Empire and Modern Turkey*, Vol. 1 & 2 (Cambridge University Press, Cambridge and New York, 1976).

Skiotis, Dennis N, 'The Greek Revolution: Ali Pasha's last gamble', *Hellenism and the First Greek War of Liberation (1821–30): Continuity and Change* (Institute of Balkan Studies, Thessaloniki, 1976), pp. 97–109.

Stavrianos, LS, *The Balkans Since 1453* (Hurst, London, 2000).

Tennent, James Emerson, *History of Modern Greece, from its Conquest by the Romans B.C. 146, to the Present Time*, Vol. 2 (Colburn and Bentley, London, 1830).

Wagstaff, Malcolm, 'Colonel Leake's knowledge of events in Greece and following Independence: the Finlay Correspondence', *British School of Athens Studies*, Vol. 17 (Scholars, Travels, Archives: Greek History and Culture through the British School at Athens, 2009), pp. 27–38.

Wiseman, James, 'Encounters with Ali Pasha', *Archaeology*, Vol. 52, No. 4 (Archaeology Institute of America, July/August 1999), pp. 10–12, 14–15.

Woodhouse, CM, *Capodistria: the Founder of Greek Independence* (Oxford University Press, London, 1973).

Woodhouse, CM, *The Greek War of Independence: Its Historical Setting* (Hutchinson's University Library, London, 1952).

Yaycioglu, Ali, *Partners of the Empire: The Crisis of the Ottoman Order in the Age of Revolutions* (Stanford University Press, Stanford, 2016).

Index